Tales of a Cardiologist

Stories by Aaron J. Feingold, M.D

BASHEVIS
PRESS

Published by Bashevis Press

New Jersey, United States of America

Paperback ISBN: 979-8-9995070-0-6

This is a work of creative nonfiction. Names and identifying details may have been changed to protect the privacy of individuals.

First Edition

Printed in United States of America

Table of Contents

III. Chambers of the Heart: Patient Stories

Clinical encounters revealing universal human truths

IV. Bloodlines: Family & Legacy

Intergenerational relationships and moral evolution

V. Beat Generation: Medicine Through Time

Technological/personal evolution across decades

VI. Vital Signs: Human Conditions

Thematic pairings exploring life's dualities

a. Mortality & Meaning

b. Humor & Healing

VII. Consultations: Ethical Crossroads

Moral dilemmas and clinical decision-making

VIII. Afterglow: Reflections at Dusk

Contemplative closure and philosophical resonance

ISAAC B. SINGER
209 WEST 86TH STREET
NEW YORK, N.Y. 10024

August 17, 1979

Dear Mr. Sullivan,

Thank you for your letter. I hope against hope that in the 80's more people and nations will come to the conclusion that killing and torturing people will not make a better world.

I really expect that humanity will make this decision or perish. It would be for me a great satisfaction to live to see it or at least to hear about it.

Cordially,

Isaac B. Singer

IBS/drm

P.S. I would also like to see the readers of the world go back to the short story which has been badly neglected all over the world.

Isaac Bashevis Singer, winner of the 1978 Nobel Prize in Literature, wrote with an intimacy and universality that made him one of the greatest short story writers of the 20th century. This letter, treasured in my personal collection, embodies the literary spirit that has shaped my own approach to storytelling.

Introduction

The Talmud teaches that a physician should hold deep gratitude for his patients, for without them, he could not practice the healing arts. This ancient wisdom resonates profoundly with my own experience in medicine.

I, too, am grateful – not only for the privilege of caring for those who seek healing, but for the profound gift they have unknowingly bestowed upon me: these stories. Each patient encounter has offered me a glimpse into the extraordinary depths of human nature and existence, moments of revelation that have shaped not only my practice but my understanding of what it means to be human.

The stories that follow are drawn from these encounters – true experiences that have illuminated the resilience, vulnerability, courage, and grace that define our shared humanity. While I have carefully altered names, locations, and timeframes to honor the sacred trust between physician and patient, the essence of each story remains intact.

These narratives have enriched my life immeasurably, and I hope they will do the same for you. They are testament to the profound truth that in caring for others, we discover ourselves. In witnessing their struggles and triumphs, we find our own capacity for both healing and being healed.

If these stories resonate with you, know that there are many more yet to be shared – each one a small window into the magnificent complexity of the human experience.

I. First Pulse: Stories Shared Online Prior to Publication

The first stories I shared online; each met with heartfelt emotion and encouragement

The Geography of the Heart

In the sterile corridors of New York Presbyterian, where life and death dance their eternal waltz, I am but a witness – a cardiologist whose stethoscope has heard more secrets than most confessors. My patient, Samuel Kaufman, was not like other men. His heart, a fragile instrument of desire and limitation, played a melody that defied medical logic.

Each year, like a migratory bird following an inexplicable instinct, Samuel would vanish. Not to rest, not to recuperate, but to meet her – a woman whose name I never knew, whose existence was as ephemeral as a whispered promise. One week in Mexico, another in Buenos Aires, then Paris, their rendezvous scattered across the world's romantic landscapes like fallen flower petals.

"It is the romance of my life," he would tell me, his eyes sparkling with a light that seemed to mock the electrocardiogram's somber lines. His heart – oh, his heart! A broken vessel held together by a defibrillator, weakened by congestive failure, with an ejection fraction so low it seemed a miracle he could walk, let alone travel.

I would watch him during our appointments, this man who lived between hospitalizations and passionate interludes. His medical chart was a testament to survival: heart failure, multiple interventions, yet always returning with stories of that one week, that singular connection.

Last week, he died in the coronary care unit. His wife of decades sat beside him, her hand folded into his, a landscape of long-suffering love. And I found myself wondering about the other woman – the one who existed in those ephemeral weeks, in those stolen moments across continents.

Would she know? How would she learn of his passing? Through some bureaucratic letter, a cold telephone call, or would the universe simply whisper her the truth, as it had whispered their annual meetings?

In my years of medicine, I have learned that the heart is more than a muscle pumping blood. It is a cartographer of human longing, mapping territories of connection that defy medical understanding. Samuel's heart, weak as it was, had found a strength beyond diagnostic measurements – a strength of memory, of anticipation, of a love that existed outside the boundaries of conventional time.

And so he passed, this man whose heart told a story more complex than any medical journal could comprehend. A story of waiting, of meeting, of a passion so pure it seemed to sustain him more effectively than any medication I could prescribe.

The mystery remains. The heart, after all, has its own logic – one that no physician can fully explain.

Forty-Three Years of Mending Hearts

Very often, I find myself behind a lectern at medical conferences, addressing audiences that vary in their technical sophistication – laypeople with their earnest curiosity, physicians with their collegial nods, fellow cardiologists with their knowing smiles. Recently, I've found my thoughts turning backward, surveying the curious landscape of my forty-three years as a cardiologist, a span of time that has witnessed nothing short of a revolution.

I try to convey to these audiences what practice was like when I first entered the profession, though I suspect my description strikes them as something closer to medieval bloodletting than modern medicine. When a patient arrived in those days, clutching their chest and wearing that particular expression of terror that accompanies the conviction one is dying, our arsenal was remarkably sparse. I would often sit at the bedside – yes, actually sit, a luxury few cardiologists today could imagine – and administer morphine. Perhaps slip some nitroglycerin under the tongue. And then we would wait. The patient either improved or didn't. Death or recovery – medicine at its most binary, it's most humbling.

I describe this primitive tableau to patients, colleagues, and families, and watch as their faces register disbelief. They simply cannot fathom it, these beneficiaries of our modern cardiac miracle factory. It's rather like describing to a teenager how we once navigated cross-country without GPS or survived without the internet – theoretically comprehensible but emotionally unfathomable.

The transformation occurred by increments. I remember when bypass surgery was not the routine procedure it is today but rather an exotic intervention, something one flew to Texas for, to place one's chest under the renowned hands of Denton Cooley or Michael DeBakey. Patients would endure months of chest pain before such drastic measures were considered. The delay alone seems barbaric now.

Today's heart attack patients encounter an entirely different medical machine. No sitting still, no waiting. Instead, a choreographed frenzy of activity ensues. We rush them to the cardiac catheterization laboratory with an urgency that is not only encouraged but measured and judged. How quickly can we remove the clot? How swiftly can we deploy an emergency stent to open the occluded vessel? Administrators time us. Insurers monitor us. Our professional reputations hang on minutes saved.

Our arsenal has expanded beyond recognition. We deploy aortic balloons, emergency stents, clot-busting agents like streptokinase and TPA. Pacemakers, which barely existed when I began practice, have undergone their own evolution. I recall the early models with their rechargeable batteries, ungainly things the size of three cigarette packs stacked together. Patients would recharge them externally, the skin growing hot beneath the device, sometimes to the point of burning. Compared to today's elegant implantable devices, they seem as sophisticated as stone tools.

What strikes me most profoundly is how heart disease has transformed from an acute killer to a chronic condition. When I began practice, it was the terror of sudden death that drew me to cardiology – the high-wire act of medicine, where decisions made in minutes determined survival. Now, even the most catastrophic heart attack can be survived. We can prevent death by promptly opening blocked vessels with stents. We can forestall lethal arrhythmias with defibrillators. We can manage heart failure with biventricular pacemakers and an ever-expanding pharmacopeia.

In my early days, our medicinal options consisted primarily of Lasix and Digoxin – a diuretic and a cardiac glycoside. Now pharmacology texts devote entire chapters to the medications available for each cardiac condition. The result? People live with heart disease rather than die from it. They live with heart failure, with angina, with stents, with bypassed vessels.

Sometimes, remarkably, they even forget they're sick. I've had patients who, the day after we've opened a blocked artery that was actively killing them, express impatience to return home, as if we'd merely fixed a minor inconvenience rather than snatched them from death's anteroom.

All in all, I've had the extraordinary privilege of witnessing the great progression of this field. It has been, in the truest sense, scientific triumph made manifest – knowledge accumulated, tested, and applied to the most practical and profound end: the extension of human life. Every day, amid the routine documentation and administrative burden that modern medicine entails, I find moments to marvel at what we've accomplished, at the lives extended, at the suffering prevented.

It has been, I must tell you, nothing short of wonderful.

A Matter of Perspective

It is nine-thirty in the morning, and I am making my rounds at Northwestern Memorial Hospital, where I have been an attending physician for nearly twenty years. The hallways are familiar enough that I could navigate them blindfolded, which is sometimes how I feel I am proceeding through life these days.

As I walk briskly from room to room, clipboard in hand, my mind is elsewhere – on the stack of bills that arrived yesterday (my daughter's college tuition has risen, again, by an implausible percentage); on the tedious staff meeting scheduled for Thursday where the hospital administration will announce yet another restructuring that promises efficiency but will deliver only paperwork; on the small leak in my office ceiling that maintenance has promised to fix for three weeks running.

These are what my late father, who sold furniture on the West Side, would have called "regular problems" – the quotidian concerns that attach themselves to middle-class professional life like barnacles to a ship's hull. Not serious in the cosmic scheme, yet they colonize one's thoughts with remarkable persistence.

I enter Room 412, where Mrs. Eleanor Pinsky has been receiving treatment for metastatic colon cancer. The disease has spread to her liver and lungs. Her oncologist and I have had several hushed conversations about time frames and palliative options. The median survival for her condition is measured in months, not years.

"Doctor! What a wonderful morning," Mrs. Pinsky says as I enter. She is sitting up in bed, her thinning hair covered by a cheerful blue scarf. "Have you looked out the window? The lake is just sparkling today."

She is right. Lake Michigan is indeed sparkling, a deep azure embroidered with whitecaps. I hadn't noticed.

Mrs. Pinsky tells me about her chemotherapy session yesterday. "The nurse – Brenda, such a dear – she found my vein on the first try! A small victory, but I'll take it." She laughs with genuine delight.

She shows me photographs of her grandchildren's recent visit. "Little Jacob lost his front tooth right here in this room! He was so proud. Said he wanted to be brave like Grandma."

As she speaks, I note her jaundiced complexion, the slight wince when she shifts position, the labored breathing. Yet these physical realities seem secondary to her buoyant spirit.

"And doctor," she adds, adjusting her scarf, "that tie is very becoming. Brings out the blue in your eyes. Your wife has excellent taste."

I did not select this tie. I did not even remember which one I was wearing until she mentioned it.

We discuss her medication adjustments. She listens attentively, asks intelligent questions, thanks me for "taking such good care" of her. As if I am doing something extraordinary by performing the basic functions of my profession.

Later, as I close her door and continue down the hallway, I am struck by the peculiar mathematics of human perception. Here is a woman whose body is engaged in the ultimate betrayal, whose future has contracted dramatically, who spends her days in a sterile room with its industrial lighting and mechanical bed – and yet she radiates an appreciation for life that makes my own preoccupations seem not merely petty but perverse.

I recall something Montaigne wrote about how we experience reality: "The defect is not in the thing but in how we see the thing." All morning I have been seeing bills, meetings, leaks – Mrs. Pinsky sees sunlight on water, the miracle of a found vein, the blue in a stranger's necktie.

The Greeks had a word, *metanoia,* which literally means "change of mind" but implies a fundamental shift in how one perceives and experiences the world. Standing outside Mrs. Pinsky's room, holding my clipboard with its charts and numbers that attempt to quantify her decline, I wonder if I have just been given a small taste of this transformation.

My watch tells me I am running behind schedule. There are twelve more patients to see before noon. The day's concerns press forward again – but now they seem less substantial, as if Mrs. Pinsky's perspective has introduced a competing gravity that pulls against their weight.

What determines how we live our lives? I suspect it is not the circumstances we encounter but the attention we bring to them. Mrs. Pinsky has taught me, without intending to do so, that there is always more than one way to inhabit a moment.

I straighten my blue tie and continue down the hall.

Through the Eyes of Others

In my thirty-three years as Chief of Cardiology at Princeton Community Hospital, I've found that the stethoscope serves as much more than a medical instrument; it has become a conduit for stories. The examining room, with its fluorescent lighting and antiseptic smell, transforms without warning into a confessional, a theater, or sometimes a battlefield.

Let me explain. My name is David Bernstein. I'm sixty-one, balding, and perpetually fifteen pounds overweight despite my wife Elaine's vigilant monitoring of my cholesterol. I am not, by training, a marriage counselor. Yet somehow, between checking blood pressure and listening to heart murmurs, I've become an unwitting witness to the erosion and occasional resurrection of countless marriages.

Our hospital staff has changed dramatically since I began practice. Over half our physicians now are Indian – brilliant doctors who have brought with them not only their medical expertise but their cultural traditions. I've been invited to more Hindu weddings than bar mitzvahs in the past decade, a fact that would have astonished my grandfather, who rarely ventured beyond the five boroughs of New York.

It was at one such wedding – Dr. Patel's daughter Meera to a young radiologist named Vikram – where I witnessed something that would become an unexpected tool in my medical practice.

The wedding was elaborate, even by New Jersey standards. It took place at the Hyatt in New Brunswick, transformed for the occasion into a riot of marigolds and silk. Vikram arrived on a white horse, bedecked in gold embroidery and looking simultaneously regal and terrified.

Meera, in a red sari that must have weighed twenty pounds, stood waiting with her parents.

What struck me wasn't the pageantry, though it was impressive, but rather the moment when the couple first saw each other. Their eyes met across the crowded hotel ballroom, and the intensity of their gaze silenced even the *tabla* drums. They looked at each other with such naked adoration that I, cynical cardiologist that I am, felt like an intruder witnessing something too intimate for public display.

The Hindu priest – pandit, I believe is the correct term – stopped the proceedings. This wasn't in the program; I checked. He turned to the assembled guests, his voice carrying without a microphone.

"Look," he said, gesturing toward the couple. "Look at how they see each other. Not just with their eyes, but with their souls." He paused, letting his words settle. "Remember this moment. Ten years from now. Twenty. Fifty. When you are old, when you argue about nothing, when you consider separation, when you can no longer remember why you married – remember that what they see in each other now will always be there. You will simply need to look deeper to find it."

I remember Elaine squeezing my hand. We'd been married twenty-seven years at that point, and had weathered our share of storms. I squeezed back, wondering if she could still see whatever it was she'd seen in me when I was a skinny resident with more hair and fewer opinions.

This morning, the Greenspans came in for their annual checkups. Morris is eighty-two with a pacemaker and a tendency to minimize his symptoms. Sylvia is seventy-nine with mild hypertension and a talent for interrupting.

"He never listens to me anymore, Dr. Bernstein," Sylvia complained while I checked her blood pressure. "Forty-seven years married, and now he acts like I'm the wallpaper."

Morris snorted from his chair in the corner. "Hard not to when you never stop talking."

Sylvia pulled out her phone and showed me a photo. "Look at us on our honeymoon. Niagara Falls, 1976. We were so happy then."

The picture showed a slender, dark-haired Morris with his arm around a beaming Sylvia in a dress that screamed disco era. Their faces were pressed together, radiating the peculiar glow of the newly married.

"Now look at us," Sylvia continued. "Two old people who can't even agree on what to watch on Netflix."

I finished noting her blood pressure (143/82, not terrible) and looked at them both. Something about their bickering reminded me of that Hindu wedding.

"Let me tell you about a wedding I attended years ago," I said, and related the story of Meera and Vikram, the white horse, and the pandit's words.

When I finished, the examining room was quiet. Morris was looking at Sylvia, really looking at her, perhaps for the first time in years.

"You still have the same smile," he said finally.

Sylvia blinked rapidly. "And you still have that cowlick," she replied, her voice softer than I'd ever heard it.

I busied myself with my computer, giving them a moment. By the time I turned back, something had shifted between them. Nothing dramatic – they weren't embracing or weeping – but the air in the room had changed.

As they left, Sylvia squeezed my arm. "Thank you, Doctor," she whispered.

In medical school, they teach us to treat the disease, not the symptoms. But in practice, I've learned that healing often extends beyond the physical. That pandit knew something important: that love doesn't disappear; it just gets buried under years of routine and resentment.

Sometimes, my job isn't to heal hearts with medicine, but to help people remember what their hearts once knew.

My nurse Jennifer has developed a running joke. When an older married couple comes in, she'll wager whether one of them will answer "too long" when I ask how many years they've been married. She wins more often than not.

But today, when the Greenspans returned for Morris's follow-up, and I asked that routine question, they looked at each other and answered in unison: "Not long enough."

Jennifer owes me five dollars.

The Luckiest Man in Miami

Dr. Weinberg had been practicing medicine in Miami for nearly thirty years, long enough to watch the art deco buildings of South Beach undergo their renaissance and the skyline sprout glass towers like exotic mushrooms after a summer rain. He had accumulated, as doctors do, a catalogue of patient stories that served him in ways medical textbooks never could.

One such story, which he found himself returning to often, concerned Howard Blumstein, a man of seventy-nine who had what insurance companies euphemistically call "a complicated medical history." Blumstein wore an ileal conduit – a plastic pouch attached to his abdomen that collected urine after his bladder had been removed due to cancer. His chest bore the zipper-like scar of coronary bypass surgery performed a decade earlier, and beneath the skin near his left collarbone sat a pacemaker, regulating the beats of a heart that had, both literally and figuratively, been through a great deal.

When Esther, his wife of fifty-two years, died from ovarian cancer, Blumstein had slumped into Dr. Weinberg's office like a man awaiting execution. "What's the point?" he had asked, not rhetorically. "Tell me, Doctor, what exactly is the point of going on?"

Weinberg, who prided himself on having answers, found none adequate to the occasion. He prescribed an antidepressant, made the appropriate referrals, and penciled Blumstein's name into his mental ledger of patients to worry about after hours.

The transformation, when it came six months later, was so complete that Weinberg at first thought the medication might have triggered some sort of manic episode. Blumstein – the same man who had previously needed assistance to rise from the waiting room chairs – practically bounded into the examination room.

"You look... different," Weinberg offered, a master of clinical understatement.

"Different?" Blumstein's laugh was full-bodied and genuine. "Doctor, I am the luckiest man in Miami. Perhaps in all of Florida!"

The source of this miraculous recovery was named Sylvia Kaplan, a seventy-one-year-old widow who had moved into Blumstein's condominium building two months earlier. They had met in the building's modest library, reaching for the same dog-eared copy of Philip Roth's "Everyman" – an irony not lost on either of them.

"You know what she said when I told her about this?" Blumstein gestured toward his urine collection bag. "She said, 'Howard, at our age, everyone's carrying something. At least yours comes with a convenient handle.'" He laughed again, a sound Weinberg realized he had never before heard from the man.

On subsequent visits, Weinberg observed that Blumstein had begun to color-coordinate his clothing with his medical apparatus. "Sylvia's idea," he explained. "She says if I'm going to accessorize, I might as well do it with style."

Weinberg found himself recounting Blumstein's story to other patients – those recently widowed, those struggling with chronic illness, those convinced that life had nothing further to offer them. He changed the names, of course, adjusted the timeline to protect confidentiality, but kept the essence intact: here was a man who, by any objective medical standard, should have been consumed by his infirmities, yet had discovered himself to be, against all odds, fortunate beyond measure.

What Weinberg never told these patients – what he scarcely admitted to himself – was how Blumstein's story had affected his own marriage of thirty-four years. How he had begun, after all this time, to notice the particular way his wife's eyes crinkled when she laughed. How he had started bringing home flowers on Tuesdays, for no reason at all. How he had realized, watching Blumstein's improbable renaissance, that gratitude need not wait for perfect circumstances.

The human heart, Weinberg had learned, was a far more resilient organ than any cardiology textbook suggested. It could falter, be bypassed, require electronic assistance, and still somehow find the capacity to fall in love anew. In Miami's relentless sunshine, this seemed to him a medical miracle worth noting – one he had witnessed not in some prestigious journal, but in Examination Room B, on a Tuesday afternoon in April, from a man who carried his bladder in a bag and his joy in every cell of his being.

A Mother's Devotion

One notices things in a hospital – small things that fill the empty moments between procedures and consultations. I had been coming to this same wing for nearly a year now, and among my catalog of observations was a nurse with remarkable hair, dark and luxuriant, the kind that advertisers might hope to feature in shampoo commercials if only they could find a woman who possessed it naturally.

I'm not particularly given to admiring the physical attributes of the medical professionals who tend to me. There's something vaguely inappropriate about it, I suppose, though I can't imagine any ethical code that forbids simple aesthetic appreciation. Nevertheless, I had noticed her hair, and in the economy of my attention, it had earned its place.

So it was with genuine surprise – something increasingly rare at my age – that I found her one Tuesday morning with that glorious mane shorn away, replaced by a pragmatic, almost severe cut that barely reached her collar. And there, on the newly exposed nape of her neck: a tattoo. A name, "Ted," rendered in an understated script.

What fascinates me about such discoveries is not the thing itself, but the immediate narrative we construct around it. In the space of seconds, I had composed a complete romance: her sacrifice of vanity for love, the symbolic gesture of permanence in both the cutting of hair and the inking of skin. How fleetingly we love, I thought with the quiet superiority of a man who fancies himself a student of human nature. How desperately we attempt to make permanent that which is, by its very essence, ephemeral.

For weeks, this little narrative entertained me during the tedious intervals of my treatment. I imagined Ted – a mechanic perhaps, or a musician, someone whose rough-hewn authenticity had pierced the professional veneer of a healthcare worker.

Yesterday, as she adjusted my IV with practiced efficiency, I finally surrendered to curiosity.

"That must be quite the love," I said, nodding toward the name on her neck as she leaned forward, "to sacrifice such beautiful hair and mark yourself permanently."

She smiled – not the polite, professional smile I was accustomed to, but something genuine that reached her eyes.

"Yes, Doctor," she said, her fingers absently touching the tattoo. "It's the strongest love there is." A brief pause, then: "He's my son."

I felt the peculiar deflation that comes when a cherished theory collapses under the weight of new evidence. My romantic fabrication dissolved, replaced by something far more ordinary and yet infinitely more profound.

We do this constantly, I realized – construct narratives from fragments, impose our expectations on the lives of others. And how often we miss the simplest truths. A mother's love for her child – perhaps the most common story of all, and yet I had overlooked it entirely, seduced instead by my own cynical romanticism.

I said nothing more about it, of course. What was there to say? But as she finished with my treatment and moved on to the next patient, I found myself wondering about the stories I had constructed about all the other small mysteries that populated my days. How many of them, I wondered, might dissolve just as quickly under the gentle pressure of a simple question?

The Menu

So I dislike so much the mechanized ritual that occurs in hospitals these days. The reduction of life's final chapter to checkboxes and protocols. Mrs. Levinson – my mother's oldest friend – now lying in Beth Israel with pneumonia at eighty-seven, and there I was, summoned by her daughter Rebecca to "discuss options."

A young nurse with efficiency in her step approached us outside the room, tablet in hand. "We need to establish Mrs. Levinson's code status," she announced, not so much a greeting as an administrative declaration.

"Code status?" Rebecca asked.

"Yes," the nurse replied, tapping her screen. "We need to determine interventions. Would Mrs. Levinson want chest compressions? Intubation? Vasopressors? Cardioversion?" She rattled off the list like specials at a diner.

Rebecca's face blanched. I placed my hand on her shoulder.

"Her mother is here for pneumonia," I said. "She was gardening last week."

The nurse nodded professionally. "Hospital policy. We need these decisions documented within twenty-four hours of admission."

And there it was – the transformation of dying into paperwork, of human dignity into institutional procedure. The nurse did her job. She completed her chart. What more could the system ask?

Rebecca turned to me later, over coffee in the cafeteria. "Mom never discussed this. How am I supposed to know?"

The coffee tasted of industrial cleaner and resignation. Outside the window, people walked by, blissfully unaware of the menus awaiting them all.

The Unexpected Jolt

Dr. Saul Bernstein had been practicing cardiology in Englewood, New Jersey, for thirty-seven years. In that time, he had witnessed the full spectrum of human frailty, both physical and emotional, that accompanies cardiac disease. His patients' stories – their fears and denials, their rationalizations and reconciliations – had provided him with what he considered a more comprehensive education in human nature than any literature course at Princeton, where he had once harbored pretensions of becoming a novelist before biology and medicine claimed him.

The human heart, Bernstein often thought, was endlessly fascinating, both as a mechanical pump and as the metaphorical seat of our deepest emotions. This intersection of the scientific and the poetic had sustained his interest through decades of practice, when colleagues in other specialties had long since surrendered to cynicism or boredom.

Monday mornings in his office typically featured a parade of weekend cardiac events – the occasional chest pain following excessive yard work, the shortness of breath after a too-ambitious tennis match. But this particular Monday brought something unprecedented even to Bernstein's experienced ears.

"So you see, Doc," explained Morris Feldstein, a sixty-four-year-old retired high school physics teacher with dilated cardiomyopathy, "neither of us knew what happened at first."

Morris had been Bernstein's patient for over a decade, ever since the diagnosis of his weakened heart muscle, likely the result of a viral infection compounded by what Morris euphemistically called his "bourbon appreciation phase." The implantable cardioverter-defibrillator had been a precautionary measure, one that had remained dormant all these years – until Saturday night.

"Ruth and I, well, we've been married forty-two years," Morris continued, his wife beside him nodding with a mixture of embarrassment and surprising pride. "You know how it is with long marriages. You develop... routines."

"Indeed," Bernstein replied, keeping his expression professionally neutral while recognizing the universal truth in Morris's diplomatic phrasing.

"Well, Saturday night was different," Morris said, his eyes suddenly animated behind his thick glasses. "At the... culmination, shall we say... I felt this incredible jolt. Like nothing I'd ever experienced before. Ruth felt it too."

Ruth Feldstein, a petite woman with carefully maintained auburn hair, adjusted her pearl necklace and cleared her throat. "We thought perhaps we'd discovered something new," she offered quietly. "At our age, you can imagine our surprise."

Bernstein nodded, already suspecting what the device readout would reveal. The interrogation of Morris's defibrillator confirmed it: a sustained ventricular tachycardia transitioning to fibrillation, promptly terminated by the device's life-saving shock. The timing of this potentially fatal arrhythmia, precisely at the moment of sexual climax, was a remarkable coincidence of physiology and circumstance that Bernstein knew would become one of those anecdotes shared discreetly among cardiologists at conferences.

"So what you're telling us, Dr. Bernstein," Morris said slowly after the explanation, "is that at the exact moment when we thought we were experiencing some kind of... late-life sexual renaissance..."

"I was actually saving your life," the defibrillator seemed to finish for him, though of course it was only a silent device doing exactly what it had been programmed to do.

The irony was not lost on any of them. Morris and Ruth exchanged a look that contained decades of shared understanding, then both began to laugh – softly at first, then with increasing abandon.

Bernstein found himself joining in their laughter, appreciating as he often did the peculiar comedy of the human condition. Here was Morris, literally snatched from death's door at the very moment he was most vigorously affirming life. The universe, Bernstein thought, had a sense of humor that was sometimes crude but never without a certain poetic justice.

As the Feldsteins prepared to leave, Ruth suddenly turned to Bernstein with an expression of mischievous inquiry.

"Doctor," she asked, "are there any... precautions we should take in the future?"

Bernstein smiled. "Just the usual cardiac guidelines, Mrs. Feldstein. Moderate exertion, adequate rest periods." He paused. "And perhaps a moment to appreciate the remarkable technologies that allow life – in all its aspects – to continue."

"Of course," Bernstein added, his tone shifting to the more formal register of medical necessity, "this incident means we'll need to schedule you for a complete cardiac workup. The fact that the device activated after all these years without incident suggests something may have changed in your underlying condition."

Morris's expression sobered. "I thought we might be done with all that testing business."

"Unfortunately, no," Bernstein replied. "We'll need a new echocardiogram, stress test, possibly cardiac MRI. The defibrillator did its job, but now we need to understand why it needed to after such a long dormant period."

Ruth placed her hand protectively over her husband's. "Whatever it takes," she said firmly.

After they left, Bernstein made his notes in Morris's file, reflecting on how the most sophisticated medical devices and the most primal human experiences could sometimes intersect in ways that no medical textbook could ever fully address. In medicine, as in life, he thought, the most profound truths often revealed themselves in moments of unexpected humor and grace – and often necessitated a battery of follow-up tests.

II. Foundations: The Physician's Formation

Early medical education, identity development, and ethical awakening

Bubula's Dilemma

The fluorescent lights of PS 217 flickered neurotically above my head as I sat, all of four years old, drowning in the vast ocean of linoleum and primary colors that was Miss Bergman's kindergarten class.

There I was, surrounded by twenty other children whose parents had given them sensible, practical names that would serve them well into adulthood. Names like Michael and Susan and David. Names that wouldn't require years of therapy or lengthy explanations at job interviews.

"Aaron Goldstein?" Miss Bergman called out, her voice cutting through the classroom chaos with the precision of my mother's kitchen scissors through a piece of lox.

I sat there, of course, saying nothing. Why would I? This "Aaron" person was clearly someone else, perhaps hiding in the coat closet or cowering behind the finger-painting station. I continued arranging my wooden blocks, constructing what I believed was an architectural marvel but what was, in reality, a mediocre representation of existential uncertainty.

"Aaron Goldstein?" she repeated, this time with the slight edge that schoolteachers develop after years of dealing with children who refuse to acknowledge their existence.

The room fell silent, as silent as my father's apartment ever got, which is to say you could still hear the radiator hissing like a disappointed relative.

"Young man," Miss Bergman said, approaching my table with the determined gait of someone who had been trained to handle small insurrections, "why aren't you answering when I call your name?"

I looked up at her, my face a perfect mixture of confusion and indignation. A face I would later perfect for dealing with film critics and ex-wives.

"My name isn't Aaron," I explained with the certainty only a four-year-old can muster. "My name is Bubula."

Miss Bergman's eyebrows performed an impressive gymnastics routine, first rising in surprise, then furrowing in confusion.

"But your registration form says Aaron."

"That's what they put on the paper," I conceded, "but everyone calls me Bubula."

"Bubula?" she repeated, the word sounding foreign and slightly dangerous on her lips, like she was ordering something questionable at a delicatessen.

"Yes. Bubula. That's my name."

I later learned that Miss Bergman had a fascinating conversation with my mother, who explained between nervous laughs that "Bubula" was a term of endearment, Yiddish for "darling" or "sweetheart," and not, in fact, my legal name.

By then it was too late. The damage was done. I had already begun my lifelong journey of correcting people's perceptions, a skill that would serve me well in both therapy sessions and movie production meetings.

Now at 74, I sometimes share this story at dinner parties, usually after the second glass of wine but before the inevitable discussion about real estate prices or colonoscopies. It's my way of saying, "Look, I came from love. I came from people who called me 'darling' so often I thought it was my name."

Which is, I suppose, not the worst inheritance for a neurotic Jewish boy from Brooklyn. Some people get trust funds. I got Bubula. And several decades of material.

Ice Skating

I was twelve years old when I decided to become a figure skater. Not in the traditional manner – with lessons, a coach, and incremental progress – but through sheer force of intellectual will. It was a Saturday evening like any other in our household; the family gathered around the television set, its blue glow illuminating passive faces. I, however, had other plans.

Earlier that day, I'd purchased a book on figure skating, complete with photographs of Olympic champions frozen in moments of grace – axels, lutzes, and camel spins captured in glossy black and white. While my parents and siblings absorbed whatever forgettable programming filled our living room that night, I retreated to my bedroom with my new treasure.

The hardwood floor of my bedroom became my personal rink. I studied each illustration with scholarly intensity, mimicking the positions with what I imagined was perfect form. Arms extended, one leg raised behind me – I was, in my mind, the very picture of balletic precision on ice. I practiced jumps from standing positions, landing with what I believed was textbook technique. I executed imaginary spins, my socked feet pivoting awkwardly on the wooden planks.

By bedtime, I had convinced myself that I possessed, if not mastery, then at least a comprehensive theoretical understanding of figure skating. The physical execution, I reasoned, would naturally follow from my intellectual preparation.

Sunday morning arrived with winter sunshine reflecting off the frozen pond in the park. I laced up the skates I'd borrowed from a neighbor and stepped onto the ice with the confidence of the self-taught prodigy I imagined myself to be. My first attempt at a jump – perhaps a single axel, though memory has mercifully blurred the specifics – ended with a spectacular introduction of my posterior to the unforgiving ice. The second attempt produced identical results, as did the third, and the fourth, until a pattern emerged that even my twelve-year-old ego could not ignore.

The day passed in a series of falls, each one a rebuke to my bookish preparation. By afternoon, I was soaked, bruised, and humbled. The distance between knowing and doing had never been so painfully evident.

Now, five decades later, as I prepare for my cardiology recertification exam, I find myself revisiting this lesson. The study materials present medicine as a series of algorithms: If A, then B; if B, then C. The patient presents with symptom X, order test Y, prescribe medication Z. Cookbook medicine, we call it – a recipe for patient care that, while not incorrect, fails to capture the art that accompanies the science.

Just as my childhood self-believed that studying pictures could translate to skating prowess, there exists in medicine the temptation to reduce complex human pathology to flowcharts and decision trees. But the patient, like the ice, has a way of humbling those who rely too heavily on theoretical knowledge.

Every cardiologist knows that moment when the textbook must be set aside, when the algorithm fails to account for the peculiarities of the human heart – both literally and figuratively – before them. It is in these moments that experience, intuition, and the accumulated wisdom of countless patient encounters guide our hands where guidelines cannot reach.

I passed my recertification exam, of course. The algorithms were dutifully memorized, the proper responses checked. But as I return to my practice, I carry with me the memory of that Sunday morning on the ice – a reminder that expertise is not found in books alone, but in the bruises earned through practice, the humility gained through failure, and the wisdom that comes from recognizing the difference between knowing and doing.

Notes from the Early Days

I find myself, on occasion, reviewing old notebooks. It's a habit developed over decades of medical practice – a quiet cataloging of cases, observations, and the occasional philosophical musing that strikes a physician who has seen too much of life and death to take either for granted. Today, leafing through a journal from March 2020, I encountered notes about the beginning of what we did not yet realize would transform our world.

The entry concerns a patient who had, over the years, become something of a friend. The sort of relationship that develops when you've monitored a man's heartbeat for over a decade, when you've seen him through one cardiac event and the subsequent years of recovery. He had suffered a heart attack some ten years prior to what I was now recording.

Nine days before his death – how clinical that phrase sounds in retrospect – he developed a fever. Following the protocols we were establishing hourly in those uncertain days, I advised him to stay home and rest. Seven days before the end, he reported shortness of breath. Hospital admission followed promptly. Then, just a day before I made my entry, his condition deteriorated significantly. Intubation became necessary.

Nine days from first symptom to death. The mathematics of this new disease were merciless and mysterious.

His wife – I recall her voice on the telephone, remarkably steady – could not be at his bedside. None of us understood enough then to know if this prohibition was excessive or insufficient. She said her goodbyes via FaceTime, that most improbable of funerary tools. Their children were scattered across the country, unable to travel as the nation ground to a halt. I called her after it was over. The burial would be immediate, minimal. "The love of my life is gone," she told me, "and this business of COVID won't even let me mourn him properly."

I've long been fascinated by the butterfly effect – that poetic notion from chaos theory suggesting a butterfly's wings flapping in China might alter weather patterns in Argentina. I had always interpreted this concept optimistically, evidence that our human and planetary equilibrium were delicately, beautifully synchronized. The interconnectedness of all things seemed a comfort rather than a threat.

Now the smallest of things – a virus invisible to the naked eye – had demonstrated this interconnection with brutal efficiency. Instead of changed weather patterns, we witnessed human death and economic devastation rippling outward from patient zero, wherever that unfortunate soul had been.

Five years later, the digital ghosts of the pandemic still haunt us. Just yesterday, Facebook cheerfully announced the birthday of one of our computer specialists who died during those dark months. The algorithm, oblivious to human tragedy, continues its programmed functions.

This digital persistence reminded me of something I'd read about Israeli soldiers being forbidden from carrying cell phones into combat zones. After bombing attacks, the bodies of the fallen would ring incessantly as desperate families called, hoping against hope to reach their loved ones. The image of those ringing phones amid the silent dead seems an apt metaphor for our time – technology connecting us across distances while simultaneously highlighting the unbridgeable gap between the living and the dead.

I close my notebook, having had enough musing for one day. Tomorrow brings new patients, new challenges. The practice of medicine continues, changed irrevocably by what we've learned, haunted by what we still don't know.

The Congressional Page

I had not expected to see him again after all these years. Twenty years, to be precise. In the psychological profession, one becomes accustomed to the revolving door of human suffering – faces appear, stories unfold, progress occurs (or doesn't), and then life moves on. Most patients fade into the blur of professional memory.

But this one I remembered. Not because his problems were particularly unusual – the standard midlife anxieties, career disappointments, marital tensions that fill the appointment books of practitioners from Hoboken to Malibu. No, what I remembered about him was his son, or rather, the way he spoke about his son.

The boy had been selected as a congressional page in Washington. How many fathers from our modest New Jersey suburb could claim such a distinction for their offspring? He had mentioned it during our very first session, and it became a leitmotif of our subsequent meetings. "My son, the congressional page," he would say, working it into conversations about entirely unrelated matters. The congressmen the boy had met, the political luminaries whose coffee he had fetched, the inner workings of government he had witnessed – these accounts flowed endlessly, polished by repetition.

I admit I found it fascinating. The halls of Congress were as remote from my consultation room as the palace at Versailles. I had never met a congressional page, nor the parent of one. His pride was palpable, almost uncomfortable in its intensity, yet I understood. In the quotidian disappointments of middle age, his son's achievement shone like a beacon.

And now here he was again, settling into the same chair where he had once regaled me with tales of his son's Washington adventures. Older, grayer, but instantly recognizable. The receptionist had brought in his chart, but I hardly needed it.

"How is your son?" I asked, after we had exchanged the necessary pleasantries. "The congressional page?"

There was a silence, longer than is customary even in a therapist's office where silences are professional currency. His face remained impassive, yet seemed to collapse inward in some subtle way I cannot precisely describe.

"My son is dead," he said finally, the words emerging with deliberate slowness.

"How?" The question escaped before professional discretion could intervene.

"HIV AIDS" he said. Then, after another pause: "They hurt him in Washington."

The last five words hung in the air between us like something physical. They hurt him in Washington. A sentence containing multitudes – of accusation, of grief, of a father's impotent rage against forces too large and impersonal to confront directly.

I said nothing. There are moments when the therapist's celebrated toolkit – interpretation, reflection, gentle redirection – seems like so many children's toys in the face of genuine human devastation. This was such a moment.

Outside my window, suburban life continued its ordered patterns. A mail carrier moved from house to house. Someone walked a dog. But in my office, time had stopped, captured in amber by those five stark words.

Seeds of Influence

After forty-three years in medicine, I sometimes find myself contemplating not the patients I've treated – though there have been thousands – but rather those individuals who shaped my approach to the profession. We doctors rarely discuss this aspect of our careers, preferring instead to focus on outcomes, procedures, and the ever-expanding body of research that demands our attention. Yet the question of influence seems increasingly relevant as I approach the twilight of my practice.

One name surfaces with particular clarity: Dr. Daniel Levin.

I encountered Dr. Levin during my studies at Chicago Medical School in the late 1970s. Five of us students were assigned to him for our pediatric rotation, an arrangement that, in retrospect, proved fortuitous beyond measure. Unlike other clinical instructors who confined their teaching to hospital corridors and classroom discussions, Dr. Levin invited us into the fullness of his professional life.

"Medicine," he would say in his accented English, "is not practiced in textbooks."

This philosophy manifested in his habit of loading us into his aging Oldsmobile – all five students crammed into the back seat, our knees touching, white coats rumpled – and driving us between his various obligations: his private practice in an unremarkable brick building on the North Side, his hospital rounds at Mount Sinai, and occasionally to house calls that had become anachronistic even then.

Dr. Levin was beloved by his patients, a fact evident in the small gifts that accumulated on his office shelves: hand-knitted items, framed children's drawings, and the occasional bottle of wine. Parents trusted him implicitly, and children, despite their natural wariness of physicians, would brighten at his entrance.

What made Dr. Levin particularly intriguing was his background, which he referenced occasionally but never dwelled upon. He was an Israeli who had fought in the 1948 War of Independence – not as a physician but as a young soldier in one of the paramilitary organizations that preceded the formal establishment of the Israel Defense Forces. Whether it was the Haganah, Irgun, or Stern Gang, I cannot recall with certainty; Dr. Levin himself seemed reluctant to elaborate on this chapter of his life.

After the war, he immigrated to America, completed his medical training, and established himself in Chicago, where he married Sarah, a nurse he met at Mount Sinai Hospital. Their union produced three sons whom I glimpsed only briefly when Sarah brought them to the office one afternoon – small, dark-haired boys with their father's intense eyes.

The rotation ended, as all rotations do, and I moved on through my medical education, carrying Dr. Levin's example with me: his attentiveness to patients, his insistence on understanding the family context of illness, his gentle but firm manner. These qualities became touchstones in my own practice, though I doubt I ever mentioned his name to colleagues. Our influences, like our doubts, are often kept private in the medical profession.

Nearly thirty years later, while scanning The New York Times one Sunday morning, I was arrested by a feature article about three remarkably successful brothers. The piece detailed their disparate but equally impressive careers: one a renowned medical ethicist advising presidents on healthcare policy, another a political powerhouse who had served in the Clinton administration and later became mayor of

Chicago, and the third a Hollywood agent of such influence that his name had become synonymous with the entertainment industry's highest echelons.

What caught my attention, however, was not their achievements but their surname: Levin. The article credited their father, Dr. Daniel Levin, with instilling in them an uncompromising work ethic and intellectual curiosity. A photograph accompanied the text – an older version of the man I had known, surrounded by his accomplished sons.

Curiosity led me to research the family further. I found interviews where the brothers mentioned their father's experience in Israel's founding war, his immigration to America in pursuit of medical training, his dedication to his Chicago practice. These fragments aligned perfectly with the Dr. Levin I had known, confirming that my mentor had indeed fathered this remarkable trio.

Five years after this discovery, I returned to my undergraduate alma mater in upstate New York for an alumni weekend. The program included a seminar on medical ethics featuring, as keynote speaker, Dr. Levin's eldest son, the bioethicist. After his lecture – a thoughtful examination of resource allocation in modern healthcare – I approached him, introduced myself, and shared memories of afternoons spent in the back of his father's Oldsmobile.

"He was an exceptional teacher," I told him, "and an inspiration to me throughout my career."

The son smiled with evident pleasure. "He would have appreciated hearing that. He always said his students were extensions of his practice."

I presented him with a copy of a book I had written on the history of Jewish physicians during the Renaissance and their contributions to medical ethics – a subject that, I explained, had interested me since observing his father's practice.

As we parted, I reflected on the curious geometry of influence: how Dr. Levin had shaped not only his sons' trajectories but, in some measure, my own. And how, through his sons' work in healthcare policy, politics, and entertainment, and through the care I have provided to my own patients over four decades, his influence has radiated outward, touching lives he never knew.

We rarely consider, when teaching medical students or treating patients, the potential reach of our actions. Yet Dr. Daniel Levin – immigrant, soldier, healer, father – planted seeds of influence that continue to bear fruit long after his rounds have ended. In my remaining years of practice, I can only hope to cultivate a fraction of what he sowed so effortlessly, perhaps passing along to others what he once gave to me: not merely knowledge of medicine, but an understanding of its deeper purpose.

The Dentist's Reunion

A very successful dentist came into my examining room. He was visibly distraught, his normally composed demeanor replaced by something resembling the anxious fidgeting of a patient awaiting the drill.

"What's troubling you?" I inquired, setting aside my clipboard.

He sighed deeply, settling into the chair not as the confident professional I knew him to be, but as a man burdened. He told me he had recently attended his high school reunion, his wife accompanying him. An evening meant for nostalgic celebration had somehow ended in domestic discord.

"My wife," he said, "is furious with me." He removed his glasses and pinched the bridge of his nose. "She observed something about me I hadn't realized myself."

It seems that when his former classmates – now balding, paunchy captains of various modest industries – began their good-natured ribbing, something curious happened. These men, whom time had transformed into unremarkable middle-aged specimens, still wielded a peculiar power over our accomplished dentist. With surgical precision, they located old wounds, extracting from him not teeth but dignity.

"She said to me afterward, 'I thought all that was decades behind you,'" he continued. "'How could you become their punching boy again in an instant? Everything you've built, everything you've become – and the moment they started in with their tired routines, you reverted to that insecure teenager.'"

The dentist looked at me, his expression a complex mixture of revelation and shame. "The worst part is, she's absolutely right. I didn't even notice the transformation. One moment I was Dr. Charles Westfield, respected periodontist with three offices across the city, and the next I was skinny Charlie with the prominent Adam's apple, desperate for their approval."

I nodded, recognizing in his story something universally human. No matter how extensively we renovate the architecture of our adult selves, the original blueprint remains, ready to reassert itself when the proper code is entered.

"That's why I'm upset," he concluded. "I've spent thirty years believing I had outgrown that boy. Turns out I've merely been renting space from him all along."

Interesting. We craft these elaborate adult identities, convinced we've left our former selves behind. Yet perhaps we never truly escape them. They remain dormant within us, waiting patiently for the right impetus – a familiar voice, a knowing glance, an old nickname – to reclaim possession of the premises we thought we owned.

The Stock Market and My Father

I'm seventy-four and thinking about my father today as the stock market crashes. The futures were down 1500 points this morning – a sight I've never witnessed before, even though decades of watching markets rise and fall. This dramatic plunge, triggered by Trump's new tariffs, stirs memories of my father that I haven't examined in years.

My father arrived in America in 1921, having been born in 1908. He began as a jeweler, but when the Depression made that profession untenable, he pivoted to owning Jewish bakeries in Connecticut and Pennsylvania. Those bakeries became the family's salvation. My older sisters tell me he carried customers on the books for pennies they owed him – eight cents here, nine cents there – gestures of kindness during desperate times.

But what I remember most vividly wasn't the bakeries. It was the stock market – that invisible, omnipresent force that functioned almost as a second parent in our household. The market's daily movements dictated our family's emotional weather: sunshine when stocks climbed, storms when they fell. I knew stock names like other children knew baseball players: IT&T, General Telephone, and Syntex. These companies were characters in our family drama.

Throughout my childhood, my father spoke of the market with a peculiar personification. When stocks rose or fell, he would attribute these movements to "they."

"They're pushing it up today," he'd announce with satisfaction when his investments gained value.

"They're pushing it down," he'd mutter darkly on bad days.

When I asked him who "they" were, he'd look at me as though I'd asked something both obvious and profound. "The big boys," he'd say, tapping his finger against the financial pages. "Always the big boys." There was something both respectful and adversarial in his tone – as though he simultaneously admired these faceless power brokers and saw himself locked in an eternal contest against them. He was determined, in his small way, to outsmart "the big boys" at their own game. This narrative gave meaning to his daily scrutiny of stock tables, his frequent calls to brokers, his careful calibrations of buying and selling.

I remember when I got my first tape recorder at around ten years old. I'd carry it around the house, capturing family moments and conversations. One evening, my father was poring over stock listings at the kitchen table, and I set the recorder beside him.

"What's going to happen with New York Central?" I asked, not because I cared about the railroad stock, but because I wanted to document his predictions.

He looked up, momentarily startled by the microphone, and then smiled. "When New York Central hits 40," he declared with magnificent confidence, "we'll go to Europe – Paris! I'll take the whole family." Then he added, with a mischievous glance toward the living room where my mother sat, "And if your mother doesn't want to go – well, I'll go myself!"

That recording became a family treasure. For the next decade, we'd replay it at gatherings, all of us laughing – even my mother, who recognized the gentle tease about her occasional recalcitrance. That tape probably still exists somewhere, tucked away in a box of memorabilia, preserving my father's voice and his magnificent dreams. But more than preserving his words, that recording captured how completely he had structured his existence around the market's promise – how he envisioned not just wealth but experiences, adventures, and family moments all flowing from the right stock hitting the right number at the right time.

In 1961, when I was ten, the market crashed. I couldn't attend sleep-away camp that summer – not that I particularly minded – but the $600 fee had suddenly become impossible. I remember margin calls taped to our front door, messengers of doom that made my stomach tighten. Every evening, my father would be on the phone with his broker, their hushed, urgent conversations carrying through our New Jersey home like prayers or curses.

When he eventually sold the bakery, my father became a stockbroker himself. He was brilliant at it, especially with options just emerging as a financial instrument. When I started my medical practice, I entrusted him with $50,000, which he quickly turned into $300,000. But then came 1987 and the great panic. I managed to sell everything just before the crash, reclaiming my initial investment, but my father and his clients rode the roller coaster down. At seventy-nine, he lost everything – his savings, his confidence, his purpose.

He couldn't execute trades fast enough as the market plummeted. This wasn't just a financial catastrophe; it was an identity crisis. The market had been his obsession, his craft, and his contribution to the world. When it betrayed him, he sank into a depression from which he never fully recovered. My brother-in-law and I bailed him out, settling a lawsuit over discrepancies in his portfolio that had driven him into negative territory.

Throughout my life, I've experienced the market's volatility – its soaring heights and stomach-churning descents. Five years ago, I nearly cashed out investments worth millions, but the broker couldn't process the transaction until the end of the business day. In my frustration, I abandoned the plan. The market subsequently boomed, climbing 30% from there. I was wrong then. Perhaps I'm wrong now too.

There's strange comfort in collective trouble. If everyone's portfolio is shrinking, mine doesn't feel so personally tragic. My sisters called this weekend, cursing politics and lamenting their diminished net worth. I shrugged outwardly but feel the inner turbulence. Still, this isn't really my money – it's wealth that will eventually be inherited by others.

What does it all mean? Is the drive to invest and accumulate wealth simply human instinct? Is the desire to ride economic peaks and troughs embedded in our nature? I don't have answers. But I know that as I watched the futures plummet this morning, I thought about my father – thought about him very hard. I remembered being eleven years old, staring at margin calls stapled to our door, feeling the weight of financial anxiety that would become a familiar presence throughout my life.

The market will likely recover as it always has. But today, as we face another crash, I can't help but see my father's face, pinched with worry yet still determined, still believing in the American promise that brought him to these shores. For better or worse, his relationship with the market shaped mine, linking us across time through the mysterious rhythms of economics that neither of us ever fully understood. And sometimes, in moments of market volatility, I find myself unconsciously echoing his words: "They're pushing it down today. The big boys are at it again."

The Lesson

There it was again, that Nietzschean phrase echoing in Dr. Levinson's mind as he scribbled notes in the patient chart: "What doesn't kill you makes you stronger." The phrase had come up during his afternoon appointment with Gennaro, a sixty-five-year-old furniture mover from Hazlet with remarkably good stress test results and an even more remarkable life philosophy.

Gennaro had sat in the examination room, his broad shoulders and calloused hands testimony to decades of hauling dressers and armoires up narrow staircases. "Every day is a stress test for me, Doc," he'd said with a laugh that shook his still-solid frame. "I outwork guys half my age. They call me crazy, but I call it living."

When Levinson had inquired about his background, Gennaro mentioned twelve years in the Marines with the casual air of someone referencing a previous address. The conversation had turned to boot camp, and Levinson – whose knowledge of military training came entirely from films – asked if it was truly as brutal as Hollywood portrayed it.

"Worse," Gennaro had replied, his face momentarily darkening. "Had a drill instructor who'd make us carry ten-gallon water jugs, arms extended, up and down steps. Twenty times. Then when we'd finally reach the top, gasping for breath, he'd kick us in the stomach, send us tumbling back down."

Levinson had winced. "Did you hate him?"

"At first, sure. But by the end?" Gennaro's eyes had softened. "Respected him. Even loved him, in a way. Man made me who I am."

"Like Nietzsche said," Levinson had offered, "What doesn't kill you..."

"...makes you stronger," Gennaro had finished with a knowing nod.

Now, sitting alone in his office, Levinson rolled the phrase around in his mind like a familiar stone. It had first entered his consciousness decades earlier, from the lips of Rachel Goldberg, a precocious girl with horn-rimmed glasses and a formidable knowledge of German philosophy that had both attracted and intimidated him during his sophomore year at Rutgers.

When she'd ended their brief romance, she'd offered those words as a parting gift: "David, what doesn't kill you makes you stronger." He'd stood there on the brick walkway outside the library, heart splintering, as she'd adjusted her bookbag and walked away.

The irony was, she'd been right. That first serious rejection had indeed strengthened him, preparing him for the subsequent heartbreaks that would eventually lead him to Sarah, his wife of twenty-seven years. Just as the punishing nights as a medical resident – the seventy-two-hour shifts, the impossible decisions made through a fog of exhaustion – had forged him into the physician he was today.

Levinson closed the patient file and glanced at the framed medical license on his wall. The certificate bore his name in elaborate calligraphy, but it might as well have listed all those who had shaped him through their demands and disappointments: the Marine who'd found strength in brutality, the intellectual girl who'd delivered wisdom with rejection, and the attending physicians who'd pushed him beyond reasonable limits.

Outside his window, the late afternoon sun cast long shadows across the medical center's parking lot. Another day of examining the hearts of others while contemplating his own. He gathered his things, thinking that perhaps tonight he would tell Sarah about Gennaro, about Rachel Goldberg, about how we are all, in our way, carrying heavy things up difficult stairs, becoming stronger with each painful step.

The Patient

In 1982, in a small medical office in Hackensack, New Jersey – one of those places where the linoleum floor had begun to curl slightly at the edges and the magazines in the waiting room were invariably three months out of date – I first encountered Mr. Goldstein. I was thirty-two then, fresh enough in my practice still to believe that a doctor's white coat conferred not merely authority but a certain wisdom.

Mr. Goldstein was fifty-five. Though merely at middle age, to my youthful eyes, he appeared weathered and worn, a man who seemed to have already traveled far along life's journey. His hands moved deliberately as he unbuttoned his shirt, revealing a chest that showed the first telltale signs of time's passage. I recall thinking, with the casual presumption of youth that his best years were certainly behind him.

"My father died at sixty-two," he told me then, his voice carrying a gravity that belied his relatively young age. "My grandfather at fifty-eight. I'm closing in on the family record." He said this not with fear but with a kind of stoic acceptance, as if discussing the weather forecast rather than the potential parameters of his existence.

What does one say to that? In medical school, they teach you about the pancreas and the pituitary, about dosages and contraindications, but they offer no instruction on how to respond when a patient presents you with the poetry of his survival.

Thirty-four years have passed. I am now sixty-six, eleven years older than Mr. Goldstein was when I first examined him. I've acquired reading glasses, a slight stoop, and the habit of forgetting names at parties. My own youth feels like a country I once visited but can no longer find on any map.

And Mr. Goldstein? He is seventy-nine and still among us. In the intervening years, he has endured two cancer surgeries, three heart procedures – both bypass and valve – and most recently, the installation of a pacemaker. His body has become a testament to modern medicine's refusal to accept the traditional boundaries of life and death, a canvas upon which surgeons have painted their determination.

When he visited my office last week, moving deliberately but with a surprising vigor, I found myself thinking not of ancient creatures but of certain oak trees – not the oldest in the forest, perhaps, but those that have weathered countless storms and emerged still standing, their roots somehow deeper for the challenge.

"You know," he said to me, settling onto the examination table, the paper crinkling beneath him, "I never thought I'd make it this far. Now I'm thinking about what the next decade might bring."

I nodded, but what I was thinking was this: when I first examined him, I had been so certain about everything – about his imminent demise, about my own boundless future, about the clear demarcation between youth and age. Now I understand that time makes fools of us all, but especially of doctors who presume to predict its effects.

Mr. Goldstein has become, without intending to, one of my great teachers. He has taught me not about medicine – though his resilience has certainly provided lessons there – but about the dangers of assumptions, about the folly of certainty, about the strange mathematics of mortality.

"See you in six months," I told him as he left.

"God willing," he replied, with the faintest hint of a smile, acknowledging the joke that time had played on both of us.

A Call from an Old Friend

The telephone rang yesterday afternoon, just as I was settling into my chair with the latest issue of *Commentary*. It was Bob Goldstein, my college roommate from more than half a century ago. We shared quarters at the University of Chicago in the early 1970s – he immersed in organic chemistry while I struggled through Aristotle's *Nicomachean Ethics*. Now, at seventy-four, we find ourselves in that peculiar stage of life where conversations inevitably drift toward laboratory results and medical prognoses.

"How are your numbers?" he asked after we exchanged pleasantries, a question that would have been incomprehensible to our younger selves. Now it stands as the secret handshake of the septuagenarian set.

Bob proceeded to detail his latest blood work with the precision one might expect from a cardiologist who has spent decades interpreting such data. Cholesterol, triglycerides, PSA – acronyms that have become as familiar to men our age as ERA and RBI were in our youth. I listened and offered appropriate murmurs of concern or relief as the values warranted.

"They found something on the scan," he said, his voice carrying that studied neutrality physicians develop when discussing worrisome findings. He wanted my opinion, though I suspect what he truly sought was reassurance – that commodity which grows increasingly precious as we age.

Our conversation meandered, as conversations between old friends do, from the clinical to the philosophical. We spoke of mutual acquaintances, some thriving, others less fortunate. We reminisced about our fiftieth college reunion two years ago, where we posed for photographs beneath the same Gothic arches that had witnessed our youthful indiscretions and intellectual awakenings.

Our conversation turned to mortality, the subject that hovers at the edges of all dialogue between men our age.

"Have you ever considered Einstein's approach to death?" Bob asked, his voice thoughtful.

Later that evening, an email arrived from Bob containing a quote attributed to Einstein. The great physicist, upon learning of the aortic aneurysm that would eventually claim his life, reportedly refused surgery, saying: "I want to go when I want to go. It is tasteless to prolong life artificially. I have done my share. It is time to go."

Bob's accompanying note indicated that Einstein's philosophical resignation was worthy of contemplation. But I found myself considering a different angle, one that speaks to the remarkable progression of medical science during our lifetime.

When Einstein confronted his diagnosis in the 1950s, an aortic aneurysm was essentially a death sentence – a ticking bomb within the body that modern medicine could neither defuse nor remove. The primitive surgical techniques of the era carried mortality rates so high that a reasoned rejection of intervention wasn't merely philosophical – it was practical. Einstein's stoicism, I realized, wasn't merely a choice but a necessity born of his circumstances. He was forced to develop this philosophy because he lived with the certainty of sudden death, never knowing when the aneurysm might rupture. His existential stance was not an abstract intellectual exercise but a vital psychological adaptation to living with mortal terror – the only way to face each day while carrying the knowledge of an unstoppable catastrophe within.

How different things are today. The same condition that forced Einstein to contemplate his mortality with stoic resignation is now often addressed through minimally invasive procedures, sometimes requiring no overnight hospital stay. What was once inevitable is now merely inconvenient.

I wonder how Einstein's reflections on mortality might have differed had he lived in our era. Would he have still found it "tasteless to prolong life artificially" if the intervention were as routine as cataract surgery? Would he have still felt it was "time to go" if continuing meant the possibility of additional years of productive thought?

These are the questions that occupy me as I reach the age where actuarial tables become less abstract and more personal. One might argue that our generation has been granted a reprieve that Einstein's did not enjoy – the luxury of deferring philosophical resignation in favor of practical intervention.

Yet I suspect Einstein's words contain wisdom independent of medical context. There comes a point – different for each of us, perhaps – when we must acknowledge that we have, indeed, "done our share." The question is whether that realization should coincide with our biological capacity to continue.

Bob and I didn't resolve this question during our call. How could we? We are still amid the experiment, still collecting data. We agreed to meet for lunch next month at the faculty club, where we'll continue the conversation amid the portraits of distinguished scholars who have already determined their own answers.

Until then, I'll keep taking my statins and checking my numbers, grateful for the reprieve that modern medicine has granted, yet mindful that even reprieves have their limits.

Massachusetts Mani

He came in with his mother, this young man of twenty-three. Palpitations, he said. I listened to his heart, examined him thoroughly, found nothing amiss. Anxiety, I told him. Not uncommon for someone his age.

"What do you do?" I asked, making conversation while updating his chart.

"I'm on social media," he said, his voice soft, almost apologetic. "I have about eight million followers."

I nodded absently, pen scratching against paper. Eight million – the number registered dimly at first. Then Sandra, my receptionist, appeared in the doorway, her eyes wide.

"You're Mass Mani," she said. "The one who dances with goats."

The boy – because despite his age he seemed still a boy – smiled shyly. His mother beamed beside him.

Within minutes, my orderly office dissolved into chaos. Staff appeared from every corner of the clinic. The phlebotomist, the x-ray technician, nurses from the second floor. They crowded in the doorway, phones raised.

"Could I get a selfie?" "My daughter loves your chicken dance!" "Is it true you have a pet goat now?"

Massachusetts Mani – this child who danced with barnyard animals and broadcast it to millions – transformed my medical practice into a mob scene. I stood against the wall, chart clutched to my chest, watching as this slender boy with anxiety became something else entirely: an icon, a celebrity, a vessel for whatever it is we worship now.

Later, alone in my office, I thought about fame in this strange new world we've built. How a boy dancing with goats commands more attention than all my years of medical expertise. How eight million people watch his movements while patients wait weeks for appointments with specialists.

What is it they see in him, I wondered, that they don't see in themselves?

A Physician's Notebook: Collected Observations

They come to me in white examination rooms, under fluorescent lights that do no favors to anyone's complexion. Patients, with their bodies that betray them and their stories that sustain them. For thirty-odd years I've practiced medicine in New Jersey, that much-maligned state that nonetheless seems to produce an inordinate number of philosophers disguised as ordinary people. I've developed the habit of jotting down their utterances – brief encounters that linger long after prescription pads are torn and vitals are recorded.

What follows is a collection of these notations, these fragments of humanity offered up between blood pressure readings and referral forms. Together they form a kind of accidental anthology of wisdom, humor, and that particular poignancy that comes when mortality pulls up a chair and makes itself comfortable in the examination room.

A seventy-eight-year-old man told me about attending a show in Lancaster, Pennsylvania. "Doc, there was stadium seating only. I felt for all those old people." The irony that he excluded himself from this geriatric contingent seemed lost on him entirely, though I noticed he gripped the arms of my office chair with spotted hands as he rose to leave.

An elderly patient with a dream of remarkable persistence: "Last night, I dreamed about a girl I saw fifty-four years ago. I experienced the same emotion that happened when I was fourteen. She was so pretty. And still unobtainable." Go figure – the heart preserves what the mind should have composted decades ago.

The democracy of travel never ceases to amaze. Every other patient has just returned from or is planning a Mediterranean cruise. "We go to Europe every year," one patient boasted. Meanwhile, my lowest-paid employee announced she was off to Italy: "Got a deal on the airfare. It's cheaper than going down the shore." The world has become astonishingly small, though our capacity for wonder remains stubbornly provincial.

A patient who had been administered anesthesia before cardioversion muttered drowsily that she wished to "meet the Cabana boy" in her dreams. "He's the one whose fantasies always bring me what I desire." A strange request before a medical procedure, but who among us wouldn't prefer to drift into unconsciousness on a pleasant fantasy rather than the sterile reality of a hospital ceiling?

One patient with a broken wrist related his wife's concern about the orthopedist's choice of cast. "Do you think there's a difference between a cast below the thumb and one that includes the thumb?" he asked. I told him the unvarnished truth: "The difference is you can only wipe your ass when it's below the thumb." Medicine occasionally requires brutal honesty in matters of basic hygiene.

My colleague was insufferably proud of sending his ninety-one-year-old patient for an abdominal aneurysm stent. She survived, against considerable odds. When I saw her the following week and congratulated her on this curative miracle, she fixed me with rheumy eyes and said, "You should have let me die. It was time." Physicians are trained to extend life, but not always to recognize when we should step aside and let nature conclude its business.

"Doc, how are you?" a patient inquired politely.

"I am getting old," I admitted.

"Doc," he replied, "only lucky people get to say that."

I have seen the curious alchemy of grief transform the past. One woman wished her husband dead for years, describing him as "the worst, an evil husband ever." Now that he has died, she is hysterical with loss. "He was so wonderful," she insists, tears streaming. Memory performs its own plastic surgery, smoothing the rough edges of the departed.

A photographer who specializes in touching up commercial advertising and magazine portraits confided the melancholy aspect of his profession: "The saddest part of my job is when I touch up actresses on magazine covers. Now nothing is real. The poor little girls who idolize these stars are looking at pure fantasy no one can ever live up to." He told me this shortly after his wife died, while we discussed the widow-vultures circling his newfound eligibility. Reality and fiction, it seems, are perpetually misaligned.

A patient called in a panic: "Doc, I am so nervous. I have two dates and I am apprehensive. I am getting prepared." I offered Viagra samples to help with his anxiety, at which point he clarified: "Doc, for what? I have two dates for cataract surgery." The misunderstandings between physician and patient can be as revealing as they are humorous.

There is profound wisdom in the observation of one woman facing a difficult diagnosis: "One minute, you're a peacock, and the next minute, you're a feather duster." I have seen no better encapsulation of life's capricious reversals.

A patient visits his father's grave daily, placing a cigarette butt on the ground with each visit "so that my father knows I was there." This ritual – touching in its simplicity – exists alongside his struggle with multiple skin cancers requiring operations, chemotherapy, and radiation. He blames his condition on Bradley Beach, New Jersey, where he spent weekends for sixty-two summers. Life exacts its toll on pleasures eventually.

A wrestling coach once told a patient of mine: "Get off the team. You can't make chicken salad out of chicken shit." The patient shared this as a joke, but such casual cruelties often lodge themselves permanently in the psyche, quoted decades later in examination rooms to physicians who serve as inadvertent confessors.

I observe certain patterns. You tell some patients they've stubbed their toe, and they'll worry about that toe for the rest of their lives. Tell others they may have cancer, and by the next appointment, they've forgotten you mentioned it. The capacity for denial and catastrophizing seems distributed without logic or fairness.

"Never waste an erection," an elderly gentleman advised me solemnly. "You never know when it's your last." This wisdom, delivered as I was leaving the examination room, struck me as applicable to more than just matters of virility. Time, love, courage – all are finite resources not to be squandered.

Facebook, that digital agora of our age, makes its presence felt even in medicine. A patient befriended me there and later messaged about suicidal intentions. I called him and an ambulance; he was admitted to the psychiatric ward. Thus, Mark Zuckerberg's empire saved a life, an accomplishment I doubt was envisioned in the company's founding mission.

Another Facebook miracle: a ninety-year-old man heading to Las Vegas asked for Viagra samples. When I inquired about his plans, expecting talk of gambling and entertainment, he replied, "Doc, I'm getting married to my grammar school sweetheart from seventy years ago. Have thought about her all these years. Found her this year on Facebook." Social media, it seems, enables reunions across decades that were once impossible.

The same platform delivers tragedy with equal efficiency. A wife's posts: "Enjoying a Caribbean cruise." Five days later: "He is in hospice." Two hours after that: "He just passed." The digital chronicle of a life's sudden end, delivered in staccato updates between vacation photos.

I told a very old patient he should no longer shovel snow. His disappointment was palpable: "Doc, I am very unhappy. I do my best praying while shoveling alone in the quiet." Who am I to come between a man and his method of communion?

An Alzheimer's patient had what he considered a revelation: "Doc, there's a problem with my butt. I have a hole and a crack there. Please help me." The same man has survived two cardiac bypass surgeries, a new aortic valve, prostate cancer, colon cancer, a large skin cancer, a ruptured gallbladder, a pacemaker, and a mini-pacemaker replacement. At ninety-one, he asks me, "Doc, why am I so tired?" The human capacity for understatement can be remarkable.

A nun visiting with her anxious sister offered this wisdom: "I tell her worrying is like sitting in a rocking chair. You rock and rock and go nowhere." The clergy occasionally dispense prescriptions more effective than anything in my pharmacopeia.

"I thought I was going to die in 1987," a patient reflected, "just before my cardiac bypass surgery. It's now thirty years later, and here I am. Go figure." The body's resilience remains the greatest mystery in medicine.

When I asked a ninety-year-old male if he enjoyed his six days on the beach, he replied, "This was the D-Day invasion, and it was Normandy Beach. Spent the first days picking up bodies." History occasionally walks into my examination room, wearing the bodies of ordinary men.

The bitter fights of an elderly Jewish couple had been the background music of their appointments for years. Imagine my surprise when the wife proudly displayed her cell phone: "Look. We just got remarried last month in Las Vegas. By Elvis. Here's the picture." Second acts are possible, even in marriages everyone assumed were terminally ill.

A woman with a terrible, aggressive brain tumor sat quietly in my office. We talked about coincidence – how she had met her husband decades ago at the same sleepaway camp my daughters attended. This man and his wife had sent birthday cards with twenty dollars to each of my daughters for twenty-eight consecutive years. Now he lay comatose on a respirator with a cerebral hemorrhage, waiting for hospice.

"Never take any peace of mind for granted," a patient told me a decade ago. "Out of the blue, God, nature, chance, or circumstances can and will throw you a blow. But just remember, these blows are certainly recoverable. You just stagger. Just remember to stagger, doc." I have thought of this advice often in my own moments of staggering.

A woman told me through tears about her grandson, a great high school athlete who suffered a sports injury playing football. He was given painkillers, became addicted, and died at twenty-three of an overdose. The casual prescriptions we write can cascade into tragedies we never imagined.

An old, very sick physician with congestive heart failure confided from his hospital bed that he wished he could trade places with his twenty-one-year-old granddaughter, recently diagnosed with T-cell lymphoma. Even in medicine, we who understand disease most intimately cannot shield our families from its reach.

"Don't worry, it's only my cancer that's vigorously coughing," a woman reassured the room as others drew back in concern about germs. Gallows humor is often the last defense of the seriously ill.

One patient compared flying private jets and using Viagra to smoking crack cocaine: "Of course, they're addictive." I marveled at the unlikely juxtaposition of transportation, pharmaceuticals, and illegal substances – the confessional nature of the examination room produces strange taxonomies.

A woman married thirteen years celebrated her husband's heart transplant anniversary: "He was on the transplant list for six hours, and we got a call that a heart was available. He is doing great. The heart belonged to a nineteen-year-old in a car accident. I really do believe in God." Faith flourishes in the borderlands between medical intervention and unexplainable good fortune.

A patient once told me that everything means something. Years later, she reminded me of this when recounting her former husband's episode of global amnesia. Though the neurologist assured them it "didn't mean anything," five years later, the man developed severe dementia. Medicine's casual dismissals often precede its humbling reckonings.

She is "so much happier," another patient reported about a widow. "It's almost inexplicable. Her husband has been dead two years, and the happiness is correlative to the death." Liberation sometimes wears the guise of bereavement.

A man burdened by multiple skin cancers requiring significant operations, chemotherapy, and radiation blames his condition on Bradley Beach, New Jersey, "where I went every weekend during the summer for sixty-two years." Our pleasures exact their tolls eventually.

A patient complains that her father-in-law suffers from "a strange dementia." In his late eighties, at family gatherings he walks around pinching the breasts of young girls. "The doctors all say it's dementia, a type of dementia, but I don't believe him," she says, seeking my opinion. Sometimes the line between pathology and depravity becomes conveniently blurred in old age.

These fragments I have shored against my ruins, to borrow from Eliot. They accumulate in examination rooms under fluorescent lights, between blood draws and prescription renewals. The poetry of ordinary lives, spoken by people who would never consider themselves poets. I collect these memos not because I fancy myself a writer, but because I have found, over decades of practice, that the truest wisdom rarely arrives in textbooks or medical journals. It comes in the offhand remarks of patients, thrown casually across the desk on otherwise unremarkable Tuesday afternoons.

A Physician's Notebook: Three Decades of Patient Encounters

One accumulates, over a medical career spanning three decades, not merely a collection of cases but a veritable anthology of the human condition. These fragments – too brief for proper stories, yet too resonant to discard – have resided in my notebooks, awaiting some purpose beyond my own recollection. Perhaps in their collective presentation, a portrait emerges not only of a practice but of our peculiar journey through illness, recovery, and mortality.

A man of sixty-two, impeccably dressed despite his hospital gown, complained, "Doctor, my wife snores terribly. We've had to sleep in separate bedrooms for years now." He paused, his expression softening into something between amusement and melancholy. "Who would have thought, thirty years ago when we met at a school dance, that our entire relationship would hinge on snoring?"

I attended a gentleman dying from a massive heart attack, who required stents, an aortic balloon pump, and a left ventricular assist device – the full arsenal of our technological interventions. Between labored breaths, he informed me that he was a Microsoft executive. "I know Bill Gates personally," he said. "Sometimes I play golf with Donald Trump." I nodded, thinking how, at this precarious moment, neither Gates nor Trump could save him. Only I might be able to, and even that prospect seemed increasingly doubtful. The mighty reduced to the merely mortal, awaiting salvation from a doctor.

A patient fell off a ladder, necessitating a CAT scan of his back. The scan incidentally revealed an early kidney cancer. Following its removal, he was fond of saying that his life was saved by his fall. I have often pondered how frequently catastrophe and salvation arrive in the same package.

"Has she fractured her ankle?" I inquired of the nurse.

The patient herself answered: "Frozen hot dogs fell out of the freezer when I opened the door. Landed right on my ankle." Then, with perfect deadpan delivery: "Never know, doc. Watch behind the door."

In thirty years, I've learned that household injuries often come with their own peculiar poetry.

A woman refused anesthesia for a minor procedure. "She thinks she knows everything," the nurse whispered to me. "She needed to be awake to tell the surgeon what to do." I have encountered no greater metaphor for the modern patient's relationship with medical authority.

A patient's granddaughter died last week in a car accident, age twenty-three. The patient told me she was comforted by the rabbi who told her that "this life is just a hallway to heaven." A hallway to heaven. I thought to myself, how does one find comfort if they aren't sure of the existence of God? Some questions medicine cannot answer.

I saw a patient in the brain trauma unit who woke from a mild stupor, smiled, laughed, and said, "Doc, no matter what happens, I will pay your bill." Even in our disorientation, we remember our obligations.

"Doctor, you gotta help me. I'm going to the funeral for my penis." This is a common complaint, in one way or another, though rarely expressed with such blunt poetry.

"Doc, forget women. Give me a car." The patient was eighty-four.

What was going on in her head just before? A twenty-five-year-old paramedic was found hanging from her bed canopy, her belt wrapped around her neck. She had been there for perhaps thirty minutes before being brought to the emergency room with no heartbeat or breath. The ER doctors worked on her and restored a heartbeat. In the intensive care unit, I examined the probably brain-dead young woman. Her mother wanted to know her daughter's chances. I keep thinking about what was going on in her daughter's mind just before.

This is the question that haunts me.

A beautiful twenty-year-old girl was admitted with bacteremia and fever. She described IV heroin use in the past, now on methadone – a narcotic substitute. She had suffered a stroke because of an infected valve that embolized, and she was waiting for her blood to be sterilized before surgery. The morning that surgery was planned, she was found unresponsive, not breathing, near death. A heroin syringe was found next to her IV antibiotic line – both lifesaving and deadly.

She was ninety-one, and I heard her Yiddish-Polish accent as we talked at her bedside. I asked if she had been in Poland during the war. "Yes," she said. "Ten of my eleven siblings were killed by Hitler. And I still believe in God." Her name was Raquiella. Some faith transcends understanding.

A patient with a mechanical prosthetic heart valve had vaginal bleeding. I refused to significantly reduce her anticoagulation because of stroke risk. I was adamant, though other doctors wished to stop it. The uterus had to be removed with a hysterectomy to stop the bleeding. She told me later that I had saved her life because the uterus was full of cancer. "After the bleeding had stopped, I never would have undergone a hysterectomy." I'm not sure about that logic, but I accepted the gratitude.

An Israeli patient said, "Doc, my brother in Israel just told me the trouble with the rockets. They are cramping his style. He can only visit two of his four girlfriends daily." Humor persists even in war zones.

An elderly lady, fifty-five, with a fifty-five-year-old son with Down syndrome: "Doctor, you must keep me alive. I'm living for my son. He is my treasure." The treasure, the Down syndrome son. I have never heard such pure love.

"Doc, am I permitted to take my medicines on Yom Kippur?" As if I am the arbiter of religious law rather than merely the prescriber of pills.

A patient took his father to France for the D-Day commemoration. His father had served in the U.S. Army during the invasion. "My father's tooth became loose, and we visited a local French dentist," the patient told me. "The dentist refused payment, thanking the American soldier for liberation." Some debts can never be repaid in currency.

A patient witnessed the bubonic plague in Dakar during World War II. "I saw many natives die in less than twenty-four hours," he told me, his eyes distant. History lives within our patients.

"Doc, never retire. My advice is, don't retire. It's like taking an endless boat cruise with your wife for the rest of your life." This from a man who had been married for fifty-two years.

"Last year, my sister, aged sixty-three, had a stem cell transplant for multiple myeloma. In the same year, her thirty-two-year-old son committed suicide. 'No meaning to it all,' she said. 'Life is not fair. There are no rules that we get, and we think we are entitled to.'" So if I learned this lesson, then: expectation, disappointment, lesson. Life is not fair, and really, no referees govern it except the natural laws. Life does not see your tears or hear your prayers. It also does not know laughter. My patient who survived her suicide attempt just told me this.

I examined a very attractive woman, a new patient, who said she was going through a recent divorce with much stress. I took an extensive medical history and learned that two years ago, she had stomach sleeve surgery to lose weight and help her diabetes. She had lost a hundred pounds in a year and a half. Her current weight was perfect. She said, "I guess my husband likes them large." The economics of attraction, it seems, can be as unpredictable as health.

"Doc, I just returned from Antarctica. The penguins really smell," a female patient told me. "I was with three other women, and I thought those three women were having their smelly menstrual days. I went around a bit and began to realize it was the penguin smell. Doc, don't go to Antarctica." The unexpected hazards of exotic travel.

He is seventy-one and told me he just set the world's record for speed in a pickup truck: a hundred and ninety-two miles per hour. I saw the written article and presentation. "So much for taking it easy with your heart condition," I remarked.

His mother sat in the corner, alternately crying that he might have to go to jail for reckless driving and vehicular manslaughter, and bragging about his huge classic car collection. "Money is no object with my son," she said, pride overcoming concern.

"Doc, I smoke two and a half packs a day. I spend $9,000 a year on cigarettes," a patient told me. "And that is after taxes," I replied. The economics of self-destruction.

A very holy and spiritual rabbi's wife developed breast cancer. He was so upset his wife just asked him, "Where is your faith now?" Faith, it seems, is more easily preached than practiced.

"I was a little child during World War II," a patient said. "And all I remember is my mother walking around the house all day for years with her rosary beads." She paused. "But all three of my brothers came home from the war." Perhaps prayer works after all.

Just heard from a patient, a theory of life: "How do you eat an elephant? One bite at a time." The key to moving forward and not stumbling is living with chaos, she said. I've heard worse philosophies from supposedly wiser sources.

I saw a patient today who wanted to go to New York for a special procedure. "We thought the care would be better," his wife explained. I told him healthcare is not like a beautiful watch. One bad link and the chain is useless. "So," I said, "That can happen also in New York." Geography is no guarantee of competence.

A patient told me yesterday an interesting parable attributed to King Solomon that I had never heard before. King Solomon had a ring designed to make him happy when he was sad and sad when he was happy. It was inscribed, "And this too shall pass." Ancient wisdom still applies to modern ailments.

A ninety-year-old patient just told me that she never cooked but was "good at other things," and then she gave me a big wink. Even in our final decades, we retain our essential selves.

An obese woman in the ICU had an equally large husband who pleaded, "Send my wife home as soon as possible. I can't sleep. We share a bed, and it feels empty." I asked how big their bed was. "Full size," he replied. "Queen is too big for us." These enormous people shared a modest bed, pressing against each other through the nights. Such is the geometry of marriage.

I said hello to a nurse in the hall whom I hadn't seen in a while. "How are you?" I asked. She answered, "Okay. One day at a time." I immediately knew what she meant. Nothing more needed to be said. That phrase – "one day at a time" – implied volumes about struggle and persistence. I subsequently found out that she had breast cancer and was undergoing chemotherapy. Some diagnoses reduce life to its simplest increments.

A patient just said to me, "Worse than the pain of a bad marriage is the pain of a great marriage when one of the beloved spouses dies." As much as I've witnessed of human suffering, I believe this observation to be true.

"The purpose of dementia is to protect the patient from pain," I told a daughter. "It is, for sure," she agreed. "Mom still asks if Dad is in the room, and he died nine years ago." Sometimes forgetfulness is a blessing.

A patient just told me, "Yes, we have been married sixty-two years, but lately it has become a little rocky." His wife has been gone for nine years. Love endures beyond reality.

An eighty-two-year-old patient just said to me, "I think she's a little older than I am – sixty-two. I feel eighteen in my head." This disconnect between our physical selves and our self-perception is perhaps what makes aging so bewildering.

III. Chambers of the Heart: Patient Stories

Clinical encounters revealing universal human truths

A Father's Grief

In the cardiology ward, where the rhythms of human hearts are monitored with clinical precision, I have found that it is often the unmeasurable arrhythmias of the soul that prove most instructive. This was particularly true on a Tuesday morning in October, some thirty-odd years ago, when I was still adjusting to the weight of my white coat and the peculiar authority it seemed to confer.

I was, at the time, a cardiologist of perhaps thirty-two or thirty-five – that awkward age when one has acquired enough knowledge to be dangerous but insufficient wisdom to recognize the fact. Youth affords us many luxuries, not least of which is the comforting delusion that we understand the mechanics of both the heart and what we casually refer to as "heartbreak."

The patient was Mr. Abramowitz, a man I had reflexively categorized as "elderly," though in retrospect he may have been merely sixty or sixty-five. Such is the tyranny of relative age; to my young eyes, anyone with white hair and liver spots belonged to a single, undifferentiated category: old. Mr. Abramowitz was the father of Dr. Simon Abramowitz, a gynecologist of some repute in our modest medical community. The elder Abramowitz had been admitted for congestive heart failure, a condition we were treating with what I then considered to be masterful pharmacological interventions.

I recall entering his room during morning rounds, armed with the casual confidence of the young physician. The room had that distinctive hospital quality of light – a sterile fluorescence that seems designed to eliminate shadows and, by extension, any hint of metaphysical mystery. Yet something was amiss. Mr. Abramowitz, normally stoic and dignified despite the indignity of hospital gowns and bedpans, was weeping. Not the performative sniffling that sometimes accompanies a difficult diagnosis, but the profound, body-shaking sobs of genuine grief.

"Mr. Abramowitz," I said, adopting what I imagined to be a tone of professional concern, "what's happened? Are you in pain?"

He looked up, momentarily startled by my presence, and attempted to compose himself. "Oh, I'm sorry, doc," he said, wiping at his eyes with the edge of the hospital blanket. "My son died."

I felt a cold shock run through me. Simon Abramowitz, dead? I had seen him just yesterday in the physicians' dining room, animated and voluble as ever, holding forth on some new surgical technique. Had there been an accident overnight? A sudden illness? And why had no one informed me?

"Your son?" I asked, my voice betraying my confusion. "Simon? What happened? When?"

Mr. Abramowitz looked at me with red-rimmed eyes. "No, no," he said. "My David. He got hit in the head with a baseball."

I stood there, perplexed. In my several months of treating Mr. Abramowitz, I had become acquainted with his family history – or so I had thought. I knew of Simon, of course, and of a daughter who lived in Phoenix. But I had never heard mention of a David.

"I'm very sorry," I said, defaulting to the physician's all-purpose expression of sympathy. "When did this happen?"

Mr. Abramowitz looked down at his hands, liver-spotted and traced with the blue map of prominent veins that cardiologists read like fortune tellers. "Forty years ago," he said quietly.

"Forty years?" I repeated, unable to mask my astonishment. "And you're crying now?"

He looked up at me then, and I saw in his face not the fragility of age but the enduring strength of a burden carried decade after decade. "Doc," he said, with the patient tone one might use with a particularly obtuse child, "I cry every day."

That moment altered the trajectory of my practice, though I didn't recognize it immediately. In medical school, we had been taught about the stages of grief – denial, anger, bargaining, depression, acceptance – as though they were stations on a commuter train, each one to be passed through on the way to some terminal called "healing." But Mr. Abramowitz had shown me that grief, true grief, doesn't move along tracks. It moves through time like a companion, sometimes walking ahead, sometimes behind, but always present.

In the examining room now, decades later, when patients relate to me the death of a child – which is, in my considerable experience, the most devastating loss a human being can articulate – I tell them about Mr. Abramowitz. I tell them that their grief is real and legitimate. That it may extend for decades. That there is no timetable for tears.

I do not tell them that grief will pass, because I now know better. I tell them instead that they will learn to carry it, and that there is no shame in the carrying. After all, what is grief but love with nowhere to go?

This is not, perhaps, what they wish to hear. They come to physicians seeking certainty, cures, and the comforting fiction that all pain can be alleviated with the right prescription. But in this one area, at least, I offer them the truth as I have come to understand it: that some wounds remain fresh despite the passage of time, and that acknowledging this fact is not weakness but it's opposite.

Mr. Abramowitz taught me this, crying in a hospital room over a forty-year-old loss. It was, I now realize, the most valuable consultation of my career – one for which I never submitted a billing code, but for which I remain, nevertheless, profoundly compensated.

A Matter of Appetite

In my forty years of practicing medicine, I've found that patients often tell me more about themselves than they intend. The gentleman who sat before me that Wednesday afternoon – a man of substantial girth, with ruddy cheeks that suggested both good humor and elevated blood pressure – had been discussing his struggles with weight.

"My appetite is insatiable, Doctor," he said, shifting uncomfortably on the examination table. The paper crinkled beneath him like a disappointed sigh. "I've tried everything."

We reviewed the parade of modern pharmaceutical interventions – Ozempic, Mounjaro, Wegovy – those injectable miracles that have transformed the landscape of weight management. But his head shook with each mention, a metronome of futility.

"Nothing works," he insisted. "Nothing."

His declaration summoned a memory from the dusty archives of my childhood. I found myself telling him about those school carnivals of the 1950s, where among the ring tosses and cake walks, one could win a goldfish in a water-filled plastic bag. How proudly I'd carry home these glistening orange prizes, these living trophies.

"I kept them in my bedroom," I told him, "and fed them with religious devotion. Each morning, I'd sprinkle those golden flakes across the water's surface and watch with satisfaction as they disappeared."

My patient nodded, perhaps wondering where this tale was headed.

"But invariably," I continued, "I'd wake one morning to find my fish floating at the surface, belly up, or later, settled at the bottom like a discarded toy. This happened repeatedly, until a kindly pet store owner explained my error. Goldfish, it seems, lack the capacity to regulate their intake. They will consume whatever is offered, eating themselves quite literally to death."

My patient's eyes widened with recognition. "So I'm a goldfish," he said softly.

"Perhaps we all are, in our way," I replied. "Our ancestors – hunting for wild boar in primeval forests – gorged themselves at every kill because scarcity was the rule. Now abundance surrounds us, yet our primitive instincts remain unchanged."

We sat in silence for a moment, contemplating this collision between ancient biology and modern life.

"The difference," I finally said, "is that you possess something the goldfish does not: awareness. The goldfish cannot know that its appetite betrays it. You do."

As he left my office that day, I wondered if our conversation would make any difference. Medicine is full of such uncertainties – seeds planted that may never sprout. But I've learned over decades of practice that sometimes the most effective medicine isn't found in a syringe or pill bottle, but in a moment of clarity, when a patient recognizes himself in the most unexpected of mirrors.

Even, perhaps, in the round, unblinking eye of a carnival goldfish.

The Memory Keeper

Dr. Michael Stein had been practicing medicine in the small town of Riverdale for over twenty years. He prided himself on knowing his patients – not just their medical histories, but their lives, their families, their stories.

"Doc, let me tell you something," said Frank Daniels during a routine check-up one spring afternoon. Frank was sixty-two, a retired machinist with a perpetual tan and calloused hands. He'd been coming to Dr. Stein for nearly a decade.

"I'm all ears, Frank," Dr. Stein replied, setting his clipboard aside.

"My wife Elaine and I, we have this little ritual," Frank began, his eyes brightening. "Once or twice a month, we pack a thermos of coffee and drive down to the Metropark train station. We sit on the bench there for hours, just watching the trains go by."

Dr. Stein nodded, waiting for the point of the story.

"But here's the thing-" Frank leaned forward. "Elaine watches those freight trains – some with a hundred cars or more – pass by completely. Then, after all hundred-plus cars have gone past, she takes out a pad and pencil and writes down every single serial number from every single car, exactly in order."

"Serial numbers?" Dr. Stein asked, confused.

"Yeah, those identification numbers on the sides. Some have eight digits, some twelve. Different for every car. She watches them pass – some trains moving pretty fast – and only after they're completely gone does she write down every single number without a mistake. We've checked."

Dr. Stein felt his eyebrows rise. “That’s... remarkable.”

“Been doing it for years,” Frank said with a shrug and a smile. “Just a game we play.”

Dr. Stein was stunned. The mental capacity required seemed almost superhuman. “Your wife must have an extraordinary mind,” he said. “What does she do professionally? Mathematics? Computer science?”

Frank laughed. “Elaine? She works in the high school cafeteria. Has for twelve years now.”

“The cafeteria?” Dr. Stein couldn’t hide his surprise.

“Yeah, we can’t afford to live on just my pension. She helps prepare the food, stacks the trays, and makes sure everything’s clean. Simple work, but honest.”

“Has she ever considered... other careers? With a memory like that-"

Frank shook his head. “People have suggested things over the years. The principal once asked if she wanted to train for an administrative position. She turned it down flat.”

“Why?” Dr. Stein was genuinely perplexed.

“She likes what she does,” Frank said simply. “Says she doesn’t want the stress. Likes working with her hands, likes the routine. She comes home, and her mind is free. No paperwork following her, no problems to solve after hours.”

As Frank left the examination room, Dr. Stein sat contemplating their conversation. Here was a woman with an extraordinary gift – the kind of memory that research institutions would want to study, that corporations would pay handsomely to employ – spending her days serving tater tots and pizza to teenagers.

For weeks afterward, Dr. Stein found himself thinking about Elaine Daniels. He even drove past the high school once, watching cafeteria workers in hairnets and aprons moving efficiently behind the counter. Which one was she? The woman with the mind that could capture and retain strings of numbers at a glance, content to spend her days in the background of teenage life?

Six months later, Frank returned for another check-up.

"How's Elaine?" Dr. Stein asked, unable to resist.

"Oh, she's just fine," Frank said cheerfully. "They offered her a supervisor position last month – more money, an office, the works."

"That's wonderful," Dr. Stein said. "Did she take it?"

Frank chuckled. "Nope. Turned it down same day. Said she's happy right where she is."

Dr. Stein tried to hide his confusion. "She didn't want... advancement?"

"Doc," Frank said, studying him with gentle amusement, "not everyone measures life the same way. Elaine's got this incredible gift, sure. But to her, it's just something she can do, like some people can wiggle their ears or touch their nose with their tongue. It's not who she is."

"But with a mind like that-"

"She uses it the way she wants to. Remembers every student's food allergies without checking the list. Knows exactly who likes extra gravy and who wants their vegetables on a separate plate. Recalls every kid's birthday and gives them an extra cookie." Frank shrugged. "To her, that's enough."

After Frank left, Dr. Stein added a note to his patient's file. But his thoughts were on Elaine, on this woman who possessed an extraordinary mental gift yet found fulfillment in an ordinary job that most would consider beneath her capabilities.

He wondered about his own assumptions – that intelligence must be leveraged, monetized, advanced. That a remarkable mind must pursue remarkable achievement. That happiness correlates with professional status.

Perhaps the real irony wasn't Elaine's contentment with her cafeteria position. Perhaps the irony was his own inability to understand it.

Later that night, as Dr. Stein drove home, he passed the high school. Through the cafeteria windows, he saw workers cleaning up after the day's meals. Just ordinary people doing ordinary work – except one of them possessed an extraordinary gift that she had chosen, with full awareness, not to parlay into advancement or achievement or recognition.

And she was happy. Completely, genuinely happy.

It challenged everything he thought he knew about potential and purpose.

What was intelligence, really? And who got to decide its proper use?

A Medical Witness

In my practice, which spans some forty years now, I have witnessed families rise and fall, marriages bloom and wither, and children grow distant and sometimes return. Such is the peculiar privilege of the physician: we become unwitting archivists of human connection.

The Goldsteins first appeared in my examining room in 1997. He swaggered in, all Italian leather shoes and Hermès tie, reeking of success and something more illicit. "You should see my new Jaguar, Doc," Marvin announced within minutes of our first meeting, jingling his keys. "Perfect ride after a little boost, if you know what I mean." He winked, then brazenly bragged about his cocaine use as if describing a sophisticated hobby rather than a dangerous habit. She followed, elegant in that particularly Manhattan way – tasteful jewelry, skillfully preserved beauty, eyes sharp with intelligence and disappointment.

"Doctor," Marvin announced, jangling his Jaguar keys, "I don't have time for this check-up business. I've got three shipments of blouses coming in from Hong Kong tomorrow."

"You'll make time," Ruth countered, settling into the chair beside my desk. "Unless you want to drop dead before you pay off that ridiculous car."

They bickered through the entire appointment – about his cholesterol, her smoking, his late nights, her overspending. Yet when I mentioned a suspicious shadow on his chest X-ray, her hand found his with an instinctive urgency that revealed everything their words concealed.

That was their peculiar choreography: public combat, private tenderness. They separated five years later – "For my sanity," Ruth told me during her annual physical – but continued to orbit one another like binary stars locked in mutual gravitation. Time worked its inevitable transformations. Marvin's strokes took his swagger, then his speech, finally his independence. Ruth's arthritis gnarled her hands; emphysema stole her breath. Their daughter, Elaine, Chicago's rising star attorney, vanished from their narrative except as a painful absence.

"She thinks I called her fat at her law school graduation," Ruth wheezed through her oxygen mask. "I said the black robe was unflattering. Twenty years ago! Now she sends checks but no cards."

When necessity forced them into separate nursing facilities, I became their reluctant messenger.

"How's the old battle-ax?" Marvin would scrawl on a notepad, his mouth twisted in what might have been a smirk or a stroke-induced palsy.

"Is that fool still watching the stock market?" Ruth would ask, pretending indifference.

They died within three weeks of each other this past winter. Ruth first, of pneumonia. Then Marvin, cause officially listed as heart failure, though we physicians know the heart can fail for reasons beyond the merely physical.

Their daughter arranged separate services. I attended both, a solitary witness to the conclusion of a love story disguised as warfare, wondering, as I often do in my profession, how much we truly understand about the mysteries that bind us to one another.

One Is Only As Happy

I keep a small notebook in my white coat pocket. Nothing fancy – just a spiral-bound affair with coffee stains on the cover and dog-eared corners. In it, I jot down the fragments of humanity that reveal themselves in my examination rooms. Not the diagnoses or treatment plans – those go in the electronic charts that have all the warmth of a tax form – but rather the moments that remind me why I became a physician in the first place.

Yesterday provided three such entries.

The first came mid-morning. Mrs. Goldstein arrived with her son David, a ritual they've enacted twice monthly for years. David is fifty now, with the mind of a child and the enthusiasm of a puppy. Mrs. Goldstein herself is well into her seventies, a testament to maternal devotion that continues long after most mothers have graduated to the lighter duties of occasional babysitting and holiday visits.

I had remembered, from previous visits, David's passionate attachment to the Yankees – his encyclopedic knowledge of batting averages standing in stark contrast to his inability to tie his own shoes. Last year, I'd attended a game at Yankee Stadium on T-shirt day, coming away with a souvenir I had never worn and had forgotten until that morning when I spotted it in the back of my office closet.

"David," I said after his examination, "I have something for you."

I presented the shirt with the casualness of offering a lollipop. What followed was a spectacle of pure joy that no prescription I've ever written has produced. David clutched the shirt to his chest, then held it out to examine the logo, then hugged it again. He ran from the examination room to the waiting area, showing every receptionist, nurse, and bewildered patient his treasure.

"Best present ever!" he kept proclaiming, his voice carrying down the hallway. "Best doctor ever!"

Mrs. Goldstein gave me a look that parents of special-needs children perfect – a complex blend of gratitude, weariness, and the quiet acknowledgment that small kindnesses mean everything in their world.

I felt good. Irrationally, disproportionately good. A forgotten T-shirt and thirty seconds of thought had created such happiness. Medicine, for all its technological marvels, rarely offers such immediate and uncomplicated rewards.

Two hours later, I sat with Elena, a young woman with hollow eyes who spoke just above a whisper.

"I lost the baby," she said, her hand unconsciously moving to her abdomen. "I was five months along."

I offered the practiced condolences that such situations call for, asked about bleeding, pain, and follow-up care.

"My husband's girlfriend kicked me in the stomach," she added, her voice flat, as if she were reporting a minor traffic incident.

I stopped writing. There are statements that render medical questions irrelevant that transform doctor-patient interactions into simply human ones. This was such a statement. I said nothing but reached out and placed my hand over hers. We sat in silence for a long moment before moving on to discuss her physical recovery. The emotional recovery, I knew, would take far longer and require different kinds of medicine than I could prescribe.

My last patient of the day was Richard, an old friend and occasional patient who had made his fortune in tech investments. Our relationship had always straddled the line between professional and personal, allowing for conversations that wandered beyond symptoms and treatments.

Richard looked impeccable as always – tailored suit, expensive watch, the confident posture of a man accustomed to being the most successful person in any room. We discussed a tech stock he'd mentioned during his last visit, one that had performed exactly as he'd predicted.

As our appointment wound down, I found myself in a philosophical mood.

"You know, Richard," I said, "For all the focus we put on financial success, it's not really what matters in the end. Stay close to your family. Don't take anything for granted."

It was the kind of platitude that comfortable doctors often offer to wealthy patients – a gentle reminder that health can't be purchased. Richard's life seemed perfect from the outside: the beach house in the Hamptons, the beautiful wife who appeared in charity gala photos, the Porsche 911 he occasionally drove to appointments.

Richard looked at me for a long moment.

"Just got back to work after thirty days off," he said quietly. "My youngest son died."

The air left the room. "What happened?" I managed to ask.

"He was nineteen. Been depressed most of his life."

I nodded, assuming without asking that it had been suicide. I recalled another father from decades ago – an ophthalmologist colleague whose daughter had hung herself in their basement. When I'd finally gathered the courage to offer condolences, he had said something that had stayed with me.

"You know what they say," I offered to Richard. "She's not in pain anymore."

Richard nodded slowly. "That's true," he said. Then added, "But what's also true is that one is only as happy as their least happy child."

I wrote that line in my notebook after Richard left. It seemed to contain all the wisdom and sorrow that thirty years of medical practice had taught me. The T-shirt joy of David, the silent trauma of Elena, the profound grief of Richard – all part of the same day, the same medical practice, the same human experience.

What else can I tell you? We are all, each of us, as fragile as we are resilient. And sometimes, a forgotten T-shirt is the best medicine I have to offer.

The Empty Chair

In all my years as a physician, I've witnessed a particular phenomenon repeatedly. It's become so familiar that I can almost sense it before the conversation begins – a subtle tension in the air when I ask certain patients about their families.

Most often, it involves a middle-aged or elderly man. The examination room feels suddenly smaller when I inquire about his children. There's that telltale pause, a slight shift in posture, perhaps a clearing of the throat before he answers.

"Three," he might say, looking somewhere past my shoulder. "I have three children."

But there's something in his voice – a hesitation, a weight to the words that suggests more complexity than a simple headcount.

When I inquire further about his relationships with them, the details flow easily about two of the children. The accomplishments, the grandchildren, recent phone calls or visits. But the third child exists only in the negative space of his narrative, conspicuous by absence.

"And your oldest?" I might ask.

The silence that follows carries years of unspoken history. Sometimes there's anger there, or profound sadness, or a resignation that has calcified into something hard and immovable.

"We don't speak," he might finally say, or "I haven't seen him in fifteen years," or simply, "I wouldn't know."

In these moments, I've learned not to press too hard. The medical history I need rarely requires excavating these particular wounds. But I've observed how these estrangements manifest physically – in the tightening around the eyes, the subtle elevation in blood pressure readings, the stress that hangs in the room like an unwelcome guest.

What strikes me most is the pattern that emerges when I do gently probe these absences. Almost invariably, it's a daughter who has withdrawn, though sometimes a son. The common denominator? A divorce that occurred during the child's formative years – the volatile landscape of adolescence.

"When did you last speak?" I might ask.

"Ten years. Maybe twenty now," they'll say with a studied casualness that doesn't quite mask the wound beneath.

It's a peculiar arithmetic, the way they round down these chasms of time, as if minimizing the years might somehow diminish the loss.

Some volunteer more. "She took her mother's side," or "Things were said that can't be unsaid." Occasionally, there's mention of a girlfriend who entered the picture around the time of the divorce, though this detail often emerges obliquely, if at all.

The estrangement is nearly always unilateral. My patients – these fathers – insist they've made overtures. Phone calls unreturned. Birthday cards sent to outdated addresses. Olive branches extended into silence. Whether these efforts were sufficient or sincere is not for me to judge from the confines of an examination room.

"There are grandchildren I've never met," one patient told me, his voice betraying no emotion while his hands twisted the wedding band of his second marriage. "I've seen pictures on Facebook. That's how I found out my daughter had twins."

I've observed a peculiar psychological adaptation in these men. They construct lives around these absences – second marriages, stepchildren, new family constellations that fill the spaces left behind. They develop a practiced nonchalance when speaking of their estranged biological children, a protective shell calcified over decades.

But occasionally, I glimpse what lies beneath. A tremor in the voice. A momentary faltering when I ask an innocent question about family medical history. The body betrays what words conceal.

As I update their charts, I think about the intergenerational nature of these ruptures. The grandchildren growing up without knowing half their heritage, inheriting absences they didn't create. These estrangements ripple outward, creating negative spaces in family narratives that span generations.

I'm struck by how unnatural this seems to me, how contrary to biological imperative. I hold my own children and grandchildren close – their absence would be a wound I couldn't fathom bearing with such apparent stoicism.

Some of these patients die without reconciliation. I've signed death certificates and known that somewhere, an estranged child was receiving news of a parent's passing as if learning about a distant acquaintance. Perhaps there's grief there, or relief, or a complex emotion for which we have no name.

In medical school, they never taught us about this pandemic of familial fracture. There's no diagnostic code for the empty chair at the holiday table that remains empty for decades. No prescription I can write to heal these particular wounds.

I just listen, note the pattern, and wonder about the silent epidemic of fathers who have become strangers to their own children – and whether what I'm seeing in my examination room reflects something fundamental about the fragility of the bonds we presume to be most unbreakable.

The Gas Station Owner

I'm driving today between hospitals, and the mind works in funny ways with remembrances.

On the corner of the highway on Route 9, I see an empty gas station that's out of business. There's a for sale sign posted, and suddenly my mind travels back thirty-five years to a patient who owned a string of gas stations. Phil – that's what we'll call him – was considered extremely wealthy then, a pillar of the community both for his philanthropy and his established presence.

I joined the practice in 1982 as a new cardiologist. In those days, we found lots of pathology that wasn't acted upon by the older cardiologist I joined – a man with less sophisticated education and fewer skills. We discovered many patients with severe valvular disease.

Phil had aortic stenosis. Back then, all surgeries were sent to New York, and Phil was transported to Mount Sinai Hospital to have his aortic valve replaced. There was no new technology such as the TAVR where the valve could be replaced through the skin. This was sophisticated open-heart surgery that hadn't been around for very long.

I remember what Phil looked like very clearly because he resembled my senior partner. Both had bald heads, both came out of Newark, New Jersey, out of the Weequahic section. Both appreciated classical music, setting them apart as sophisticated Jews who had risen from the Jewish ghetto. Both carried a certain arrogance that they were above others in their community – a trait of the educated Jewish professionals of that time who had emerged from fathers and mothers who were ordinary shopkeepers or tailors or even pushcart owners. They had risen to become professionals but kept that arrogance with them. I had some cousins exactly the same and recognized it immediately.

The surgery went as well as a surgery could go at that time. Phil returned home. But perhaps a year, a year and a half later, he became very sick. Liver failure. Opportunistic infections. Rare infections. We weren't used to this in the community.

It turned out he had full-blown AIDS, as they called it then. Now it's rare to see "full-blown" because of the excellent treatments available. Apparently, he had received blood with his heart valve replacement. And lo and behold, he developed HIV. Blood wasn't screened back then as it is now. This was one of the first HIV cases I'd seen.

Shortly after Phil died, his wife came down with the same disease. Obviously, she contracted it through probable intercourse with her husband. She died much more slowly.

This morning, driving up Route 9, looking at a gas station for sale, these memories returned to me – memories of an era when HIV was very much in the minds of physicians and the community. An era where we all had to take care of these patients. We gowned up. We worried that we'd prick ourselves with needles. We saw myriads of people die in the hospital: nurses who were stuck by needles, drug addicts, homosexuals.

For some reason, that abandoned gas station brought it all back to me.

The Final Curtain at Morty's Deli

In the pantheon of New York delicatessen owners – a particular breed of men who combine the talents of showman, chef, and benevolent despot – Morty Feldstein stood apart. His establishment, Morty's New York Deli, had for decades been the cathedral where worshippers of excessive sandwiches made their pilgrimages from across the Tri-state area. The pastrami at Morty's wasn't merely a sandwich; it was an architectural achievement, a testament to abundance that required both hands and a strategic approach to consumption.

I came to know Morty first as his physician and later as his friend, a relationship that spanned more than twenty years. He was, in every sense, larger than life – a man whose personality matched the scale of his menu offerings. My own daughters once returned from a visit to his deli with tales of sandwiches taller than their school textbooks. Their teacher, naturally skeptical of children's propensity for exaggeration, made a special trip to verify these claims. She left not only convinced but converted, becoming yet another regular at the counter.

Morty's personal life mirrored the controlled chaos of his restaurant: several ex-wives, an assortment of children and step-children scattered across various households, and a girlfriend young enough to raise eyebrows among the older clientele. Money flowed through his life as freely as mustard at his condiment station – always in abundance, often distributed with cavalier generosity, and occasionally messy in its application.

His medical chart read like a catalog of serious afflictions: an aortic valve replacement, a bout with lymphoma that he dismissed as "a little cancer problem," a defibrillator installed in his chest that he referred to as his "interior doorbell," and most recently, severe prostate cancer. Through each medical crisis, he maintained the same brash humor that had made his deli a landmark. "Doc," he once told me after a particularly grim prognosis, "the only thing worse than dying would be running out of corned beef on a Sunday morning."

When he was hospitalized a few weeks ago with a brain bleed, I found myself in the unexpected position of being his healthcare proxy. There was no blood relative suitable for the role – his children were either estranged or unreliable, his current girlfriend too new to the cast of characters in his life. And so it fell to me, his doctor and friend, to make decisions that no medical school training adequately prepares one for.

His decline was swift and merciless. Pneumonia set in, followed by heart failure. The defibrillator he had joked about implanted in his chest fired repeatedly, each shock a desperate attempt to maintain rhythm in a heart that had served generously but was now failing. The hospital corridors seemed to grow longer with each visit, the elevator rides to his floor increasingly solemn.

The medical facts eventually became unavoidable. My colleague – another physician who had known Morty for years, a man with the bedside manner of a bookie and the moral compass of a rabbi – joined me in the difficult conversations with the hospital staff. The pressure to move toward hospice care mounted. The ventilator was prolonging not life but the inevitable conclusion to it.

Yesterday afternoon, we made the decision to remove the breathing tube. I signed the forms with a hand that felt leaden, wondering how one summarizes the moral calculus of such a moment in a mere signature. The nurses were kind, the room was prepared, and family members – those who were speaking to each other – were called.

But Morty, true to the independent spirit that had built a deli empire from a counter with six stools, had other plans. Within fifteen minutes of our decision, before the procedure could even begin, he summoned whatever strength remained in his failing body, rolled to his side, and pulled out the tube himself. Within five minutes, he was gone.

One of my office nurses called me later that evening. "He knew you were grappling with this decision, doctor," she said. "He made it himself and helped you make it, so you wouldn't have to carry that burden."

In the delicatessen business, timing is everything – knowing precisely when the brisket is perfect, when the rye bread has cooled enough to slice but is still warm enough to enhance the sandwich. Morty's final act demonstrated that his timing remained impeccable to the end.

The deli will continue without him, of course. The sandwiches will still tower over the plates, the pickle bar will remain abundant, and customers will still debate whether to attempt their pastrami in sections or compress it to manageable proportions. But those of us who knew the man behind the counter understand that something substantial has been removed from the menu of life in our corner of the world.

I find myself wondering if somewhere, in whatever follows this life, Morty is already setting up shop, instructing celestial beings on the proper thickness for slicing corned beef, and arranging for deliveries of rye bread that meet his exacting standards.

The Veteran's Hat

It was a Tuesday morning in October, the kind of crisp autumn day when the light slants in through office windows at just the right angle to make dust motes visible, dancing in the air like miniature planets. Mrs. Goldstein, a new patient, had arrived with her husband, a thin man with careful posture who waited patiently in a chair by the wall. What caught my attention was his cap – navy blue with gold embroidery, announcing his status as a World War II veteran.

I've always found that a doctor's waiting room has its own peculiar sociology. The magazine readers, the phone scrollers, the nervous leg-bouncers, and occasionally, the silent companions who seem to have perfected the art of courteous invisibility. Mr. Goldstein was of this last variety.

While his wife filled out her forms, I approached him, thinking to make the sort of innocuous small talk that oils the machinery of professional interactions.

"That's a fine veteran's cap," I said. "Where did you serve?"

It's remarkable how quickly the human face can transform. His expression shifted from placid waiting to something ancient and raw in the span of a heartbeat. His eyes – pale blue and suddenly liquid – met mine.

"Italy," he said, his voice steady despite the emotion I'd inadvertently excavated. "Outside Rome. I caught some shrapnel in the leg in '44."

He paused, and I sensed that whatever would come next had not been spoken aloud in some time.

"My sergeant died right next to me. Johnson was his name. Good man from Minnesota." He gestured with his hand, measuring an invisible distance. "I was standing maybe five feet to the right when the shells came in. Just dumb luck."

Mrs. Goldstein, having completed her paperwork, glanced over at us. There was something in her look – not surprise, but a gentle acknowledgment, as if she were witnessing a familiar ritual.

"And here I am," Mr. Goldstein continued, "sixty-five years later, with my Esther. Three children. Seven grandchildren now. One great-grandchild on the way." He made a small, encompassing gesture with his hands. "A whole universe that wouldn't exist if I'd been standing five feet to the left."

I nodded, suddenly aware of the inadequacy of any response I might offer.

"Amazing," I managed to say.

"Yes," he agreed, as if we were discussing nothing more consequential than the weather. "Amazing."

Later, examining Mrs. Goldstein's arthritic knees, I found myself thinking about her husband in the waiting room. How many times had he sat in waiting rooms, government offices, anniversary dinners, and graduation ceremonies carrying this knowledge with him? How many ordinary Tuesday mornings had been silently measured against that single moment outside Rome?

We construct elaborate professional facades – the white coat, the careful questions, the practiced hands – but what I've learned over years of practice is that we are all like Mr. Goldstein. Just below the surface of our most casual interactions lies the entire architecture of a life: its terrors and mercies, its arbitrary boundaries, its blind, stunning luck.

You never know.

The Window Tree

Dr. Samuel Rosen settled into his desk chair and glanced, as he had every morning for thirty years, at the sycamore outside his office window in Old Bridge. The tree stood like a patient sentinel, its bare branches etched against the February sky. Soon, he knew, the first buds would appear – those small promises of renewal that never failed to move him.

"Doctor?" His nurse Helen stood in the doorway. "Mrs. Goldfarb is here for her follow-up."

"Send her in." But he lingered a moment longer at the window. That tree had marked more seasons than calendars ever could. When he'd opened this practice, fresh from residency, it had been smaller, struggling. Now its branches reached past his second-floor window, and each spring its revival felt like a personal vindication of some cosmic order.

Mrs. Goldfarb, wrapped in a winter coat despite the office warmth, sat down heavily. "So, Doctor? Any good news?"

"Your tests are better. Much better." He turned his chair to face her. "See that tree?"

She looked puzzled but followed his gesture.

"Thirty years I've watched it. Every winter it looks dead. Every spring it comes back. There's something to that, don't you think?"

"You're getting philosophical on me, Dr. Rosen?"

"Maybe." He smiled. "Sometimes I think Spinoza had it right – God is in the natural order of things. That tree doesn't question its purpose. It just... continues."

"My mother used to say something like that," Mrs. Goldfarb said, relaxing slightly. "Everything in its season."

After she left, he remained at his desk, thinking about seasons – not just nature's, but life's. The morning mail had brought news of Rabbi Eliezer Teitz's death. The rabbi had led the Elizabeth congregation for decades, but it was his father, Rabbi Pinchas Teitz, whom Samuel remembered from childhood.

He must have been eight or nine when his friends had dared each other to approach the grand rabbi for a blessing. Samuel had hung back, shy, but the old man had noticed him, beckoned him forward with a gentle hand. The Hebrew words had flowed over him like warm water, and though he hadn't understood them, he'd felt... protected. Chosen, somehow.

Sixty-five years later, he could still feel those hands on his head.

His receptionist buzzed. "Your daughter's on line two."

"Sarah?"

"Dad, did you hear about Rabbi Teitz?"

This morning, yes."

"Remember how you used to tell me about getting that blessing from his father? How you always said it stayed with you?"

"I was just thinking about that."

"Funny how some moments just... stick."

After the call, he found himself at the window again. A red-tailed hawk circled overhead, riding the winter thermals above Route 18. Below, cars streamed toward the Turnpike, their occupants rushing to their own appointments with life.

The mention of Elizabeth had triggered another memory – that converted bus on Morris Avenue that had served as a doughnut shop throughout his childhood. The Doughnut Man, they'd called the owner, though no one knew his real name. The aroma would hit you a block away, sweet and yeasty, making your mouth water even if you'd just eaten.

His father would drive him there Sunday mornings, ostensibly to get the sports final with the closing stock prices, but they'd always stop at that bus. "Don't tell your mother," his father would say, buying them each a warm glazed doughnut, the sugar melting on their fingers.

Even now, whenever he passed a Dunkin' Donuts, that scent would transport him back to Morris Avenue, to his father's Oldsmobile, to those stolen moments of sweetness before the rest of Sunday – before Hebrew school, before family dinner, before Monday and another week of being careful and responsible – could claim them.

His last patient of the morning was Mrs. Berkowitz, there for a medication check. As he reviewed her chart, she noticed his distraction.

"Everything alright, Doctor?"

"Oh, yes. Just... remembering things. Did you ever notice that tree?" He gestured toward the window.

"Every time I come here. It's beautiful in spring."

"It is. You know, I didn't choose this office for the tree. Could have been any office, with or without a window. But sometimes I think that tree chose me."

"My mother always said there are no accidents," Mrs. Berkowitz offered.

"Your mother," Samuel said, writing her prescription, "sounds like she was a wise woman."

After Mrs. Berkowitz left, he thought about his own mother. After his father died, she'd insisted on buying him the exact same granite headstone that Jerry Gottesman – the real estate mogul who'd rebuilt half of Edison after escaping Poland – had chosen for his own plot. "If it's good enough for the richest man in New Jersey," she'd declared, "it's good enough for your father."

Even in her grief, that peculiar pride. As if death itself could be democratized by the right grade of granite.

The intercom buzzed. "Your one o'clock cancelled. Want me to hold your calls for lunch?"

"Please."

He stood at the window, hands in his pockets, watching his tree. Somewhere in Elizabeth, that doughnut bus had long since disappeared. Somewhere in the cemetery, his parents rested under their Gottesman-grade granite. But here in Old Bridge, the sycamore held its ground, bare but alive, waiting for spring.

And surely, he thought, that blessing from sixty-five years ago still hovered somewhere in the air around him. Like the scent of those doughnuts. Like the memory of his father's hand on his shoulder. Like all the moments that refuse to leave us, even when everything else does.

The seasons turn, but some things remain. Thank God for windows. Thank God for trees. Thank God for the ordinary miracles that remind us, daily, that we're still here.

The Angels' Request

Dr. Himmelfarb had been practicing medicine on the Lower East Side for thirty years. His office, a small suite above Goldstein's Delicatessen on Delancey Street, had seen all manner of human suffering. The wallpaper was yellowed from decades of cigarette smoke, and the leather of his examination table was cracked like the face of an old man. But still the patients came, day after day, with their aches and pains, their worries and their secrets.

On a Tuesday in November, when the sky hung low and gray over Manhattan like a wool blanket, Mrs. Feinberg came for her regular appointment. She was a widow of sixty-five, with dyed black hair and fingers twisted by arthritis. I had been treating her for high blood pressure for many years.

After I checked her pressure and renewed her prescription, she remained seated on the examination table, smoothing her skirt over her knees. There was something troubling her, something beyond blood pressure and arthritis pills.

"What else is bothering you, Mrs. Feinberg?" I asked, settling into my creaking chair.

"Dr. Himmelfarb," she began, her voice lowered as if the walls themselves might gossip, "I met a man."

I raised my eyebrows. "At your age? This is good news, no?"

"At my age," she said with a little snort. "That's exactly what my daughter said. 'At your age, Mama, what do you need with romance?'"

"And what did you tell her?"

"I told her the blood doesn't cool just because the hair turns gray." Her cheeks flushed. "But that's not why I mention it. This man, Mr. Brodsky, he's very learned in the old ways. We were talking, you understand, about intimate matters..."

I nodded professionally, though I confess I was amused. In all my years of practice, patients had shared with me their most private bodily functions, yet they still blushed when speaking of what happened between a man and a woman.

"He told me a story," Mrs. Feinberg continued. "A very old story that he learned from his grandfather in Lodz. I can't stop thinking about it."

She leaned forward, her voice dropping even lower. "He said that many centuries ago, perhaps even thousands of years ago, the angels in heaven gathered before God with a complaint. 'Master of the Universe,' they said, 'the people of Earth are consumed with idolatry. Everywhere they build statues and bow to wood and stone. This abomination must end.'"

"And did God listen to the angels?" I asked, glancing at my watch. My next patient would arrive soon, but I found myself curious.

"God did listen," she said. "He removed from mankind the urge to worship idols. And the angels rejoiced." She paused, looking at me meaningfully. "Then, emboldened by their success, the angels approached God again. 'Master of the Universe,' they said, 'the people of Earth are consumed with lust. They think of nothing but the pleasures of the flesh. This too must end.'"

I smiled. "Let me guess. God granted this request as well?"

"Exactly so!" Mrs. Feinberg's eyes widened. "God removed from all living creatures the desire for physical love. The angels were pleased and flew back to Earth to see a world purified of carnal thoughts."

Her arthritic fingers gripped the edge of the examination table. "But what did they find? The world had stopped. No one went to work. No one planted fields or baked bread. The markets were empty. Even the chickens stopped laying eggs."

"Without desire, there is no life," I said, more to myself than to her.

"That's what Mr. Brodsky said! The very next day, the angels rushed back to God. 'Master of the Universe,' they begged, 'please restore what you have taken away. Without desire, the world cannot continue.'"

She sighed and looked out my small window at the gray sky. "And God, in His wisdom, returned the urge to mankind. Because without it, what would be the purpose of anything?"

We sat in silence for a moment. Outside, a siren wailed in the distance, and the smell of fresh rye bread drifted up from Goldstein's below.

"A nice story," I said finally. "Your Mr. Brodsky sounds like a wise man."

"Dr. Himmelfarb," she said, her eyes suddenly direct, "I am sixty-five years old. My Morris, may he rest in peace, has been gone for eight years. Is it wrong that I still feel... desire?"

In that moment, she wasn't my patient of thirty years but a woman asking a fundamental question about life itself. I thought of my own wife, gone now for three years, and the emptiness of my apartment each evening.

"Mrs. Feinberg," I said, "even God understood that without desire, the world stops turning. Who are we to argue with such wisdom?"

She smiled then, the lines around her eyes deepening like the cracks in my examination table. She nodded once, decisively, and stood to gather her purse and coat.

As she left, I made a note in her chart about her blood pressure medication. But I was thinking of the angels in their presumption, and of God in His wisdom, and of the endless, complicated dance of desire that keeps us all – even widows and widowers, even the old and the lonely – somehow moving forward in this difficult world.

That night, as I walked home through the crowded streets of New York, I looked at the faces passing by – young lovers holding hands, old men playing chess in the park, mothers calling to their children – and I thought: here is God's answer to the angels. Here is life, continuing.

The Awakening

It is a curious thing, the invisibility that descends upon the elderly. We see it daily in our hospitals, where the machinery of medicine proceeds with cool efficiency, where vital signs are monitored but personhood often goes unremarked. I encountered this phenomenon last Tuesday while making my rounds at Princeton General.

I had been summoned to the emergency department's holding area – that purgatorial space where patients linger between crisis and admission – to examine one Walter Thornton, age 91, presenting with an acute exacerbation of congestive heart failure. The name registered dimly in my consciousness as I approached the curtained bay.

Drawing back the thin fabric barrier revealed a figure so diminished that he seemed to disappear into the institutional linens. His skin, the color of weathered mahogany, hung loosely on a frame that had once, I knew, carried itself with dignified authority. Oxygen cannula in his nostrils, IV line in his arm, monitor leads trailing from beneath his gown – all the usual apparatus of modern medicine at work on a body that had, by all appearances, nearly completed its journey.

The nurses moved about him with professional detachment, adjusting his pillows, checking his fluids, recording data in their electronic charts. Their efficiency was beyond reproach, yet something was missing – a recognition, perhaps, that this frail vessel had once contained multitudes.

"You know," I said, speaking to no one in particular but loud enough for all to hear, "Mr. Thornton here was once a prominent labor organizer in central New Jersey. He marched with Dr. King in Selma in 1965. There's a photograph of him crossing the Edmund Pettus Bridge."

The effect was immediate and rather astonishing, like witnessing a chemical reaction in a laboratory. The elderly man's eyes, which had been half-closed and unfocused, suddenly widened. His breathing, labored a moment before, found a new rhythm. One nurse, who had been mechanically recording Mr. Thornton's blood pressure, stopped and really looked at him for the first time.

"You marched with Dr. King? At Selma?" she asked, her voice carrying a note of reverence.

Mr. Thornton nodded, a small movement but definitive. "Front line," he whispered, his voice a dry leaf rustling. "Got hit... but kept walking."

Within minutes, the news had spread through the department's staff. Five nurses and aides – all African American, all previously occupied with the countless tasks that fill a hospital shift – gathered around his bed. They were no longer merely healthcare workers attending to a geriatric case of cardiac failure; they were bearing witness to history embodied.

"My grandmother told me about Selma," said a young aide, leaning closer. "She watched it on the television and cried."

"Tell us what it was like," urged another, a woman whose badge identified her as a charge nurse.

And remarkably, Mr. Thornton began to speak. His voice, initially faint as distant radio static, gathered strength with each sentence. He described the tension before the march, the eerie quiet as they crossed the bridge, the shocking violence that followed. His hands, previously lying motionless on the blanket, now rose to gesture, to emphasize, to bring the past into this sterile present.

I stood back, observing this transformation. The medicines we had ordered – the diuretics, the beta blockers, the ACE inhibitors – would address his failing heart. But what I had witnessed was a different kind of treatment altogether: the restoration of personhood, the acknowledgment of a life that extended beyond the confines of this hospital bed and the limits of this failing body.

Later, reviewing his chart, I noted with clinical satisfaction that Mr. Thornton's vital signs had stabilized. His oxygen saturation had improved, his heart rate had settled into a more regular rhythm. These were the metrics by which we measure medical success.

But I had witnessed something our instruments cannot record: how a man nearly erased by age and illness had briefly stepped back into himself through the simple act of recognition. How the telling of his story had awakened not just him but those around him to the complexity that resides in every patient, waiting only for someone to inquire.

Mr. Thornton was admitted to the cardiac unit and stayed with us for six days. I am told that during his stay, staff members would often linger in his room during their breaks, listening to his stories of the civil rights movement, of labor organizing in the factories of New Jersey, of a life lived at the intersection of significant historical moments.

He was discharged to a rehabilitation facility last Monday. His prognosis, given his age and the condition of his heart, remains guarded. But I find myself thinking that we had given him something as valuable as medical treatment: we had restored, however briefly, his visibility.

In the vast, impersonal machinery of modern medicine, this strikes me as no small accomplishment.

The Science of Heartbreak – "Broken Heart Syndrome"

Long before our modern medical taxonomy categorized every human affliction with clinical precision, the sages of antiquity knew a thing or two about matters of the heart. What we now label with the sterile nomenclature "Takotsubo cardiomyopathy" was, for centuries, simply called lovesickness – a condition no less real for its poetic name.

I was reminded of this recently when Mrs. Abernathy, a widow of three months, arrived in my examination room clutching her chest. Her EKG showed the characteristic pattern, and the echocardiogram confirmed what I already suspected: her left ventricle had ballooned at the apex, taking on the shape of a Japanese octopus trap – a "tako-tsubo" – from which this syndrome derives its unwieldy name. Science, in its relentless pursuit of precision, had managed to transform poetic suffering into something diagnosable.

Yet in my medical library at home – the one my colleagues find quaintly archaic – I have translations of medical texts dating back to medieval physicians who described this condition with remarkable accuracy, if lacking our modern imagery. Doctor Zahalon of Rome, that forgotten giant of Renaissance medicine, wrote eloquently of "a severe melancholy when an object of desire cannot be gotten," describing physical symptoms we would recognize instantly on today's cardiac ward.

What would Zahalon make of our modern "discovery"? Would he find amusement in our pride at having "identified" what he and his contemporaries had already documented in meticulous detail? Medicine, like all human endeavors, suffers from historical amnesia – each generation believing itself the first to truly see what generations before had already mapped.

In the paintings of the 15th century, we find numerous depictions of the lovesick patient, hand placed precisely where the anatomical heart sits, and face drawn with the same pallor I observed in Mrs. Abernathy. Artists captured what they saw; physicians treated what they recognized, even without our elaborate diagnostic tools.

Today, I prescribe beta-blockers and monitor ejection fractions. My notes contain phrases like "stress-induced cardiomyopathy" and "transient ventricular dysfunction." But I know – as does Mrs. Abernathy, who never finished high school but understands her condition perfectly – that her heart is, quite literally, broken.

Six months later, her follow-up echocardiogram shows near-complete resolution of the ventricular dysfunction. Medicine would say she has recovered. Zellan would have said her heart has mended – not from any potion or bloodletting, but from time's inevitable passage.

Some truths about the human condition require no modern validation, though we insist on providing it anyway. The wisdom of the ages often awaits our rediscovery, patiently enduring our pretense that we are the first to see what has always been there.

The Refrigerator Truck

It occurs to me now, looking back on those early months of what we called the pandemic, that medicine had become, suddenly and without notice, a profession of helplessness. We physicians, trained in the confidence of modern science, found ourselves thrust back into medieval times, when doctors could do little more than observe, classify, and record the progression of an illness they were powerless to treat.

The hospital where I worked in March 2020 was located in what quickly became one of the epicenters. I had practiced medicine for nearly thirty years by then, considered myself something of a veteran, had seen my share of difficult cases, tragic outcomes, even the occasional public health scare. Nothing prepared me for this.

Information arrived in fragments, contradictory reports, rumors disguised as facts. One day masks were unnecessary, the next they were essential. One day the virus lived on surfaces for hours, the next for days. One day it affected only the elderly, the next it was striking down healthy young people. The only constant was death – relentless, efficient, and impersonal.

I remember the first time I noticed the refrigerator truck. It appeared overnight in the physicians' parking lot, a large white rectangle with no markings except for a small sign taped to the door. The hospital administration had ordered it with minimal discussion; our morgue had filled to capacity within the first ten days. The truck's refrigeration unit emitted a constant mechanical groan, a bass note of despair that formed the soundtrack to our coming and going.

Each morning I would park my car as far from the truck as possible. I developed a ritual before entering the hospital: check the seal on my N95 mask, adjust my face shield, pull on fresh gloves, and try not to think about the colleagues who had already fallen ill. Three doctors from our staff were hospitalized within the first month. Two would never return.

The truck's groan followed me across the parking lot. The low, steady vibration seemed to rattle something loose in my imagination. I would find myself thinking of the bodies inside, stacked on shelves, waiting for overwhelmed funeral homes to claim them. Some mornings there would be attendants in hazmat suits wheeling gurneys toward the truck's rear doors. I learned to time my arrival to avoid these encounters.

One particularly difficult morning – after a night shift during which we lost five patients – I found myself stopped before the truck, staring at its blank metal exterior. The unit groaned. I imagined the cold inside, the bodies growing stiff, the stillness. I imagined myself there, another casualty, another physician who had come too close, made one small error in the elaborate choreography of self-protection we had all learned to perform.

"You coming in today, Doc?" A security guard called from the hospital entrance, breaking my trance.

I have always prided myself on emotional detachment, what some would call professional distance. My wife used to complain about this quality, saying I brought it home with me like hospital antiseptic still clinging to my hands. But standing before that truck, I felt something crack in me, a fissure in the professional persona. Fear, yes, but something else – a recognition of my own profound vulnerability, my ordinariness in the face of extraordinary circumstance.

Now, years later, the pandemic has receded in its virulence if not in memory. Our medical journals have categorized the disease, outlined treatment protocols, documented outcomes. The science has caught up. But sometimes at night, in the space between wakefulness and sleep, I hear it still – that mechanical groan, the sound of industrial refrigeration keeping death in a state of temporary suspension, waiting just beyond the parking lot.

I never saw inside that truck. It disappeared one day in late summer, replaced by an ordinary dumpster, as if the hospital administration were eager to erase the evidence of our overwhelming. But I can conjure it still – the cold stillness inside, the rows of bodies, the absolute silence beneath the mechanical groan. The sound reminds me of what we rarely acknowledge in medicine: that our control is illusory, our knowledge limited, our distance from those we treat measured in luck and circumstance rather than any fundamental difference.

Thank God I never made it inside that truck. But in a way, I carry it with me still.

The Toe that Launched No Marriage

There are moments in life that hang suspended like a drop of mercury – seemingly inconsequential, yet bearing the quiet potential to alter entire trajectories. Such was the case with Martha Holloway's aborted engagement, a story that whispered of the most delicate and mysterious of human vulnerabilities: the inexplicable.

The beach that day was unremarkable – sand, surf, the usual maritime choreography of waves and wind. Her fiancé, a young man whose name would later become little more than a footnote in her personal history, had removed his shoes and socks with the casual unselfconsciousness of youth. And then it happened: the moment. Those toes – those ghastly, unforgivable appendages – emerged, and with them, the swift, merciless death of a potential marriage.

One might assume some grotesque deformity, some horrific podiatric anomaly. But no. It was simply... *the toes*. Their shape, their alignment, their very *essence* spoke to Martha with a clarity that brook no argument, no negotiation. In that instant, marriage became impossible.

Twenty years would pass. Twenty years of solitude, of wondering, of that single moment echoing like a pebble dropped into a still pond. Her friends would marry, divorce, remarry. Children would be born, grow, leave home. And Martha? Unmarried. Not bitter, precisely, but marked – branded by that singular moment of aesthetic revulsion.

It was in a doctor's examining room – that most clinical of confessionals – where she found herself compelled to unburden this story. The sterile environment, with its paper-covered examination table and walls the color of institutional resignation, became an unlikely sanctuary for her long-held secret. What drives a person to unveil such an intimate narrative to a medical professional? Perhaps it is the tacit understanding that doctors inhabit a realm beyond judgment, trained to listen with a detachment that borders on the sacred.

What does one make of such a decision? In an age of calculated compromises, of pragmatic partnerships, Martha's choice stood as a monument to something more primal: an instinct, a visceral understanding that some things – however inexplicable – cannot be unseen.

The toes had spoken. And she had listened. And now, decades later, she sought – what? Absolution? Understanding? Confirmation that some inexplicable moments of certainty are, in fact, perfectly human?

The Jelly Transgression

It's peculiar how the mind returns to certain moments of adolescent transgression, not the predictable sexual fumbling or academic cheating that mark most Jewish boys growing up in the stifling corridors of Newark in the 1950s, but rather the minor rebellions against paternal authority that, in retrospect, reveal something so fundamental about the American character that one wonders why Tocqueville never wrote about jelly doughnuts.

My father – a man whose hands bore the honorable calluses of labor and whose back was perpetually dusted with flour – operated Zuckerman's Bakery on Springfield Avenue, a business my grandfather had established after fleeing the pogroms of Galicia with nothing but a few recipes memorized and an inexplicable faith in American opportunity. The bakery stood as our family's monument to assimilation, a place where goyim and Jews alike lined up for challah, rye bread, and those goddamn jelly doughnuts that would become, for me, objects of both tedium and transgression.

During those endless New Jersey summers, while other boys my age were discovering baseball and masturbation with equal enthusiasm, I was conscripted into service behind the counter. The heat was relentless – a punishing combination of July humidity and the perpetual fire of the ovens that turned our back room into something approaching the theological concept of Gehinnom. Sweat collected in the hollows of my adolescent frame, pooling at the small of my back as I executed my primary function: the filling of doughnuts.

The jelly injector was a peculiar contraption, two metal spouts extending like surgical implements from a reservoir of viscous red goo that the packaging optimistically called "raspberry filling." The machine required minimal skill to operate – position the doughnut, apply pressure, dispense filling, repeat. The banality was crushing. With each squirt of jelly, I felt the narrowing of possibility, the mechanization of ambition.

And so, on one particularly sweltering afternoon, as my father argued with Mr. Liebowitz about an order of Kaiser Rolls and my mother manned the cash register with her practiced efficiency, I committed my small act of rebellion. I took a perfectly innocent doughnut – still warm from the fryer, its golden skin glistening with a sheen of oil – and I violated it. Not once, not twice, but perhaps twenty-five times I plunged those metal spouts into its yielding flesh, pumping it full of that blood-red industrial jelly until it sat heavy in my palm, a grotesque parody of its former self, gorged beyond all reasonable capacity.

The doughnut – now a bloated, obscene thing – I placed carefully on the tray destined for the display case. I imagined its fate with the perverse fascination particular to sixteen-year-old boys: some unsuspecting customer, perhaps Mrs. Goldstein with her immaculate white gloves, or maybe old Mr. Perlman who came in every Thursday for a half-dozen assorted, would select this monstrosity. They would carry it home in one of our white paper bags, the grease already beginning to seep through in familiar patterns. And then, in the privacy of their kitchens or dining rooms, they would bring this instrument of chaos to their lips and...

For sixty years I've told this story. To my daughters when they were small and demanded bedtime tales not of princesses but of their father's youth. To my patients in the examining room as I prepare to deliver diagnoses both benign and devastating, using this anecdote as a bridge between professional distance and human connection. To my wife in the early days of our courtship, presenting it as evidence that beneath my medical school propriety lurked a streak of mischief.

"What happened to that doughnut, Dad?" my daughters would ask, eyes wide with conspiratorial delight.

"What do you think happened to the poor soul who bought it, Doc?" my patients query, momentarily distracted from their ailments.

I never answer directly. The truth is, I don't know. The doughnut disappeared into the world beyond the bakery, carrying with it my small rebellion.

Perhaps it exploded spectacularly in someone's lap, a sudden eruption of sticky red violence.

Perhaps it was discovered by my father, who quietly disposed of it while adding this to the mental ledger of my imperfections.

Or perhaps – and this is the possibility that has sustained my smile for six decades – it was purchased by some neighborhood kid who, upon discovering its excessive filling, recognized it not as a mistake but as a miracle, a rare instance of getting more than what life typically allows.

Now, in my seventy-seventh year, as New Jersey fades in my rearview mirror and that bakery exists only in the increasingly unreliable archive of my memory, I find myself returning to that jelly doughnut with surprising frequency.

It has become, in its way, a metaphor for all the small rebellions that define us – the moments when we assert ourselves against the machinery of expectation, even if no one ever witnesses the results of our defiance.

And I smile. God help me, I smile.

The Bald Truth

It happened just this morning. I walked into the examining room where my patient, a man in his mid-eighties, sat waiting. My attention was immediately drawn to his hat – a souvenir piece celebrating the Amish country of Pennsylvania, with its characteristic simplicity that somehow managed to convey both earnestness and kitsch.

"Nice hat," I said, more as a pleasantry than a genuine aesthetic judgment.

"Yeah, doc," he replied with that particular forthright charm of the elderly who have outlived the need for pretense, "I'm starting to wear a hat because I'm starting to be bald."

The comment, delivered with such matter-of-factness, transported me across decades to a family gathering – was it really sixty years ago? We were preparing for dinner, everyone dressed in the slightly formal way families once did for such occasions. A cousin's husband – not really an uncle but occupying that nebulous space in family taxonomy – was notably absent.

"Why isn't Harold joining us?" I had asked my mother.

She lowered her voice, though we were alone in the kitchen. "He feels funny about going out. He's losing his hair."

The absurdity of it struck me even then, though I lacked the vocabulary to articulate it. A grown man, refusing the pleasure of company and food because of something as inevitable as the movement of continents.

How curious, the constellation of responses men have to this most democratic of physical diminishments. Some embrace their gleaming pates, cultivating the look with razors and oils, wearing baldness like a deliberate choice rather than biology's decree. They strut through the world as if their hairlessness were a badge of virility, a testament to excessive testosterone.

Others engage in elaborate architectural projects, constructing precarious arrangements with the few remaining strands, defying both gravity and dignity in desperate attempts to maintain appearances. The comb-over, that most tragic of coiffures, suggesting that the observer might be fooled by what amounts to a gossamer veil draped across bare scalp.

And then we have those who resort to the most outlandish of hairpieces – contraptions that sit atop their heads with all the subtlety of neon signs. I once saw a man at the symphony wearing what appeared to be a distant cousin to Davy Crockett's famous raccoon hat. It perched there, defiant and implausible, drawing far more attention than the baldness it was meant to conceal. These toupees, with their uniform density and suspicious perfection, announce their artificiality to everyone but their wearers, who seem to believe they've achieved some sort of follicular sleight of hand.

Still others turn to medical intervention, harvesting follicles from more fertile regions of the body and transplanting them to the barren north. They endure pain and expense, all to avoid the condition that awaits most men should they live long enough.

And what of myself? My own hairline has been in strategic retreat for years now. I've chosen the middle path of neither celebration nor concealment. I simply allow it to be what it is – a natural progression, unremarkable as rain.

All these thoughts, crystallized in that moment in the examining room, where an octogenarian and I contemplated the curious vanity that persists even as other faculties fade. How strange we humans are, I thought, as I proceeded with the examination – concerned with appearances even as the machinery beneath them gradually fails.

The Aortic Dilemma

Medical certainties have the peculiar quality of being both absolute and mutable. What we physicians know with conviction in one decade becomes quaint medical history in the next. Yet the human stories that accompany these shifting certainties remain fixed in memory with a clarity that defies the passage of time. Such is the case with young Elaine Mercer.

I was reading just yesterday about Marfan syndrome in the *New England Journal* – they're calling it "Marfan" now, not "Morphan" as we did in my day, another small evolution in the medical lexicon. The article emphasized the current protocol that women with aortic aneurysms should undergo repair before contemplating pregnancy. Perfectly sensible advice in 2025, backed by excellent surgical outcomes and recovery statistics.

But in 1983, when Elaine first came to my office, medicine inhabited a different universe.

She arrived wearing a pearl necklace that seemed too formal for her age, her slender fingers adorned with only an engagement ring. I noticed her height immediately – she must have been six feet tall, with the long, elegant limbs characteristic of Marfan's. My nurse had scheduled her for a routine examination of a heart murmur, something her college physician had detected during a campus physical.

The echocardiogram was still a relatively new procedure then. We medical practitioners regarded it with the mixture of reverence and skepticism reserved for technological novelties. The grainy images revealed what I had begun to suspect: an ascending aortic aneurysm of alarming proportions. Her aorta resembled an overinflated balloon, stretched to the threshold of rupture.

"I'm getting married in June," she mentioned, as I prepared to deliver my diagnosis. On her lap rested a leather-bound wedding planner, its pages marked with color-coded tabs – the organized dreams of a young woman with expectations of a long future.

When I explained what Marfan syndrome meant, Elaine nodded with the polite attentiveness of someone receiving complicated directions to a place they don't really need to go. When I reached the part about pregnancy being categorically contraindicated – that the strain of labor would almost certainly cause a catastrophic rupture of her aorta – her expression shifted almost imperceptibly.

"Richard wants children," she said simply. "We've talked about having three."

Elaine returned a week later with her fiancé, Richard Steinman, a serious young man with the confident bearing of someone accustomed to solving problems. He asked precise questions about surgical options, mortality rates, and alternative approaches while Elaine sat quietly beside him.

"So there's a surgical option," he concluded after our discussion. "It's risky but possible."

"Technically, yes," I admitted. "But the consensus would strongly favor management without surgery at your age, Elaine. The surgical mortality for this procedure is significant – around thirty percent at the centers with the most experience."

Richard turned to Elaine. "You need to have the operation," he said with a certainty I found troubling. "I can't marry you if you're just going to die during childbirth."

It wasn't an ultimatum delivered with cruelty, but rather with the matter-of-fact logic of a certain kind of mind. He loved her, I believe, but could not accommodate the intrusion of medical uncertainty into his planned life.

Two days later, Elaine called my office. "I've decided to have the surgery," she said. "Can you help me find the best surgeon?"

Against my better judgment, I made calls to colleagues at Stanford, where they were doing groundbreaking work on aortic repair. I secured her an appointment with the department chairman, a surgeon whose technical brilliance was matched only by his confidence.

Elaine died on the operating table three weeks later. The surgeon called me personally – a professional courtesy that felt wholly inadequate to the circumstance. "The tissue was more friable than the imaging suggested," he explained, using our medical jargon to describe the unspeakable: that her aorta had torn like wet paper when he attempted to repair it.

For years afterward, her mother, Mrs. Mercer, continued to see me for her hypertension and arthritis. During each visit, at some point, her eyes would fill with tears. We never spoke directly about Elaine – what was there to say? That her daughter had died pursuing a future that someone else had insisted upon? That medical science had offered an option that wisdom should have withheld?

Eventually, Mrs. Mercer stopped coming to the office. I heard she had moved to Arizona to live with her sister.

The *New England Journal* article I read yesterday cited a surgical mortality rate of less than two percent for elective aortic repair in Marfan patients. It recommended pre-pregnancy intervention with such casual confidence that I found myself wondering about the physicians who would read it – young doctors who might never understand how dramatically the risk-benefit equations of medicine have shifted over a mere forty years.

I find myself thinking about Elaine often these days. Not with the sharp sting of regret – I had, after all, advised against the surgery – but with the dull ache of recognition that medicine, for all its scientific pretensions, remains an enterprise inseparable from the human condition, with all its hopes, fears, and tragic miscalculations.

In my filing cabinet, I still have the handwritten thank-you note she sent after I arranged the Stanford consultation. "Whatever happens," she wrote, "I wanted you to know how much I appreciate your help in making this possible." Her handwriting was neat and forward-slanting, the script of someone leaning into a future she would never reach.

The Equilibrium

In my examination room, time often feels suspended between the ticking of the wall clock and the soft hum of medical equipment. Today, Mr. and Mrs. Krishnamurthy sat before me – he with his silver-rimmed glasses perched on a prominent nose, she with her hair pulled back in a tight bun, the vermilion dot on her forehead as precise as it must have been for decades.

"Blood pressure is normal for both," my nurse Janine announced, removing the cuff from Mrs. Krishnamurthy's arm. "Though Mr. Krishnamurthy's cholesterol remains slightly elevated."

I nodded, making notes in their charts. The Krishnamurthys had been my patients for nearly seven years, ever since they moved to be closer to their son's family. There was something about their synchronized movements that always intrigued me – the way they answered questions almost in unison, the subtle glances they exchanged before responding.

"Forty-one years of marriage," Mr. Krishnamurthy mentioned proudly when Janine asked how long they'd been together. "Arranged marriage. Very good life."

Janine's eyes widened with interest. She was young, recently engaged, and endlessly fascinated by cultural differences in romance.

"You never met before your wedding day?" she asked, her voice tinged with the particular fascination of someone who couldn't imagine such an arrangement.

Mrs. Krishnamurthy shook her head. "No. Not allowed."

"Were you nervous?" Janine pressed. "What if... I mean, when you saw each other for the first time, were you disappointed?"

I was about to interject – to redirect the conversation back to medical matters – when Mrs. Krishnamurthy answered with unexpected candor.

"Yes," she said softly. "A little."

The word hung in the air like a diagnosis I hadn't prepared them for. I watched Mr. Krishnamurthy's face carefully. In seven years, I had never seen his expression change so dramatically. His eyes, usually bright with quiet dignity, dimmed. His shoulders curved inward almost imperceptibly.

"I thought she was very beautiful," he said quietly. "Still do."

The examination room seemed to shrink around us. I felt suddenly that I was witnessing something private unfolding, a small tear appearing in the fabric of their shared history. For forty-one years, this man had believed in a mutual contentment with their arrangement. For forty-one years, this woman had kept a small disappointment folded away, perhaps forgotten until this unguarded moment.

"Did anyone ever refuse to go through with the marriage after seeing their partner?" Janine asked, oblivious to the subtle shift that had occurred.

"No, no," Mr. Krishnamurthy answered quickly. "That does not happen. I never heard of such a thing."

But his certainty seemed forced now, a recitation of cultural expectation rather than personal conviction.

I completed their examination with efficient precision, prescribing medication refills and scheduling follow-up appointments. As they prepared to leave, I noticed they no longer moved in synchrony. Mr. Krishnamurthy held the door open, but his gaze remained fixed on the floor tiles. Mrs. Krishnamurthy adjusted her sari with fingers that seemed to tremble slightly.

Three months later, their son called to transfer their medical records. They were moving back to Chennai, he explained. After forty-one years, they had decided to live separately – Mrs. Krishnamurthy with their daughter, Mr. Krishnamurthy alone in the family home.

"It was very sudden," their son said, confusion evident in his voice. "They won't explain. They just say sometimes equilibrium, once disturbed, cannot be restored."

I never told their son about that day in my examination room. About how a casual question had excavated a truth buried beneath four decades of accommodation. About how revelation, even of the smallest disappointment, can sometimes crack the foundation of an entire life built upon mutual pretense.

Sometimes I think of them in their separate lives, and wonder if the fractured equilibrium might have held for another forty years, had we simply checked their blood pressure and sent them on their way.

The Midwife's Ancient Wisdom

In the ever-accelerating race toward what we're pleased to call progress, we tend to discard the old with casual indifference. Our contemporary presumption is that newer must invariably be better, a conceit that infiltrates everything from our technological gadgetry to our medical practices. As a man who has spent the better part of six decades observing human foibles, I find this particular vanity among the most persistent – and occasionally the most misguided.

Last evening I had dinner with my cousin Eleanor, a woman I had scarcely seen in nearly a decade, though in our youth we had been as close as siblings. The intervening years had etched fine lines around her eyes, but her laugh remained unchanged – a staccato burst of genuine delight that still carried echoes of our shared childhood summers in Michigan.

Eleanor practices midwifery in Boston, where she has delivered, by her own rough estimation, somewhere north of two thousand babies. She possesses that particular blend of professional confidence and personal modesty that I've often noted in those who regularly witness the profound spectacle of birth. Over our second glass of cabernet, she shared an anecdote that struck me as worthy of contemplation.

"Do you remember that old midwifery text you gave me?" she asked. "The one with those peculiar illustrations?"

Indeed I did. Some twenty years prior, indulging my habit of collecting antiquarian medical texts – a hobby that my late father would have dismissed as "intellectual antiquing" – I had come across a midwifery manual dating back to the 1820s. The volume was remarkable primarily for its detailed engravings depicting maternal positions that, to modern eyes, appeared somewhere between absurd and torturous. I had presented it to Eleanor with the kind of ironic amusement that accompanies gifts of curious obsolescence.

"Last month," she continued, "I had a patient in distress. Nothing was working – not the standard positions, not the gentle coaxing that usually suffices. After two hours of what appeared to be a hopeless impasse, I suddenly recalled one of those preposterous illustrations from your book."

She proceeded to describe a position so awkward and undignified that I shall not attempt to render it here. Modernity, with its sanitized approach to the messier aspects of our corporeal existence, prefers its medical procedures to maintain at least the veneer of dignity.

"In desperation," Eleanor said, "I suggested we try it. My colleagues looked at me as though I had proposed bloodletting or trepanation."

The expectant mother, however, beyond caring about the orthodoxies of contemporary obstetrics, was willing to attempt anything. Eleanor arranged her according to the ancient diagram, and within minutes – after hours of struggle – the baby emerged without further complication.

"That maternal position isn't used anymore," Eleanor remarked with quiet satisfaction. "Nobody has even heard of it or used it. Until now."

"Well," I replied, raising my glass slightly, "so much for my old book collecting."

We shared a knowing smile across the table, acknowledging the peculiar irony that sometimes the discarded wisdom of yesterday contains solutions to the problems of today. I could not help but wonder what other forgotten knowledge slumbers in the pages of antiquated volumes, awaiting rediscovery by those humble enough to recognize that progress is rarely a straight line, and wisdom often circuitous in its journey.

In our headlong rush into the future, we are perhaps too quick to assume that what has been superseded has been improved upon. My cousin's story suggests otherwise – that occasionally the path forward requires a glance backward, and that true innovation sometimes consists of remembering what we have collectively forgotten.

As I drove home that evening, I found myself contemplating the strange economy of knowledge: how some information is treasured and preserved, while other insights – no less valuable – fall by the wayside, victims of fashion or the peculiar prejudices of the age. My collecting of old medical texts, previously a mere curiosity, seemed suddenly imbued with purpose. Perhaps in those forgotten pages lie answers to questions we have not yet learned to ask properly.

Or perhaps I simply need to justify the space my collection occupies in the spare bedroom. Either way, I shall continue to gather these fragments of abandoned knowledge, if only to pass them along to those, like Eleanor, who might someday find in them unexpected utility – and in doing so, stitch together the unraveling threads of our collective memory.

Sundays in Brooklyn

The word "uncle" never passed my lips when I spoke of Morty. He was always "my mother's brother," a designation that provided a slender hyphen of distance from a man whose very existence was a source of family complexity. In the rotogravure of memory, I see him now, leaning against his cream-colored Cadillac Eldorado, tie loosened, the gleam of a diamond pinky ring catching afternoon sun.

I was in my second year at Northwestern Medical, buried in the arcane rituals of anatomy, when the phone rang in my dingy student apartment.

"Go outside," Morty said, his Brooklyn accent having never surrendered to elocution lessons.

"It's midnight," I protested.

"Just go outside and tell me which way the wind is blowing."

When I returned to the phone, I reported the lake breeze, crisp and coming from the east.

"Perfect," he said. "That's five runs, maybe six."

"What are you talking about?"

"You're not far from Wrigley," he explained, as if addressing a particularly slow child. "When the wind comes off the lake like that, it carries the ball. More homers, higher scores. This is how we make a living, college boy."

I hadn't realized that meteorology was a crucial element in the calculation of odds. My medical textbooks had failed to mention this particular intersection of science and commerce.

The relationship between Jewish bookmakers and Italian "businessmen" was never explained to me directly. Like many things in our family, it existed in the realm of the unsaid, a penumbral reality acknowledged through oblique references and knowing glances at holiday gatherings.

Years later, when I had established my practice in New Jersey, Morty called again. We met at a small club in Greenwich Village where the waiters knew him by name. He introduced me to a man with hooded eyes and an expensive suit. "This is my nephew, the doctor," Morty said, with a pride that momentarily disarmed me.

The man – whose name I had seen in newspaper headlines – needed medical attention. I arranged for him to be admitted to a New Jersey hospital, a simpler proposition in those days when insurance companies hadn't yet assumed their role as medicine's prosecutorial branch.

During his examination, I noted a constellation of scars across his abdomen.

War wounds," he explained.

"Korea?" I asked.

He smiled. "The Appalachian war."

I nodded sagely, pretending comprehension, though it would be months before I understood the reference to a notorious gathering of crime figures in upstate New York. There are some things they don't teach you at Northwestern Medical School.

Our professional relationship ended when he asked me to prescribe diet pills for his wife. "Those will damage her heart," I said firmly.

He accepted my refusal with surprising grace. Later, I learned that this man provided what was euphemistically called "protection" for Morty's enterprise – a business arrangement I was evidently part of without knowing it, like finding oneself an unwitting shareholder in a questionable venture.

Family Sundays had their own liturgy: the rustle of racing forms, the staticky voices of announcers calling football games, the phone ringing at precise intervals. Once, I glimpsed a closet in Morty's house that contained what appeared to be stacks of currency. Three months later, Morty told me it was gone, lost on what he called "a streak where the midget went cold" – the midget being his source for tips, a person I never met but who assumed mythological proportions in family lore.

When I married, Morty approached me at the reception, glass of whiskey in hand. "I need your wedding money," he said. Not a request but a statement of fact. He had gambling debts in Las Vegas. I learned later that this was a familiar pattern, the feast-famine cycle of his profession.

There was the time in Las Vegas when I sat at a dollar blackjack table, a medical student's modest recreation. Morty appeared with $5,000 in chips. "Cash these for me at the cage," he instructed. This, I discovered, was a method of taking a marker – essentially a loan from the casino – without having to repay it. A small financial conjuring trick.

Morty was generous in his way. He paid for my cousins' educations, bought a beach house where we gathered in summers, and regularly appeared with mysterious gifts: unopened record albums, dress shirts still in their packaging, premium cuts of meat. These items had stories behind them that no one discussed.

In the end, Morty died as most old men do, the extraordinary details of his life compressed into the same biological conclusion awaiting us all. At his funeral, I noticed several men standing at a distance from the main gathering, their respect paid from a perimeter that seemed both physical and symbolic.

What stays with me now is not the colorful trappings of his profession but the essential plainness of his concerns: family, security, status, and survival. The bookmaking, the connections, the Cadillac – these were just the particular vocabulary of his ambition, no different in essence from my medical practice or anyone else's means of navigating the world.

Perhaps this is why, even now, I refer to him as "my mother's brother." Not out of shame, but from a recognition that his life contained multitudes I never fully comprehended, existing in a parallel universe to my own, connected by blood but separated by choices neither of us could fully explain to the other.

The Rug

One gradually comes to accept, after decades of practice, that the psychiatrist's notebook becomes a curious repository of human mysteries. Not the grand philosophical questions that occupied Aristotle or Kant, mind you, but those small, almost imperceptible moments where human nature reveals itself in ways that defy our ready explanations.

I was thumbing through these notebooks recently – leather-bound journals filled with my meticulous if increasingly illegible handwriting – when I came across an entry about Bertha K. that has haunted me since I first recorded it some fifteen years ago.

Bertha K. was Hungarian, originally from Budapest, a Holocaust survivor who had endured the camps and emigrated to New York in her early twenties. By the time she became my patient, she was in her seventies, a woman of formidable dignity who never arrived for a session without being impeccably put together. Her silver hair was always arranged in a helmet-like coiffure that suggested liberal application of hairspray. She favored well-tailored suits, usually in navy or charcoal, and carried handbags that whispered of Madison Avenue boutiques rather than shouted their designer origins. Her husband, a prominent New York City real estate developer, had amassed considerable wealth, allowing Bertha to furnish their Park Avenue apartment with the finest furnishings money could buy. She could, as she once mentioned with a dismissive wave of her bejeweled hand, "afford to purchase dozens of rugs each week if I desired."

On this particular Tuesday in April, Bertha arrived in a state of unmistakable agitation. Her hands trembled slightly as she placed her handbag beside her on the couch – a gesture she performed with the same precision each visit, as if placing a valuable artifact in a museum.

"Doctor," she began, her accent still pronounced after all these decades in America, "I am terribly upset. Terribly upset."

I waited, as is my professional habit.

"This morning my granddaughter visited. Six years old, a lovely child. And she spilled her breakfast – oatmeal and milk – all over my new rug." She paused, her voice catching. "My new rug! It was delivered only last week. Persian. Beautiful. Now it is ruined."

I observed her genuine distress – the slight flush on her cheeks, the unusual animation in her gestures.

"Bertha," I said gently, invoking the familiarity earned through years of sessions, "you survived Auschwitz. You rebuilt your life in a foreign country. Why does this rug trouble you so deeply?"

She looked at me then with an expression I can only describe as a mixture of self-awareness and confusion.

"That is precisely why I am here today, Doctor. That is exactly what troubles me." Her hands smoothed an invisible wrinkle from her skirt. "I know – I know better than most – what true suffering is. I have seen things that..." She shook her head, dispensing with the need to elaborate. "And yet here I am, genuinely distraught over a rug. A mere object that can be cleaned or replaced."

She leaned forward slightly. "I am upset, and then I am upset that I am upset. I cannot reconcile these things. How can I, who has endured what I have endured, be so disturbed by something so trivial? What does this say about me? About human nature?"

I have carried this question with me since that session. What indeed does it say about human nature that a woman who survived humanity's darkest hour can find herself genuinely distressed over a soiled carpet? Is it a triumph of the human spirit that we can eventually care about small things again? Or is it evidence of some fundamental flaw in our emotional architecture that we cannot maintain perspective?

I have no definitive answer to offer. Perhaps that is why this vignette remains in my notebook, unmarked by the marginal notes and theoretical references that adorn most of my case studies. It stands alone, a riddle about resilience and the curious elasticity of human concern.

What I do know is that Bertha's question reveals something essential about self-awareness – that rare capacity to step outside one's emotions and question their validity while simultaneously experiencing them in full force. Few of my patients ever achieved such clarity about their own psychological paradoxes.

The rug was eventually cleaned, though never to Bertha's satisfaction. She mentioned it occasionally in subsequent sessions, but always with a small, self-deprecating smile. "My famous rug," she would say, shaking her lacquered head. "Such a small thing to make such a big fuss about."

Is this not, in the end, the story of most of our distresses? Small things that make big fusses in our hearts, even as we recognize their insignificance against the grand tapestry of human suffering? Perhaps this is simply what it means to be human – to contain these contradictions, to recognize them, and to carry on nevertheless with our small concerns and our grand awareness side by side, neither canceling out the other.

The Chrysler Chronicles

There are people who regard automobiles as mechanical marvels, others who see them as status symbols, still others who perceive them merely as conveyances from point A to point B. And then there are those – I count myself among them – who understand cars as repositories of memory, as four-wheeled time capsules containing fragments of our personal histories.

Dr. Benjamin Goldstein (not his real name, though he insisted with that particular vanity common to successful physicians that I mention he is indeed a cardiologist) belongs decidedly to this last category. We met at a charity event where the wealthy and well-meaning congregate to exchange tax deductions for rubber chicken. Goldstein approached me after recognizing my name from the back jacket of a book he claimed to have enjoyed, though he couldn't recall its title – a common enough occurrence that I've learned to find flattering rather than insulting.

"Cars," he told me, after we'd exchanged the usual pleasantries, "have been the punctuation marks in the sentences of my life."

What followed was a monologue so laden with automotive nostalgia that I suspected he'd rehearsed it many times before. The central character in his narrative was not himself but a 1948 Chrysler New Yorker with what car enthusiasts call "suicide doors" – rear-hinged portals that open backwards, a design feature discontinued largely because of the dangers they presented at speed.

"My father was in the Jewish bakery business," Goldstein explained, sipping at a scotch that cost approximately what I earned for a thousand-word essay. "The Depression hit him late – many immigrant businesses showed remarkable resilience until the late thirties – but the post-war years brought him back. That Chrysler was his declaration of victory."

The first car accident of Goldstein's life occurred in this very vehicle, with his sister – fourteen years his senior – behind the wheel. He was four; she was eighteen. The details of the accident itself were conspicuously absent from his telling, suggesting either that the memory had faded or, more likely, that the incident itself mattered less than its function as a bond between siblings.

"I mentioned this in her eulogy last week," he said. "She was eighty-nine. Strange to think she went from driving that '48 Chrysler to seeing cars that can practically drive themselves."

Goldstein's narrative jumped to May 21, 1955 – his fifth birthday – when he returned home to discover the beloved '48 Chrysler replaced by a gleaming 1955 model. For most people, such a childhood memory would remain precisely that: a memory. But Goldstein, with the financial means that accompany a successful medical practice and the sentimental inclinations that no amount of scientific training can eradicate, has transformed memory into something approximating time travel.

"I found the grille from a '55 New Yorker," he told me, displaying on his phone a photograph of an enormous chrome automotive face mounted on a hillside. "Installed it on my property so I see it when I come home. Recreates that birthday feeling."

This struck me as either magnificently eccentric or borderline pathological. I have known collectors of first editions who display their treasures behind glass, but Goldstein's automotive fetishism suggests a relationship to the past that transcends mere appreciation.

His collection expanded to include a fully restored 1948 Chrysler identical to his father's original – a vehicle that has become a sort of mechanical ghost at family occasions. He arranged for this resurrected Chrysler to be parked prominently outside the "chateau" (a word he pronounced with just enough self-awareness to acknowledge its pretentiousness) where both his daughters were married.

"It was as if my father was visiting," he said, and I noticed his eyes glistening slightly. The scotch, perhaps.

The walls of Goldstein's medical office are adorned with photographs of the '48 Chrysler. Several patients, discovering his automotive passion, have presented him with oil paintings of the car – a currency of gratitude in the peculiar economy between doctors and those whose lives they've extended.

"Cars are a universal denominator in conversation," he concluded. "Like weather or sports. But better."

What I found most striking about Goldstein's automotive obsession was not the obsession itself – we all have our peculiar attachments – but rather the transparent way it served as a connection to his father. The suicide doors of that '48 Chrysler had somehow opened a pathway through time, allowing the son to visit the father and the father to attend moments his actual lifespan denied him.

There is, perhaps, something quintessentially American about locating one's heritage not in ancient soil or ancestral homes but in the manufactured products of Detroit. For immigrants and their children, like Goldstein's father and Goldstein himself, the automobile represented not merely transportation but transformation – evidence that one had, indeed, arrived.

As we parted, Goldstein mentioned casually that he was considering purchasing a contemporary Chrysler to complete what he called his "collection," though three vehicles hardly constitute serious collecting. I suggested that modern Chryslers bear little resemblance to their historical namesakes.

"That's precisely the point," he replied. "The past, present, and future – all in my garage."

Such is the peculiar comfort of nostalgia: it allows us to preserve the past while simultaneously reminding us how far we've traveled from it.

The Grandmother's Tale

It was in the offices of my small medical practice in Morganville where I first encountered Mrs. Abigail Goldstein – a woman who carried her ninety-two years with the casual elegance of someone who had long ago made peace with time. She settled into the chair across from my desk not as a patient seeking treatment but as a repository of wisdom waiting to be unpacked.

"You'll forgive an old woman for taking your time," she said, adjusting her wire-rimmed glasses. "But I've found at my age that stories are sometimes better medicine than pills."

I nodded, setting aside the chart I had been reviewing. In an age of electronic medical records and fifteen-minute appointments, there was something almost rebellious about simply listening.

"I was married at fourteen," she began, her voice carrying no trace of regret or defense, merely stating a biographical fact. "Had my first baby by fifteen. My husband – first husband, I should say – was twenty-two at the time."

She must have noticed my professional mask slip for a moment.

"There was no jail back then, Doctor," she said with a wry smile. "Not for that sort of thing, anyway. Not in New Jersey in the forties."

The morning light through the venetian blinds cast alternating shadows across her face – this woman who had been born when Woodrow Wilson was president, who had lived through the Depression, World War II, and watched men walk on the moon from her living room in suburbia.

"Just three children in all," she continued. "Eight grandchildren. Twenty-five great-grandchildren." She enumerated her descendants with the satisfied precision of an accountant tallying assets. "I've had a great ninety-two years. With more to come."

There was something in her delivery – a studied casualness that suggested these weren't merely facts but arguments in some larger case she was building.

"My grandchildren have master's degrees," she added after a pause. "They've done everything right, according to what society tells them. None married before thirty." She leaned forward slightly. "And not a one of them is happy, Doctor. Not a one."

The implicit question hung in the air between us: Had progress delivered on its promises? Had education and delayed gratification – those pillars of middle-class aspiration – yielded their advertised results?

I considered Mrs. Goldstein and her inadvertent anthropological study. Three generations of a family tree whose branches told contradictory stories about fulfillment. She had violated every contemporary prescription for female success – married as barely more than a child, motherhood before adulthood, limited formal education – and yet sat before me radiating a serene satisfaction that seemed increasingly rare among my younger patients with their carefully curated life trajectories.

"What's the lesson there, do you think?" I asked.

"Oh, I wouldn't presume to say," she replied with the false modesty of someone who has arrived at precisely the conclusion she wishes you to reach independently. "I'm just an old woman telling stories."

But her eyes – sharp and mischievous behind those glasses – suggested otherwise. They seemed to say that perhaps our modern metrics for a life well-lived deserved more scrutiny than we were willing to give them. That happiness might be found in places our sociological studies rarely thought to look.

As she rose to leave, I realized she hadn't actually required any medical attention. Mrs. Goldstein had simply delivered her oral memoir and subtle critique of contemporary values under the guise of a check-up.

"Same time next month?" she asked, gathering her purse.

"I'll put it in the books," I replied, knowing full well that insurance would never cover "philosophical consultation" as a billable service.

But some forms of healing aren't found in pharmaceuticals or procedures. Sometimes they arrive in the form of an elderly woman from Morganville who married at fourteen and lived to tell about it with absolutely no apologies.

The Bagman's Daughter

There exists a category of patients one never forgets, not for their illnesses – those blur with time – but for the private dramas they inadvertently reveal. My profession grants me unwelcome intimacies, confessions never meant as such.

Among these was Mrs. D——, daughter of what is euphemistically called a "political operative" from the Garden State's Democratic machinery of the postwar years. Her father, if neighborhood lore is to be credited, served as bagman for party bosses, a human conduit for cash that required no receipts. The polite term might be "financial liaison." Whether true or not, the family's subsequent prosperity suggested some foundation to these whispers.

She was childless, married to a man whose occupation – installing windows, I believe – seemed at odds with their lavish acquisitions. Every third visit or so brought casual mention of a new shore property in Avalon, or perhaps it was Stone Harbor. Names of architects were dropped. Square footages cited. On another occasion, it might be a foreign automobile, inevitably described by its full hyphenated name: Jaguar XK-Convertible. The pride of these announcements carried a curious formality, as if reading from a script of how the prosperous ought to behave.

I admit a certain low fascination with their finances. The mathematics never quite worked – a public school teacher's salary, a glazier's wages, even supplemented by what must have been a substantial inheritance. But one doesn't ask. The professional distance between physician and patient allows for many secrets to remain undisturbed.

The cervical cancer, when it appeared, moved with terrible efficiency. Six weeks from diagnosis to death – an unusually swift progression even for that unforgiving disease. Her husband seemed genuinely bewildered by it all. The speed of her decline permitted no proper accommodation to grief.

Nine years passed. My nurse informed me one morning that Mr. D—— was on the schedule. I had not seen him since his wife's passing. The chart noted early dementia, which became immediately apparent when I entered the examination room. His eyes, still quite blue but watery now, searched past me toward the door.

"Is she in the waiting room?" he asked.

The professional response would involve orientation: gentle correction, a reminder of reality's harsh contours. Instead, I heard myself say, "Yes, she's waiting for you."

He nodded, seemingly satisfied, and we proceeded with the examination. Afterward, my nurse and I watched him shuffle toward the exit, his gait unsteady but purposeful. We waited until the automatic doors parted for him, admitted him to the bright afternoon where, in his mind at least, his wife stood waiting with news, perhaps, of another purchase, another acquisition against which to measure a life's progress.

Some mercies are small, unethical, and necessary. I do not regret mine.

IV. Bloodlines: Family & Legacy

Intergenerational relationships and moral evolution

Consistency of Conviction

There is nothing, absolutely nothing, as malleable as a moral conviction. This particular revelation came to me not during the endless nights of medical school at the University of Chicago, where I first learned to catalog the infinite varieties of human frailty, but rather four decades later, when my sister's grandson – a boy I hardly know, the son of her eldest daughter – sent me a wedding invitation embossed with two male names.

Let me take you back. Chicago, 1985. I am freshly graduated from medical school, awash in debt and the particular brand of exhaustion that comes from having memorized every bone, muscle, and artery in the human body. Sarah – my girlfriend, now my wife – and I are living together in an apartment near the hospital. Second floor, a walk-up with a kitchen so small we can barely open the refrigerator door without hitting the stove. We are unmarried, a fact that troubles neither of us. My parents, lapsed Reform Jews who gave up religion along with their European accents, couldn't care less about the arrangement. But my sister Ruthie – sixteen years my senior, and by that time already fully immersed in the suburban respectability that would define the rest of her life – she cared.

She came for the graduation ceremony, of course. Ruthie, with her perfectly coiffed hair and her husband Morton, that interchangeable man in the gray suit who sold insurance and voted Republican and somehow supported my sister's transformation from the rebellious teenager who once pierced her own ears with an ice cube and a sewing needle into this paragon of middle-class propriety.

"I'll wait here," she said, standing on the sidewalk outside our building. She was clutching her purse with both hands, as if our sin might be contagious, transmittable through the doorknobs and banisters of our moral squalor.

"It's ninety degrees out here, Ruthie," I told her. "Come upstairs. Have some iced tea."

She shook her head, her lacquered hair not moving an inch despite the humid Chicago breeze. "I can't condone what you're doing, David. Living like this, without the sanctity of marriage. What would Mom say?"

Mom would say, "Are you eating enough?" and Dad would have slipped me a twenty-dollar bill with a wink, but I didn't argue the point. Instead, I stood there on the sidewalk with my sister, sweat dampening my new doctor's shirt, while Sarah watched from the window above, no doubt wondering what kind of family she was marrying into.

"I'll go get my wallet," I said finally. "We can meet you at the restaurant."

And that was that. My sister, the moral arbiter, the guardian of familial respectability, stood on principle that day. She would not cross the threshold of sin. She would not sit on our couch or use our bathroom or drink from our glasses. Our unmarried cohabitation was an affront to God, to decency, to the natural order of things.

Fast-forward forty years. I am a semi-retired physician with arthritic hands and thinning hair. Sarah and I have been married for thirty-eight of those years, producing two children who have given us grandchildren who remind us, with their technological savvy and progressive attitudes, how quickly we're becoming obsolete.

The invitation arrives in the mail. "Jonathan Goldman and Michael Chen request the pleasure of your company as they join in marriage..." Jonathan Goldman – Ruthie's grandson, my great-nephew, whom I've met perhaps three times in his life. Getting married to a man.

I call my son, who understands these things better than I do. "Is this legal now?" I ask, and he laughs at me, calls me a dinosaur in that affectionate way that stings nonetheless.

"For ten years, Dad. Where have you been?"

Where indeed? Apparently not at the barricades of moral revolution like my sister Ruthie.

A week later, my nephew Daniel – Jonathan's father – posts a picture on Facebook. There is Ruthie, now eighty-two years old, her hair still impeccably dyed a shade of brown not found in nature, making a bed in what is clearly a young person's apartment. There are concert posters on the wall, IKEA furniture, a guitar in the corner. And reflected in the mirror on the wall, there they are: Jonathan and Michael, arms around each other, grinning at Ruthie as she tucks in hospital corners with military precision.

I stare at the image for a long time, this digital evidence of my sister's moral flexibility. The same woman who wouldn't set foot in my apartment because Sarah and I were living in sin is now making the marital bed for her grandson and his male fiancé. There is something so profound in the contradiction that I find myself laughing alone in my study, a bitter sort of laughter that has nothing to do with humor and everything to do with the realization that moral certainty is the most temporary of human conditions.

I call her that night.

"I saw the picture of you with Jonathan and Michael," I say, after the usual pleasantries. "Making their bed."

"They're such sweet boys," she says, and I can hear the genuine affection in her voice. "Michael is a pediatric nurse. Can you imagine? So good with children."

"Ruthie," I say, and I can feel forty years of petty resentment bubbling up in my throat. "Do you remember when I graduated medical school? When you wouldn't come up to my apartment because Sarah and I weren't married?"

There's a pause on the line. Long enough that I wonder if she's hung up on me. But then she says, with a simplicity that is either profound or profoundly infuriating:

"Times change, David."

Three syllables. Times change. As if morality is a fashion, like hemlines or hairstyles, subject to the whims of cultural evolution. As if her refusal to enter my apartment wasn't a statement about the fundamental nature of right and wrong, but merely a reflection of temporary cultural norms, as changeable as wallpaper patterns.

I want to argue with her, to point out the hypocrisy, to demand acknowledgment of the pain her judgment caused all those years ago. But what would be the point? We are both old now, our convictions worn smooth by time, like river stones. What matters more – consistency of belief or the capacity to evolve? Is her embrace of her grandson's homosexual relationship a betrayal of her earlier principles or their natural evolution?

"Yes," I say finally. "I suppose they do."

And they have changed, these times we live in. But what strikes me most, as I hang up the phone and sit in the gathering darkness of my study, is how we all insist that our moral convictions are timeless and universal, etched in stone by divine hands, when in truth they are as changeable as the weather, as malleable as clay, shaped not by eternal verities but by the simple, human need to love and be loved by those closest to us.

Ruthie loves her grandson more than she loves her principles. Perhaps that is the most human thing about her after all.

A Mother's Absence

The snow had been falling since dawn, thick white flakes that accumulated with surprising speed. The radio announced school closings, recommended against unnecessary travel, and predicted another eight inches before nightfall. I expected the day's appointments would be canceled, one after another, as reasonable people chose to remain safely at home rather than venture out into the blizzard for matters that could, in most cases, easily wait.

Yet some patients came nonetheless. Mrs. Abramson, seventy-six, with her arthritic hip; young Mr. Peterson, plagued by migraines; and then, at two o'clock, Sarah Levine.

I had been treating Sarah for mild depression for perhaps three years. A competent accountant approaching fifty, never married, she lived alone in an apartment on the North Side and maintained, as far as I could tell, a small but adequate social life. She was neither particularly happy nor particularly unhappy – until that day.

I found her sitting on the edge of my office couch, still in her snow-dampened coat, weeping. Not the quiet, dignified tears that occasionally appeared during our sessions, but deep, convulsive sobs that seemed to come from somewhere ancient within her.

"Sarah," I said, taking the chair opposite her, "what's happened?"

She looked up, her face blotched and swollen. "How," she asked, "how can you find out why someone died?"

The question caught me off guard. In my profession, one becomes accustomed to questions about how to live, not about the reasons for death. "Who died?" I asked.

"My mother," she said.

I waited, confused. Sarah's mother had never been mentioned in our sessions except in passing.

"When did this happen?" I asked gently.

"1945," she said. "When I was three years old."

The calendar on my desk showed February 1990. Forty-five years had passed since this death, nearly half a century of carrying this weight.

"I think she committed suicide," Sarah continued, her voice steadier now. "My father had a girlfriend. That's what my aunt told me years later."

I nodded, encouraging her to continue.

"But what I need to know is this," she said, looking directly at me for the first time since I'd entered the room. "Why would she do it three days before my birthday? Before my third birthday?" Her voice broke again. "I think about it every day."

The room fell silent except for the muffled sound of snow against the windows and the occasional creak of the old radiator in the corner. What could I possibly say to this woman who had carried this question through childhood, adolescence, and into middle age? What answer could satisfy the three-year-old girl still living inside my patient, the child who had awakened on her birthday to find her mother gone forever?

I said nothing for a time. Sometimes silence is the only appropriate response to the deepest human questions.

"Memory is strange, isn't it?" Sarah finally said, wiping her eyes with a tissue. "How it holds onto certain things with such... tenacity."

"Yes," I agreed. "Particularly the memories we form as children."

"I can barely remember her face," Sarah said. "But I remember the cake she had ordered for my birthday. It sat in our refrigerator for days after she died. No one thought to cancel it." She smiled sadly. "It had yellow roses made of frosting."

I wrote her prescription, scheduled our next appointment, and watched her button her coat to face the storm again. As she left, I made a note in her file about our session, knowing that this revelation might be a breakthrough or merely a moment of unusual candor that would be sealed over by our next meeting.

Later that evening, as I drove home through streets made unfamiliar by snowdrifts, I found myself thinking about Sarah's question. Not the explicit one about her mother's death, but the implicit one that lay beneath it: How do we continue to live with unanswerable questions? With absences that never resolve themselves? With the knowledge that some wounds remain eternally fresh, some questions eternally open?

I have no answer, of course. After thirty years of practice, I've learned that the most profound human sufferings rarely yield to explanation. They are simply there, like weather, like landscape, like the delicate pattern of frost that had formed on my windshield while I was inside tending to the sorrows of others.

I turned onto my street, where the porch light of my house glowed dimly through the falling snow, and thought about the yellow frosting roses on a three-year-old's uneaten birthday cake, preserved perfectly in memory while everything else – the mother's face, her reasons, the possibility of answers – had long since faded away.

The Two Pockets

Dr. Gerald Weiss made his morning rounds through the corridors of St. Joseph's Medical Center in Paterson, his white coat flapping gently with each purposeful stride. The familiar antiseptic smell, the soft squeak of rubber soles on polished floors, the distant beeping of monitors – all of it felt both routine and profound, as hospital life often does. As he passed the nurses' station, where Sheila was bent over charts with her reading glasses perched low on her nose, Gerald found himself thinking of that old Hasidic saying his grandfather used to quote. "A man should carry two pieces of paper," the old man would say in his thick Brooklyn accent, "one in each pocket. On one should be written 'I am but dust and ashes.' On the other, 'For my sake was the world created and I am the center of the universe."

Gerald had always carried those words with him – not on paper, exactly, but somewhere deeper. In medicine, you lived between those two pockets daily. Just this morning, he'd pronounced Mr. Horvath in 314, watching as life slipped away despite all their interventions. Dust and ashes, indeed. Yet twenty minutes later, he was examining the Newman baby, born six weeks premature, now thriving and ready for discharge. The whole universe contained in those tiny, perfect fingers curling around his own.

He paused at the window overlooking the parking lot, where morning rain was beginning to fall on Jersey City spread out below. The hospital sat on a hill – Paterson's modest elevation offering a view of hardware stores, diners, and brick apartment buildings that had weathered generations of immigrants. Each building below housed its own dramas of mortality and meaning.

"Dr. Weiss?" It was Sheila, holding out a chart. "Mrs. Rodriguez in 402 is asking for you. Says her pain is worse."

"Thank you." He took the chart, glancing at the notes. Mrs. Rodriguez, seventy-three, metastatic pancreatic cancer. Another reminder of that first pocket – the dust that awaits us all.

But as he walked toward her room, he remembered something else his grandfather used to say: "The left pocket keeps you humble, Gerald. The right pocket keeps you going."

He knocked softly on Mrs. Rodriguez's door. Time to reach into that right pocket again, to act as if this moment, this patient, this small act of care might be the very reason the universe exists at all.

Silver Memories

There are certain patients who remain with us long after their medical charts have been filed away. Such was the case with Herbert Keller, whom I met a decade ago during what should have been a routine cardiology consultation on our hospital's rehabilitation floor.

Keller had been transferred from Columbia University Medical Center, where he had undergone one of those procedures with an acronym that impresses colleagues but means little to laymen – a TAVR, or transcatheter aortic valve replacement. The procedure had been performed by Dr. Lawrence Singer, one of those physicians whose name is spoken with reverence in medical circles.

During our initial examination, I took the standard history and performed the perfunctory assessment that my profession demands. But as often happens in medicine, the clinical encounter soon gave way to something more interesting than the mere mechanics of the human heart.

"You know," Keller said, adjusting himself against the hospital pillows, "I live in that house with the stone wall on Larchmont Road."

I knew the property immediately – a grand estate surrounded by an imposing stone fence that I had driven past countless times, always wondering about its occupants.

"I built that wall myself," he continued, though not in the sense of physical labor. "Had it constructed in memory of my father. He was a stonemason in the old country."

Keller had no children. He had married a German woman named Elsa whom he met on a Lufthansa flight decades earlier when she was working as a flight attendant – "stewardess," he called her, using the terminology of his generation. Their marriage had the quality of a romantic film, but like many such stories, produced no heirs.

Perhaps it was this childlessness that prompted his confession, or perhaps it was simply the peculiar intimacy that sometimes develops between doctor and patient. Whatever the reason, Keller began to unfold a narrative that extended far beyond his medical concerns.

"I suppose you're Jewish," he said suddenly, not as an accusation but as a simple observation.

I nodded.

"Then you'll find this interesting." He leaned closer. "I've spent half my life negotiating between Arabs and Americans. Oil, mostly."

What followed was a remarkable account of a man who had somehow inserted himself into the machinery of international diplomacy. According to Keller, he had been mentored by a former Secretary of State and had facilitated oil negotiations throughout the Middle East at a time when such relationships were delicate and often fraught.

"I was in Oman in '73," he said. "Helped reestablish relations between Saudi Arabia and Oman. The Sultan was grateful."

The rehabilitation process afforded us many conversations. Our professional relationship evolved into something resembling friendship. I found myself accepting an invitation to his home – that mysterious estate behind the stone wall – where he presented me with two gifts that now sit in my living room as I write this.

The first is a large silver camel, tarnished in places but still magnificent. "From the Sultan of Oman," Keller explained as he handed it to me. "After I helped with King Faisal. The Sultan came to Washington, had dinner at the White House. I was there."

The second gift was more striking: a silver dagger with an intricately carved handle. According to Keller, King Hussein of Jordan had presented it to him following the Six-Day War. "The President sent me to reassure Hussein that America still supported Jordan, despite everything. Spent two weeks with him. This was his personal dagger."

I display both pieces prominently, conversation pieces that inevitably lead to the telling of Keller's story. Visitors express appropriate skepticism, as would I in their position. Yet the conviction with which Keller related these tales, the specificity of his details, and his casual references to historical figures gave his accounts an air of plausibility that was difficult to dismiss entirely.

Our friendship continued for several years. Keller mentioned his position on Columbia University's board of trustees and, in the manner of the well-connected, offered assistance with admissions for the children of friends – an offer I reluctantly accepted on one occasion.

I learned of his death secondhand. Upon calling his residence, his widow informed me that they had suffered a house fire and had been living in temporary accommodations while awaiting reconstruction.

"Herbert was never the same after the fire," she said. "He seemed to lose his will. I'm glad he gave you those silver pieces. They would have been lost otherwise."

Curiosity eventually led me to search for Keller's name online. To my astonishment, newspaper archives from the 1970s confirmed much of what he had told me. There he was in a yellowed photograph from The Washington Post, standing slightly behind the Sultan of Oman during the White House visit he had described. Another article mentioned his role in diplomatic channels between Jordan and the United States following the Six-Day War. His tales, it seemed, were not the fabrications of an elderly man seeking to impress, but genuine recollections of an extraordinary life. The silver camel and dagger were not merely beautiful artifacts but authentic tokens of historical moments in which he had participated.

The practice of medicine affords us unique glimpses into the lives of others. We see people at their most vulnerable, not only physically but emotionally. Some patients, like Keller, open themselves to us in ways they might not with others. Whether his stories were true or embellished hardly matters now. They were true to him, and in sharing them with me, he ensured that some version of his life would continue.

The silver pieces catch the afternoon light in my living room. I find myself occasionally polishing them, not just to maintain their luster, but as a ritual of remembrance for a patient who became something more. In doing so, I am reminded of one of medicine's unexpected privileges: becoming, however briefly, the custodian of others' stories.

The Reunion

The ballroom of the Paramus Hilton had been transformed into a shrine to the Ridgewood High School Class of 1975. Crepe paper in the school colors of green and white hung in sad festoons from the ceiling, while enlarged yearbook photos of teenage athletes – now unrecognizable in their current incarnations – adorned the walls. A DJ who appeared to have missed the memo about our demographic played music at a volume suggesting he believed hearing loss might be a blessing for this particular crowd.

I stood near the bar, observing the choreography of septuagenarians performing rituals of recognition. "Is that you?" followed by squinting at name tags, followed by the obligatory "You haven't changed a bit!" while privately calculating the depreciation of human tissue over five decades.

"There he is! The man who saved my life!"

The booming voice belonged to Stanley Berkowitz, formerly our class treasurer, now my patient with a history of cardiac arrhythmia and a talent for hyperbole. I had merely adjusted his medication six months ago, but in Stanley's retelling, I had dramatically intervened while his heart was making a break for freedom.

"Dr. Goldstein performed an emergency procedure right in his office!" Stanley announced to a gathering crowd, embellishing with each sentence. "If I'd waited for the ambulance, they'd be displaying my urn at this reunion!"

I attempted to correct the record, but Stanley had already moved on to another cluster of classmates, his voice carrying across the room like a carnival barker's. "Did you hear about what Dr. Goldstein did for me? A medical miracle!"

The evening took an unexpected turn thereafter. Women who had once been the gatekeepers of high school social hierarchies began approaching with alarming frequency. These former cheerleaders and prom queens – now grandmothers with orthopedic shoes and retirement plans – suddenly found me fascinating.

Judith Weiss, who had once returned my biology notes with a dismissive "thanks, nerd," now pressed against me with alarming familiarity.

"I always had a crush on you," she insisted, her breath suggesting a significant relationship with the open bar.

Marsha Silverman maneuvered her considerable posterior next to mine by the buffet table, reminiscing about conversations we had never actually had.

"Remember when we talked about going to the winter formal together?" she asked, refreshing my drink without invitation.

I remembered quite clearly asking Marsha to that dance. I also recalled her laughter, followed by a detailed explanation of why such a pairing would violate several unwritten but apparently inviolable social laws.

As the evening progressed, the pattern became unmistakable. Patricia Levine touched my arm while suggesting coffee next week. Susan Cohen slipped me her phone number on a napkin. Barbara Finkelstein, who had once changed seats when I sat next to her in the cafeteria, now wanted to know if I enjoyed opera.

"We should continue this at Vinnie's Bar down the street," suggested Elaine Katz, who in 1975 had pretended not to know my name despite twelve years of shared education.

They gathered around me – a collection of variously preserved faces with uniformly predatory expressions.

"Ladies," I said, finishing my scotch, "where were you back then?"

The question hung in the air like smoke.

"I don't recall such enthusiasm when I offered to help with your trigonometry homework," I continued, reaching for my coat. "Or when I asked you to the spring dance. Or when I sat alone at lunch while you discussed which parties I wasn't invited to."

Their silence contained multitudes.

"Where were you back then?" I repeated, making my way toward the exit. "Because I was exactly where I am now – just without the prescription pad that suddenly makes me so interesting."

I waved goodbye to these women who had once defined my social worth and found it wanting. There was no anger in my departure, merely the quiet satisfaction of witnessing time's perfect sense of irony – how it reshuffles the deck of human desirability with unexpected thoroughness.

As I drove back to my empty house – my wife of thirty years having departed for a more spiritually aligned dental surgeon – I reflected that perhaps the most sophisticated revenge is simply to survive long enough to see the recalibration of social currency. In high school, it had been measured in athletic prowess and inherited beauty. Now it was calculated in reliable coronary care and a still-valid medical license.

I wondered briefly if I might have accepted one of those invitations for drinks, whether some sort of closure or vindication might await at Vinnie's Bar. But closure, like youth, is overrated. Better to leave with the question unanswered, hanging between us like the crepe paper decorations – a reminder of gravity's inevitable pull on all things once elevated.

The Torn Jacket

I have, for the better part of my life, maintained that coincidence is seldom coincidental, and that mysticism, that slippery cousin of religion, appears most vividly to those who least expect its visitation. So it was with Dr. Silverman – a cardiologist by profession, and, as I would come to learn, a closet humanist by disposition.

Silverman – who asked that I use only his surname – practices medicine in a gleaming tower in Manhattan, but his story begins at a small liberal arts college nestled in the rolling hills of upstate New York. He had attended this institution in the 1970s, before medical school summoned him away to more practical matters. The college, which shall remain nameless (though I will note it appears with distressing frequency on lists of America's most expensive), had maintained a curious hold on him.

"I'd send them a check each year," he told me over lunch at a midtown restaurant where the waiters affected European accents and the menus listed no prices. "But writing checks is the laziest form of philanthropy."

When the college's president approached him about funding a rather unusual summer program – one in which students would travel to Eastern Europe to restore desecrated Jewish cemeteries – Silverman found himself writing a considerably larger check than usual. He also, somewhat to his surprise, accepted an invitation to join the expedition.

"I'm not particularly observant," he said, dabbing at his lips with a napkin. "Two days of synagogue a year, at most. But my grandparents came from Lithuania. My presence on the trip made sense on multiple levels. I was a donor, a physician, and I suppose, a link to the very history we were attempting to preserve."

The group consisted of seven students, an English professor with a specialty in Holocaust literature, and Silverman. They were to begin in Poland before continuing to Lithuania, where they would restore a small cemetery outside Vilnius.

Silverman, who approaches even casual dinners with a certain formality, had packed accordingly for the journey. "I brought a suit jacket – navy blue, Italian-made. Not to impress anyone, you understand, but out of respect. I had decided I would not visit Auschwitz dressed as a tourist."

It was at Auschwitz that the incident occurred.

"The evidence of systematic murder is everywhere there," he said, his voice dropping slightly. "But what caught my attention were these white porcelain insulators scattered along the fences. They're part of the electrical system that powered the barbed wire. Most visitors probably don't notice them. I found myself fixated on their pristine whiteness against the rusted metal."

Silverman moved closer to photograph these objects. What happened next has occupied his thoughts for over a decade.

"I slipped – the ground was uneven – and fell against the fence. The barbed wire caught my jacket and tore it rather dramatically, perhaps four inches along the back shoulder. My first reaction was dismay. It was an expensive jacket, after all."

His second reaction is what prompted our conversation.

"In Judaism, we tear our clothing as a sign of mourning – it's called 'kriah.' And here was my garment, torn not by my hand but by the very architecture of death itself. It was as though Auschwitz had imposed mourning upon me."

Silverman keeps the jacket, unworn but unrepaired, in his closet. "Occasionally I take it out, look at it, and remember. Not just the camps, but how mourning sometimes finds us whether we're prepared for it or not."

I suggested that perhaps his unconscious mind had orchestrated the entire episode – that he had, in some sense, wished for this symbolic tearing to occur.

"That's entirely possible," he acknowledged. "But it's equally possible that some forces exist beyond our understanding. I prefer to leave the question open."

As we finished lunch, I couldn't help but note that Silverman – a man who spends his days interpreting the electrical patterns of human hearts – found himself marked by the electrical apparatus of humanity's darkest hour. Whether coincidence or cosmic message, the torn jacket remains his most tangible souvenir from a journey undertaken with the best intentions of restoration and remembrance.

The Cameo's Memory

In the examination room of my Edison office, where I've practiced medicine now for more than thirty years, I found myself momentarily distracted from my patient's chart by a gleam at her daughter's throat. The woman – perhaps fifty, with hair just beginning to silver at the temples – wore a cameo brooch of exceptional quality. The carved ivory face in profile stood in elegant relief against its darker background, and a small diamond nestled within the delicate necklace depicted on the cameo itself. These Russian-doll jewels – adornments wearing adornments – have always struck me as particularly civilized objects.

"What a beautiful brooch," I said, gesturing with my pen toward it.

The daughter's hand rose reflexively to touch it, her fingers caressing its edge with the gentle familiarity reserved for talismans. "It was my grandmother's," she explained, smiling at her mother, my patient, who nodded with the satisfaction of a woman who has successfully transferred something of value to the next generation.

"I cherish it," the daughter added. "I wear it whenever I can."

The sight of the cameo unlocked a chamber of memory I hadn't visited in some time. I told them about my mother's collection – her several cameos, the enamel bangle bracelets with their intricate floral patterns, my grandfather's pocket watch with its heavy gold chain, and various other pieces accumulated across decades.

"Much of it came from Canal Street," I explained, remembering those New York afternoons of my youth when I'd accompany my mother to the district. The jewelers' shops lined up one after another, their windows prismatic with possibilities. I was her consultant in these matters, offering opinions with the unearned confidence of a child. "Those were different times in New York," I added, though neither woman needed this explanation. New Jersey residents understand the city's evolutions without elaboration.

My mother kept her treasures in an elegant train case, midnight blue with brass fixtures that clicked open with satisfying precision. This detail I remember clearly, though I didn't know then – as I later learned – that she kept this case near her bed or sometimes beneath it, her collection never far from her sleeping form.

The story might have ended there, a pleasant exchange of familial histories prompted by a piece of jewelry. But something in me wished to complete the circuit, to share the darker coda that had transformed my mother's collection from a present pleasure to a past regret.

"My father was in his mid-eighties," I continued, "still living in our family home in Hillside, New Jersey." I described how he was alone that day, perhaps reviewing stock listings at the kitchen table or making a simple lunch. The doorbell rang – that mundane domestic sound usually signaling nothing more than a package delivery or a neighbor's visit.

The woman at the door claimed to be my mother's dearest friend. She embraced my father with what he later described as overwhelming affection, enfolding him in her arms with a vehemence that should have signaled danger. Then nothing – a blank space in his recollection.

My mother returned home to find him on the floor, conscious but disoriented. The intruder had made her way directly to the master bedroom and removed the train case containing my mother's entire collection – decades of accumulated treasures, each with its own story. One swift act of theft erased a lifetime's worth of memory-laden objects.

"Insurance covered almost nothing," I told them, watching their expressions shift from engagement to dismay. "The police called it the work of a gang of gypsies – a ring targeting elderly homeowners, somehow knowing exactly where to look."

My father's bewilderment was profound, but it was my mother's grief that lingered in the household. The jewelry's monetary value, while not insignificant, paled beside its emotional worth. Each piece had been a repository of memory – the occasions of their acquisition, the events they had adorned, the histories they had witnessed.

"How terrible," the daughter said, her hand once again moving protectively to the cameo at her throat.

I finished my examination, made my recommendations, and watched them leave – the cameo catching the light once more as they passed through the doorway. That small artifact of continuity seemed suddenly precious to me, not for its material worth but for its successful journey through time, from one generation's safekeeping to the next.

Later, driving home along the Garden State Parkway as evening descended over the Raritan Bay, I considered how objects become vessels of memory, and how their loss can feel like the disappearance of the memories themselves. Yet here I was, decades later, able to recall with perfect clarity my mother's pleasure in her collection, despite its physical absence from the world. Perhaps memory, unlike jewelry, cannot be stolen after all, only temporarily misplaced in the crowded storerooms of the mind, waiting to be rediscovered by chance encounters with the past – a cameo glimpsed in an examination room on an otherwise ordinary Tuesday in New Jersey.

The Constancy of Mothers

Very often, I see patients in my examining room after a parent has passed away. One of the most difficult times for a person is the death of their mother. I have a story that I've thought about many times over the years – one I tell not only to those in mourning but also to patients who still have their mothers with them. I consider it a small gift, a perspective that might help them appreciate what they have before it's gone.

I tell it in this way: Your mother is your best friend. Not in the contemporary sense of the word, where friendship requires mutual entertainment and perfect understanding, but in the deeper, more fundamental sense of being the one person who remains when others have departed.

Fathers can disappear, I explain. They go out into the world, sometimes physically, sometimes emotionally. Your brothers and sisters, I continue, occasionally pursue their own interests with such vigor that they seem to vanish from your life for long stretches. And your children – here I pause to let the irony sink in – your children also can disappear, pursuing their own lives as they must.

But mothers, I say, looking directly at my patient, mothers are there. In fact – and here I lower my voice slightly – you could be a serial killer, and your mother would just say, "You've had a bad day."

At this point, patients invariably nod with affirmation. Sometimes they laugh, sometimes their eyes well up with tears. But they understand. The truth of it resonates beyond any scientific fact I might offer them.

When I'm fortunate enough to have a patient who is accompanying their mother, or whose mother is still alive and well, I watch their faces as they consider this. There's often a moment of recognition, a subtle shift in expression that suggests they're seeing their relationship anew. It's a very graceful and elegant moment, one that reminds me why, despite all the paperwork and bureaucracy of modern medicine, I continue to practice.

The patient usually leaves my office thinking about their mother, which is exactly what I intended. In our rush to grow up and away, we sometimes forget the one constant in our lives. My little story is merely a reminder of what most of us already know but perhaps don't acknowledge often enough.

The Day's Notations

Dr. Aaron Goldman's notebook – a small, leather-bound affair with a slight indentation where his thumb had, over the years, repeatedly gripped it – contained what he called "the collected wisdom of the unwittingly wise." He had maintained this practice for twenty-seven years, jotting down fragments of dialogue, patient observations, and occasional insights gleaned from his daily rounds. The notations served no particular purpose beyond his own edification, though he sometimes imagined that his son, also a physician, might someday find them interesting. More likely, Aaron thought, they would be discarded during the inevitable clearing out of his office – the gentle archaeological excavation that follows a retirement or, less optimistically, a death.

Nevertheless, Aaron persisted. The ritual provided a kind of closure to each day, a literary nightcap before he removed his reading glasses and set them on the nightstand.

Today, a Tuesday in late October, Aaron opened his notebook and began to write.

Three conversations worth preserving:

The Goldman family brought in their patriarch, Bernard, age eighty-four, a man who had once possessed what Aaron considered the quintessential Jewish intellectual's disposition: skeptical, mordantly funny, and possessed of an almost Talmudic reverence for argument. Now Bernard lay in the hospital bed, unresponsive to his surroundings, having crossed some invisible threshold from which few return.

The family huddled around Aaron in the hallway, their faces etched with that particular blend of anticipatory grief and guilt that he had witnessed a thousand times before – the former because they knew what was coming, the latter because a part of them wished it would come quickly.

"What's happening to him?" asked Bernard's daughter, Sarah, a woman who had inherited her father's analytical mind but not, thankfully, his capacity for acerbic commentary.

Aaron found himself reaching back fifteen years to a conversation with his friend, Dr. Nathanson, a psychiatrist whose professional demeanor concealed a deeply mystical view of consciousness.

"I once had a similar patient," Aaron told them, "and I was quite distressed. A psychiatric colleague of mine – brilliant man, terrible dresser – said something I've never forgotten. He told me, 'Aaron, don't be upset. This patient isn't here anymore. He's up in the country, sitting on the porch with his parents, drinking lemonade. He's escaped. He's not in pain.'"

Aaron watched as the family processed this metaphor. He had worried it might seem dismissive, too folksy for this family of accountants and attorneys. But instead, something softened in their collective expression. Sarah even smiled slightly.

"Dad did love the country house," she said. "And he was devoted to his parents."

It wasn't exactly a medical explanation, Aaron knew. It certainly wasn't provable by any empirical standard. But sometimes what families need isn't information but a narrative – a way to reimagine their loved one's experience that doesn't involve only loss and diminishment.

Later that afternoon, Aaron encountered Elena Martinez in the hospital corridor. Elena, a phlebotomist whom he had known for nearly two decades, had recently learned that her breast cancer had returned. She would undergo a bilateral mastectomy the following week.

"Dr. Goldman," she said, her voice carrying that particular hospital-corridor hush, "you remember when I had cancer eighteen years ago?"

Aaron nodded, but what came to mind wasn't the medical chart or treatment protocol. It was a brief exchange in this very hallway.

"I do," he said. "In fact, I remember meeting you before you were officially my patient. I asked how you were, just making conversation, and you said, 'One day at a time, doc.' Just that. And I knew immediately that you were dealing with something serious. That phrase – it's a kind of shorthand among the initiated."

Elena's eyes widened slightly. "You remembered that? All these years?"

Aaron shrugged. "The things patients say often tell us more than what's in their charts. 'One day at a time' – it's not just a platitude. It's a philosophy of survival."

She touched his arm briefly. "Well, I'm back to that philosophy now."

"And you survived before," Aaron said, though he knew better than to make promises.

"Yes," Elena replied. "One day at a time."

Aaron's last patient of the day was Mr. Abramowitz, an eighty-nine-year-old Holocaust survivor who had endured Auschwitz and, somehow, emerged with a gentle disposition that bordered on saintly. He came in monthly for management of his diabetes and hypertension – relatively minor concerns given what his body had already withstood.

As Aaron completed his examination and reviewed the medication list, Abramowitz reached out and patted Aaron's hand with his own – a hand that still bore the faded tattoo of numbers Aaron had never asked about.

"You know, doctor," Abramowitz said, his accent still heavy despite seven decades in America, "I think maybe the most important thing is for us to treat people the way we want to be treated ourselves."

Aaron nodded, fighting the urge to dismiss this as merely a cliché. From another patient, perhaps it would have been. But from Abramowitz, who had witnessed the absolute negation of this principle, the golden rule was not a platitude but a hard-won philosophical position.

"Thank you, Mr. Abramowitz," Aaron said.

"For what?" the older man asked, genuinely puzzled.

"For the reminder."

Later, at home, Aaron finished his notations and closed the notebook. These fragments of wisdom – a metaphor for the consciousness of the dying, the coded language of chronic illness, and the ethical stance of a man who had seen the worst of humanity – would likely never be published or praised. They would not appear in medical journals or textbooks. But they constituted, Aaron believed, a kind of alternative medical education, one that occurred not in lecture halls but in hospital corridors, examination rooms, and quiet conversations.

In the morning, there would be more rounds, more patients, more fragments to collect. Aaron set his notebook aside, removed his glasses, and turned out the light. One day at a time, indeed.

The Final Message

One develops friendships over the course of a life that defy the usual categories. My friend Lisa and I met at the University of Chicago in the fall of 1973. She was studying art history; I was in the philosophy department. We were not, as the current vulgar phrase has it, "involved." We were something at once less and more: intellectual companions, fellow travelers in the realm of ideas.

After graduation, as happens with such youthful connections, we drifted. She to Boston for curatorial work at the MFA, I to New York for a thankless job at a small publishing house that specialized in books that even libraries didn't want. Thirty years passed with only Christmas cards and the occasional birth announcement to mark the trail of our separate lives.

Then email arrived, that curious technology that allows one to be simultaneously intimate and distant. We reconnected without the awkward business of explaining the intervening decades. Her messages arrived with characteristic directness, mine with what I hoped was wit. Sometimes weeks would pass between exchanges; other times, we'd volley back and forth for days about a book or political development.

Three years ago, she suffered a stroke. Her doctor, a young man with improbable confidence, recommended something called a loop recorder. I, having just read an article on cardiac diagnostics, suggested she ask about a transesophageal echo – medical terms that reminded me why I had abandoned my brief flirtation with pre-med studies. The transesophageal echo revealed a tumor on her heart valve. She had surgery immediately.

"You saved my life," she wrote afterward, a declaration I found both flattering and absurd. All I had done was send her an article about cardiac symptoms that can mimic neurological events. That she credits me with her survival says more about her generous nature than my medical acumen.

We settled back into our comfortable pattern of sporadic communication until Tuesday last, when my phone lit up at 7:39 pm with a message that I read three times before its meaning fully registered:

"Hi, David. Things are coming to an end for me. I have an end of life date of May 10th. It's hard for me to talk on the phone. So I want to let you know how much you mean to me. We always have a unique connection. You are an interesting, smart, and funny man. You will always have a special place in my heart. Have a wonderful and healthy life. Love, Lisa."

ALS – Lou Gehrig's disease – had been her diagnosis six months earlier. She had mentioned it almost casually in an email, as if reporting a change of address. I had not understood then what she understood all too well: that the disease offers no reprieve, no possibility of remission, only a relentless progression.

What does one say to a friend's farewell? The philosophers I've studied for forty years offer precious little guidance on this point. I wrote back what felt inadequate even as I typed it:

"Wow. I am sorry to hear such news. You are a brave and beautiful soul and I wish you peace, serenity, and love! We have a special relationship, so I hope to see you upstairs. When we can resume our fun. You are in my prayers!"

The exclamation points strike me now as desperate attempts to inject life into a situation defined by its approaching absence. My reference to "upstairs" seems particularly naive, a childish euphemism for whatever may or may not await us. But what vocabulary exists for such moments?

There is a special province of friendship that exists beyond regular contact, beyond shared activities, beyond even the need for sustained conversation. Lisa and I occupied this territory for most of our lives – connected by something as durable as it was indefinable. Now I find myself contemplating what remains when even the possibility of communication is gone.

May 10th. The date sits in my calendar unmarked, because what notation would be appropriate? On that day, somewhere in Boston, Lisa will exercise the final dignity left to her. And I, in New York, will look out my window at a spring afternoon and think about the curiosity of human attachment – how it persists across decades and distance, how it resists the usual metrics of intimacy, how it leaves its mark even in absence

V. Beat Generation: Medicine Through Time

Technological/personal evolution across decades

"Rounds"

There is something about the practice of medicine in New Jersey that reminds me of a carnival funhouse mirror – everything appears slightly distorted, yet somehow more truthful for the distortion. After thirty-one years of making rounds, examining patients, and listening to their peculiar wisdom, I have come to believe that the human comedy reveals itself most clearly in the doctor's office.

Take, for instance, the patient who announced with great indignation: "Doc, I have given up. I eat Ben and Jerry's ice cream every single night for dinner" Then, in the same breath: "Also, doc, why do I have the diabetes?" The cognitive dissonance would be remarkable if it weren't so utterly human.

Or the elderly woman who confided that she puts on her bathing suit to wash her dog in the shower. When I inquired about this curious modesty, she replied with perfect logic: "You can't be naked in front of the dog." In moments like these, one glimpses the elaborate rituals we construct to maintain our dignity, even when no one – save perhaps a wet spaniel – is watching.

The waiting room of a cardiologist's office serves as a kind of theater where life's essential dramas play out in miniature. A patient tells me he's lost thirty pounds since June. "My dog died," he explains, "and I stopped eating. I didn't feel this bad when my mother died." The hierarchy of grief defies conventional wisdom, yet who am I to judge the depths of a man's attachment to his faithful companion?

Then there's the retired English teacher who lifted her sleeve to show me the tattoo she got for her eightieth birthday – a raven, in honor of

Edgar Allan Poe. I discovered this while taking her blood pressure, a reminder that surprises lurk beneath even the most routine procedures.

The human capacity for dark humor never fails to astonish. A patient returning from a funeral remarked that "the dead man was lucky because his grave had a lake view." Another, when asked about vacation plans, replied: "Doc, the only place I'm going is the bathroom." And my personal favorite: the husband who said of his wife's vacation, "I hope she went to the Thousand Islands and spends a week on each island."

Sometimes the ironies are too perfect for fiction. After performing a nuclear stress test on a cardiac patient, I watched through the window as he relaxed afterward with a cigarette. The rabbi who owns the local Jewish bookstore also holds the contract for the hospital's scent producing machines. Walking through the men's room, I caught a familiar scent I couldn't quite place until it hit me – it was the exact smell of his bookstore.

Love manifests in the strangest ways. I have two patients, husband and wife, engaged in what I can only call a joint suicide pact. Each smokes two packs a day. He has multiple heart attacks and a defibrillator; she has life-threatening emphysema. Yet they continue, bound together in their self-destruction like some modern Romeo and Juliet.

The hospital corridors teach their own lessons. A beautiful nurse I didn't recognize stopped me with a cheerful greeting. "Don't you know me?" she asked. "I've lost forty pounds since my mother-in-law came to visit. Although I hate her, I want her to stay so I won't start eating again."

Life's sudden reversals humble us all. The cocky hematologist who needed an emergency stent during an acute myocardial infarction. The physician's wife who tripped carrying quilts to the basement and is now paralyzed from the neck down. "Plans for life are now new and different," as she put it with devastating understatement.

Perhaps the most American sight I've witnessed: an Orthodox Jewish physician in his yarmulke working seamlessly with his nurse practitioner in Muslim garb, her Palestinian name badge gleaming under the fluorescent lights. Smiles all around. In the cardiac unit, at least, peace in the Middle East has been achieved.

My patients offer their own philosophy. One woman, whose son died at thirty-two, told me: "It's like having a leg amputated. You wake up every day knowing it's gone, but somehow you can live without it." When another complained of constant aggravation, I suggested it only ends when we die. "Doc," he shot back, "how do you know that?"

After three decades of practice, certain truths emerge. We are, as the old saying goes, walking around with two pockets – in one, we are dust; in the other, the center of the universe. The art of living, like the art of medicine, lies in reconciling these two realities.

And sometimes, just sometimes, happiness arrives in unexpected forms. The man who left his six-million-dollar mansion for a tiny house with his "new honey" claims he's never been happier, having conveniently forgotten his pacemaker, prosthetic heart valve, and two cancers.

Perhaps that's the real secret – not the forgetting of our ailments, but the remembering of what makes life worth living, even as we shuffle between the examining room and the EKG machine, between Ben and Jerry's and the dialysis unit, between dust and the center of the universe.

The urgent calls that punctuate a physician's day often reveal more about human nature than any textbook. Take the gentleman with the defibrillator, prosthetic heart valve, congestive heart failure, and two cancers – the same one who left his mansion for love. He called demanding an immediate callback. Emergency, his message said. My mind raced through the possibilities until I reached him. "Doc," he said urgently, "my wife thinks my back is too hairy. With this defibrillator, can I have laser hair removal?" His new bride, thirty years his junior, had priorities that transcended mere mortality.

The mysteries of human behavior never cease. One patient arrives each visit with a large shopping bag, and afterward, every bathroom in the office is stripped bare of toilet paper – even the spare rolls vanish. When confronted by my nurse, she became so upset she needed to use the bathroom again. Some compulsions defy explanation.

Love reveals itself in peculiar ways. A man fell on his wife, breaking her arm and wrist while he emerged unscathed. "She saved me," he said with genuine gratitude. Another couple spent $14,000 from their retirement fund on cancer treatment for their fourteen-year-old dog. "We had to dip into our retirement," they explained, as if there were no question about the choice.

The waiting room philosopher returns periodically. This time he shared a poem his father wrote as a boy: "Days of old when nights were bold, and toilets were not invented, They left their load in the middle of the road and went away quite contented." He paused. "Ponder that thought, Doc."

Some stories cut to the bone. A woman with cerebral palsy, confined to a wheelchair, spoke of her twin sister who died of multiple myeloma. "I was the sick one," she said. "Sixteen surgeries, learning to walk. She was always the strong twin, helping me. She had a wonderful family. And now she's gone." The universe's cruel arithmetic – taking the healthy and leaving the afflicted.

The Vietnam veteran still wakes screaming from war dreams forty-eight years later, terrifying his longtime wife. When I complimented an elderly patient's wife on her new hairdo, he immediately piped up: "I'd go for her again." How long have you been married? "Seventy-one years," he said, then added with theatrical timing, "Doc, it's all about the hair."

The human libido finds its outlets where it may. A young woman schedules annual appointments insisting on echocardiograms – not for her heart, but for her long-standing crush on the male technician. An elderly gentleman demands frequent scrotal ultrasounds, refusing referral to an urologist. Under questioning, he admits the beautiful female technician "never fails to bring about an orgasm" during her professional manipulations. "Doc, she never breaks stride, acts as if she doesn't notice. It's the only fun I have all year."

I've noticed that patients who speak most passionately about their dogs often have no children. One woman confided that her dog's death was worse than her father's passing and "much, much worse" than when her husband died. The heart has its own hierarchy.

An older couple in their seventies came for examination. "When did you meet?" I asked. "Age fifteen or sixteen." "When did you marry?" "Eighteen." "When did you know she was the one?" He paused, then deadpanned: "I'm still waiting. I'm not sure." Their laughter filled the examination room.

Perhaps the harshest sentence I've ever heard from a patient after hearing a diagnosis "I have no future." After speaking about having dinner with my daughter, "Doc, I would give anything in the world to have dinner with my father. He is long gone "Time's one-way arrow pierces us all.

The hospital corridors teach their own lessons about mortality and pride. The former chief medical officer, once the terror of the hospital who "ruled over all," now shuffles through the halls bent with Parkinson's, carrying a small shopping bag that probably contains his lunch. "No one even knows his name," a colleague observed. "It is the future for all of us powerful people."

After three decades of practice, I've learned that dignity and absurdity dance together in the examination room. We are all of us – doctors and patients alike – caught between our pretensions and our realities, between our hairy backs and our defibrillators, between the toilet paper we hoard and the love we squander, between the dust in our pockets and the universe we imagine we command.

And tomorrow, the phone will ring again with another emergency, another story, another glimpse into the strange, terrible, beautiful comedy of being human. In New Jersey, of all places, where even the rabbis smell faintly of scent machines and the cardiologist's patients step outside for a post-stress-test smoke, the examined life continues, one heartbeat at a time.

A Modern Surveillance

The patient arrived at my office in a state of considerable agitation. His face bore that particular look of the hunted – eyes darting, posture tense – that I've come to recognize in my thirty years of practice. One sees it in the faces of men caught in various nets of their own design.

"Doc," he said, settling uneasily into the chair opposite mine, "my wife has put a tail on me."

I raised an eyebrow. "You mean she's hired someone to follow you?"

"No, no," he waved his hand dismissively. "Nothing as quaint or straightforward as that."

He proceeded to explain that some fifteen or twenty years ago – the kind of marital infidelity that has become so tediously common in our age of diminished self-restraint – he had engaged in what he called "a fling" with another woman. His wife, naturally, discovered his indiscretion.

"Now," he continued, leaning forward, "if we go to a restaurant and I so much as smile at an attractive waitress, she pulls me aside and demands to know, with a vulgarity I find particularly distressing, if I want to engage in relations with the poor girl."

The patient's hands trembled slightly as he described this long-festering wound in their marriage, this constant presence lurking just beneath the veneer of domestic tranquility. The sort of thing that makes one wonder about the true nature of forgiveness in the modern marriage.

"I understand," I said. "But what exactly do you mean by a 'tail'?"

"That's just it, doc," his voice dropped to a near whisper. "If I go to the grocery store, visit my relatives, attend a baseball game – she knows.

She knows exactly where I am, always. I've searched everywhere – my cell phone, underneath the car, even my clothing. I cannot discover how she tracks me. This has been going on for two years, and it's driving me to distraction."

How interesting, I thought, this collision of ancient marital suspicion with the invisible mechanisms of our digital age. The patient sat before me, a man undone not by the heavy footsteps of a private detective in a rumpled suit, but by the silent, frictionless surveillance made possible by some bit of modern sorcery he couldn't comprehend.

"What should I do, doc?" he pleaded.

What indeed? I might have suggested he simply ask his wife how she monitors his movements, but that would deprive him of the peculiar drama he seemed to have constructed around this situation. Or perhaps I should advise him to examine his Apple account, check for shared location services, or look into whether his car has GPS tracking – the mundane explanations for what he experiences as a profound invasion.

Instead, I merely observed that technology has given jealousy new tools, but the underlying condition – the breach of trust that occurred years ago – remains unhealed. Modern surveillance merely provides new expression for ancient doubts.

Digital Diagnosis

It struck me today, while examining a patient in my Short Hills office – a New Jersey town where prosperity sits comfortably if not ostentatiously on the leafy streets – that medicine has become less about the laying on of hands than a choreography of electronic devices, each beeping and humming in its own particular dialect of digital language.

My patient, a man in his mid-fifties with thinning hair and the slightly distracted look common to those who spend their days managing other people's money, was engaged with a Kindle when I entered the room. He had, he informed me with a touch of pride, just finished reading the morning's Wall Street Journal on the device and had seamlessly transitioned to a novel – something about finance and betrayal, topics that I imagine afforded him both professional insight and the comfort of familiar terrain.

I myself was not without my technological accoutrements. My computer accompanied me, of course, operated by a scribe (a recent innovation in my practice) who translated the spoken dance of questions and answers into the cold precision of an electronic medical record. Simultaneously, I dictated notes into an application on my phone, another electronic amanuensis transcribing my observations directly into the same record. The redundancy struck me as both necessary and slightly absurd, like wearing both belt and suspenders to prevent the embarrassment of fallen trousers.

The electronic stethoscope I placed on his chest did more than merely amplify the sounds of his heart; it analyzed those sounds through some algorithm developed by engineers who had perhaps never witnessed a human heart beating beneath their fingers. The device projected an electrocardiogram rhythm and heart rate onto a small monitor. I had the option – though I declined to exercise it – to transmit these sounds via Bluetooth to a medical student waiting in another room, a kind of cardiac eavesdropping that would have seemed magical, or perhaps vaguely sinister, to the physicians who trained me.

My patient, not to be outdone in this symphony of gadgetry, wore an insulin pump that sensed glucose levels in his blood and delivered insulin accordingly – a mechanical pancreas attached to his abdomen, managing with circuits and programming what his body had forgotten how to do. On his wrist, a digital watch displayed not merely the time (that ancient and increasingly superfluous information) but a two-week history of his blood pressure readings, neatly graphed in blue and red.

The ordinary telephone mounted on the wall seemed almost quaint in this context, a reminder of a simpler technological era, though it too received calls from laboratories, pharmacies, and occasionally anxious family members inquiring after their loved ones.

In the midst of this remarkable collection of devices – each one representing thousands of hours of engineering, programming, and design – we discussed his decidedly analog complaints: backaches that woke him at night, shortness of breath when climbing stairs, the need to urinate more frequently than seemed reasonable, and chest pain that manifested in ways that defied easy categorization.

The irony was not lost on me that with all this digital assistance – the amplified heart sounds, the automated insulin delivery, the instantaneous transcription of our conversation – we were still engaged in the most ancient of medical rituals: a human being describing discomfort to another human being who was expected, somehow, to make sense of it.

What would Hippocrates have made of this scene? Or even the physicians who trained me, for whom the stethoscope was an instrument of brass and rubber rather than circuits and algorithms? I suspect they would have recognized the fundamentals: a patient seeking relief, a doctor attempting to provide it. The rest – the beeping and humming, the transmission of data through the air itself – they might have regarded as elaborate stage dressing for the essential human drama of suffering and attempted healing.

As I completed my examination and promised to call with the results of his blood work, I found myself both marveling at and slightly unnerved by this collection of digital machinery, all of it arrayed in service to the same complaints that have brought patients to physicians since medicine began. Here we were, in 2025, with all the technological wizardry the age could provide, still puzzling over backaches and shortness of breath.

Perhaps this is as it should be. The human body, despite our best efforts to digitize, quantify, and remotely monitor it, remains stubbornly analog – a collection of cells and fluids and electrical impulses that occasionally malfunction in ways that all our devices can only imperfectly detect. We have, it seems, improved our ability to listen to the body without necessarily enhancing our capacity to hear what it is telling us.

As my patient gathered his Kindle and departed, his insulin pump quietly maintaining his blood glucose within acceptable parameters, I made a note to myself – handwritten, in a small leather notebook I have carried for twenty years – to remember that medicine, for all its digital trappings, remains a human conversation about pain, fear, and the hope for relief. The rest is merely assistive technology, however impressive its beeps and readouts may be.

Curbside Diplomacy

It was a Thursday afternoon in late October, the kind that New Yorkers prize – clear, crisp, with a light breeze that carried intimations of the coming winter without its bite. The afternoon light slanted through my office windows on East 68th Street, casting long rectangles on the oak flooring that I had insisted upon when renovating the practice ten years earlier. In medicine, as in literature, I find that attention to setting matters; patients reveal themselves differently in rooms that suggest permanence.

Mr. Adelson was seated in the chair opposite my desk, waiting for me to review his most recent blood work. He was seventy-one, trim, with the erect posture of a man who has spent his professional life being noticed. A retired investment banker who now served on various philanthropic boards, he wore his prosperity with the understated confidence of those who no longer need to advertise their success: a navy blazer that I suspected was bespoke, loafers buffed to a quiet gleam, a watch that signaled discernment rather than ostentation.

"Your numbers look excellent," I told him, turning the screen so he could see the results. "The statin is doing its job."

He nodded, satisfied but not surprised. Mr. Adelson was a man who expected favorable outcomes, though not in the entitled manner of many of my Upper East Side patients. There was something in his demeanor that suggested he understood good fortune as contingent, perhaps even accidental.

"You know, Dr. Bernstein," he said, as I made notes in his electronic chart, "I was reading about that American journalist they just released from detention in Damascus."

I murmured noncommittally, my attention divided between his comment and documenting his prescription renewal.

"Brings back memories," he continued. "I spent two months in a Syrian jail myself. In 1973."

My fingers paused over the keyboard. In fifteen years as his physician, this was the first I had heard of any such episode. I looked up, recalibrating my understanding of the man before me.

"I had just graduated from Columbia," he went on, seemingly unaware of my surprise. "Decided to do some traveling before starting at the firm. Crossed over from Turkey, and was arrested as soon as I entered Syria."

"On what charges?" I asked.

He shrugged, a gesture that contained multitudes. "They never said, specifically. It was the height of the Cold War, Middle East tensions, Yom Kippur War brewing. I was an American, I was Jewish – either would have been enough, I suppose."

I tried to picture Mr. Adelson as a young man in such circumstances – removed from the comfort and predictability of New York, thrown into a cell in a country where the rule of law was, at best, a casual suggestion. How does such an experience reshape one's expectations of the world?

"Were your parents able to get help from the State Department?" I asked.

A small smile appeared. "Oh, they tried. My father knew someone who knew someone at State. After a month with no word from me, they received a letter."

"From the State Department?"

"From Henry Kissinger himself. The great Henry Kissinger," he added, with a hint of irony. "It said, in diplomatic language of course, that the United States government believed I was dead, and they shouldn't hold out much hope."

He related this information with the same equanimity he might use to describe a delayed flight or a minor investment loss – events that register as inconveniences rather than catastrophes. This, I thought, is what true sophistication looks like: not the acquisition of luxury goods or cultural knowledge, but the ability to hold the world's absurdities at a slight remove.

"So how did you get out?" I asked, genuinely curious now, the blood work forgotten.

"My Uncle Morrie," he said, his smile widening. "He was a New York sanitation man. Had the route that included the Syrian consulate on East 79th Street."

I waited, sensing there was more to the story.

"One day, he's collecting the garbage outside the consulate. Sees a Syrian diplomat coming out. And my Uncle Morrie..." here Mr. Adelson paused, savoring the memory, "...who had no formal education past high school, who'd never traveled farther than Atlantic City, he calls out to this diplomat."

"What did he say?"

"He said, 'Hey, my nephew's in your jail. He's a good kid. Let him out.' Just like that, between bags of trash."

I tried to imagine the scene: a New York City sanitation worker in his uniform, probably wearing heavy gloves, addressing a foreign diplomat on a Manhattan sidewalk with the directness that is our city's most reliable currency.

"And it worked?" I asked, incredulous.

Mr. Adelson spread his hands. "Two weeks later, I was on a plane home. No explanation, no apology. Just suddenly released and escorted to the airport."

"You think it was because of your uncle's intervention?"

"What else could it have been? The State Department had already written me off. Kissinger himself had more or less sent my parents a diplomatic condolence card."

I considered the extraordinary serendipity of it all – that of all the sanitation routes in New York City, his uncle had the one that included the Syrian consulate; that he happened to see a diplomat at precisely the right moment; that his simple, direct appeal somehow penetrated layers of bureaucracy and international tension.

"So here I am, forty-three years later," Mr. Adelson concluded, glancing at his watch. "Alive because a garbage man spoke to a diplomat."

I thought about the thousands of decisions, large and small, that constitute a life. Mr. Adelson had gone on to have a successful career, raise three children, and become a significant philanthropic presence in the city. All of it contingent on that brief curbside exchange.

"One never knows where help can come from," I offered.

"Indeed," he agreed. "One never knows."

I completed my notes on his chart, renewed his prescriptions, and scheduled his next appointment. As I walked him to the door, I found myself wondering how many of my other patients carried similar stories – experiences that had brushed them against history or mortality in ways their outward appearances gave no hint of. How many lives had been redirected by chance encounters, unlikely interventions, or the simple human impulse to speak across divides?

"See you in six months," I said, holding the door.

"God willing," he replied with a slight smile, and stepped into the hallway.

I returned to my desk, still thinking about the young man in a Syrian cell, the diplomat on a New York sidewalk, and the sanitation worker who, without knowing it, had altered the course of history – not world history, perhaps, but the no less significant history of a single human life. Medicine teaches us to look for patterns, for the predictable progression of disease and recovery. But Mr. Adelson's story reminded me that we are all, in the end, at the mercy of accidents and coincidences, the unplotted coordinates where lives unexpectedly intersect.

The Patent

In a doctor's office in Newark, New Jersey, where the sun barely penetrates through venetian blinds coated with thirty years of urban grime, I found myself performing the modern ritual of patient intake. This new patient – Goldstein or Goldblatt, one of those names that would have marked him in the old neighborhood – sat across from me, legs crossed, revealing argyle socks above leather loafers that cost more than my father earned in a month at his glove factory in Elizabeth.

"Doc," he began, with that familiarity that makes me wince, that immediate collapse of professional distance that my generation was taught to preserve. "I googled you."

Of course he had. They all do now. My life's work, my publications, my embarrassments – all indexed and catalogued by algorithms indifferent to human dignity.

"Your credentials, your reviews – they're excellent. That's why I chose you." He leaned forward, a conspiratorial gleam in his eye that I recognized from countless patients before him. "But I also saw something interesting. A patent."

I nodded, knowing precisely where this conversation was headed. In my forty-three years of practice, this particular digression had become as predictable as death certificates and insurance forms.

"Which patent?" I asked, though I already knew. There's only one they ever mention.

"The condom patent," he replied, barely suppressing a smile. "The one that keeps the erection going."

How many times had I heard this? How many patients had sat in that same chair, leaning forward with that same mixture of prurient curiosity and awkward deference? As if I were some sexual innovator rather than a physician with a momentary flash of entrepreneurial delusion.

"That was a long time ago," I said, retreating to my standard response.

We proceeded with the examination – hypertension, diabetes, minor cardiac issues. All the standard decay of American middle age, the slow collapse of flesh nurtured on processed foods and suburban inertia.

But the patent. Yes, the patent.

It came from a time when Newark still had its edges, before the developers had scrubbed away its essential character with their glass-fronted condominiums and artisanal coffee shops. I had a patient then – let's call him Buonarotti, though that wasn't his name – who owned several establishments that euphemistically called themselves "gentlemen's clubs" but were, in the harsh light of medical reality, venues for the exchange of sexual services for cash.

Buonarotti would send his "dancers" to me. Young women with stage names like Cinnamon and Destiny would sit in my examination room, their makeup garish under fluorescent lights, speaking of urinary tract infections and unusual discharge in the flat, affectless tones of those who've surrendered all privacy.

This was during the AIDS crisis, when every sexual encounter carried the shadow of mortality. I lectured them on prophylactics with the fervor of a Talmudic scholar, but they had their commercial concerns.

"The condoms make them go soft," one told me, a redhead with the sad eyes of a Newark childhood. "And if they go soft, they don't come back. No return business."

Another complained about Viagra's recent emergence on the market. "These old guys come in, popped a pill, thinking they're nineteen again. They want an hour when before they could barely manage five minutes."

These consultations – half medical, half confessional – occupied a space no medical school had prepared me for. I found myself contemplating the mechanics of commercial sex with the detached interest of an engineer examining a faulty bridge.

The solution came to me during a fitful sleep in my Livingston home, in the bed my wife had vacated two years prior for a podiatrist in Montclair. An elastic band at the base of the condom – what the sexual accessories catalogs discreetly termed a "ring" – that would restrict venous return while maintaining arterial inflow. The erection would persist, the prophylactic would remain in place, and disease would be prevented.

In the morning light, the idea retained its elegance. I sketched diagrams on my kitchen table, between bites of toast grown cold with neglect. I contacted a patent attorney, paid his exorbitant fees, and submitted the application with the pride of an artist unveiling a masterpiece.

The Patent Office, in its bureaucratic wisdom, rejected my application. "Prior art," they called it, that crushing phrase that reminds us how few truly original ideas exist in the world. Someone, somewhere, had already conceived of my innovation, had already committed it to paper, had already staked their claim to that particular solution to that particular problem.

But the application remains, digitized and eternal, my name forever linked to this footnote in the history of sexual commerce. A curio for patients to discover and inquire about with poorly disguised titillation.

As I completed the examination of Goldstein-or-Goldblatt, checking his carotid pulse with fingers grown sensitive from decades of such palpations, I wondered what he would tell his wife about me. "Nice doctor," perhaps. Or maybe: "Did you know he invented a special condom?"

And she would laugh, or frown, or merely nod. And my professional life would once more be reduced to this single, failed attempt at invention.

In Newark, in America, we are all eventually reduced to our most marketable oddities. Even physicians. Even me.

Rachel from Long Island

In the autumn of 1968, our previously monastic upstate New York College admitted its first class of women, and among them was Rachel Goldstein from Roslyn, Long Island. The campus transformed overnight. Young men who had spent their freshman year discussing Kierkegaard and shooting pool suddenly developed an interest in personal grooming.

I was a sophomore then, another Jewish transplant, though from the less prestigious terrain of northern New Jersey. My accent still carried the nasal inflections of Newark, while Rachel's speech had the refined lilt of Nassau County privilege. Her father would arrive on parents' weekend in a gleaming Mercedes sedan that looked wildly out of place among the Volkswagens and dented Chevrolets that populated our campus parking lots.

Rachel was beautiful in that particular Long Island way – dark hair falling in perfect waves, cashmere sweaters, and an ease that spoke of tennis lessons and summer houses. My roommate Jerry fell immediately and catastrophically in love with her. "She's from another world," he would say, staring at the ceiling of our dormitory room. "Her family belongs to a country club."

I became Rachel's friend through what I can only describe as an accident of proximity and shared background. We were both taking Professor Bernstein's seminar on Saul Bellow, both familiar with the rhythms of Passover Seders and the taste of proper lox. We were not romantically involved – this was important to establish early – but there was a comfort between us that sometimes borders on intimacy.

That same year, I abandoned my studies of pre-medicine to form what we called the Plastic Island Band. Rachel joined as a vocalist, her voice surprisingly soulful for someone who had likely never experienced genuine hardship. I wrote earnest, sophomoric songs with titles like "Love Is on My Big Toe" and lyrics about meeting one's destiny on Cape Cod beaches. We performed at campus coffeehouses to moderate acclaim.

After graduation in 1972, our lives diverged in the way that lives do. I trudged off to medical school in Chicago, returning eventually to New Jersey with a cardiology practice and a family. Rachel, I heard through alumni newsletters, had married a scientist from General Electric, a man twenty years her senior who had patents and a house in Palo Alto. California seemed right for her somehow – the sunshine and the wealth without the Long Island insularity.

Nearly two decades passed before our paths crossed again. She reached out, seemingly from nowhere, and reconnected with Jerry, who had never fully recovered from his undergraduate infatuation. Together they attended my twin daughters' bat mitzvah in 1994. Rachel looked essentially unchanged – perhaps more elegant, with a certain California sleekness, but still unmistakably herself.

I introduced her to my friend Cy Kessler, himself twenty years our senior and recently widowed. Cy, predictably, was smitten, but Rachel was by then separated from her inventor husband and not interested in replacing him with another man of the same vintage.

Life continued its forward march. My cardiology practice thrived; my daughters went to college; Rachel again receded from view. Then, perhaps five years ago, an email arrived with her name in my inbox. She had suffered a stroke, and her doctors in California were recommending a loop recorder to monitor for atrial fibrillation.

I suggested, almost casually, that she might also benefit from a transesophageal echocardiogram. This was not revolutionary thinking on my part – merely standard protocol for someone with a cryptogenic stroke.

The test revealed a myxoma – a tumor in her heart that had almost certainly embolized and caused her stroke. The cardiac surgeons at Stanford removed it promptly, and afterward, Rachel told anyone who would listen that I had saved her life. Alumni publications carried the story; former classmates called to congratulate me. I demurred as doctors do, saying I had merely suggested a standard diagnostic test. But secretly, I was pleased.

We kept in sporadic contact after that. She reconciled with her husband; I continued seeing patients and playing occasional guitar at my synagogue's fundraisers. Then last month, another call. Rachel's voice was steady as she told me she had been diagnosed with amyotrophic lateral sclerosis – Lou Gehrig's disease. The prognosis was six months.

"Strange, isn't it?" she said. "You saved my life so I could receive this diagnosis."

Life unfolds with a peculiar narrative logic that we only recognize in retrospect. The beautiful girl from Long Island, the college band, the careers and marriages and reunions, the medical crisis and rescue, and now this final, cruel twist. If I were still writing those earnest songs from 1969, I might find some profound meaning in it all. But I am a cardiologist now, and I know that bodies are fragile, and destinies rarely follow the paths we imagine for them.

Rachel laughed a little before we hung up. "Remember that song about the big toe? God, we were young."

We were. And now we are not. And that is the simplest and most complicated story there is.

The Cardiologist's Symphony

After forty-three years as a cardiologist, I have developed what might be called a musical ear. Not for Bach or Beethoven, though I enjoy them well enough, but for the peculiar symphonies produced by the human heart. I estimate that I have listened to somewhere north of one million hearts, each with its own timbre and signature, each telling its own story through a language of lubb-dupps and whooshes that, to the untrained ear, might seem monotonous but to mine contains all the variation and nuance of a Mahler composition.

My colleagues often marvel at my diagnostic accuracy without the benefit of echocardiograms or stress tests. "Just let me listen," I tell them, tapping my ancient Littmann stethoscope, its tubing long since hardened with age. The younger cardiologists, raised on imaging technology, regard this as a quaint parlor trick. They don't understand that I'm not merely hearing sounds but interpreting a complex musical piece that reveals everything about its composer.

Mrs. Abramowitz came to me last Thursday, a widow of seventy-six with complaints of fatigue and shortness of breath. Before she had finished easing herself onto the examination table, I could hear her mitral valve prolapse – a slight disorder of rhythm, like a violinist who consistently misses the same note in an otherwise flawless performance. But there was something else there too, an arrhythmia that spoke not of physical pathology but of emotional distress.

"When did your daughter stop calling?" I asked after my examination.

Mrs. Abramowitz looked startled, then tearful. “Three weeks ago. We had a fight about her husband. How did you know?”

I merely smiled and wrote a prescription for a mild beta-blocker. The medication would help with her palpitations, but what she really needed was reconciliation. Hearts in emotional distress develop their own particular dissonance, recognizable to those who have cataloged the many variations of human cardiac disturbance.

I sometimes think about how we begin our lives attuned to this most fundamental music. The first concert we ever attend is in utero – our mother’s heartbeat surrounding us like an orchestra in the round, establishing not just rhythm but expectation and security. For nine months, the maternal heart and the fetal heart beat in tandem, not synchronized but harmonic, establishing a pattern that I believe remains with us as a template for what feels right and comforting in this world.

Young Dr. Patel, my newest associate, caught me once with my eyes closed in examination room three, not listening but almost conducting with small movements of my free hand as I attended to the heart of Mr. Gutierrez, a sixty-two-year-old with a recently implanted pacemaker.

“What are you doing?” he asked afterward, equal parts amused and concerned.

“Listening to how the mechanical rhythm interacts with his natural one,” I said. “It’s like when you splice a digital beat into an acoustic recording. There’s an authenticity gap.”

Dr. Patel nodded politely, but I could tell he thought I was becoming eccentric in my advancing years. Perhaps I am. But I maintain that there is wisdom in this approach that the textbooks don’t teach and the imaging can’t capture.

I have a patient, a pianist with the city symphony, who comes to me not because I am particularly convenient to her home or covered well by her insurance, but because, as she put it, "You're the only doctor who understands that a heart is an instrument." When she developed a concerning murmur last year – a distinctive regurgitation that suggested moderate aortic stenosis – her first question wasn't about surgical options or mortality statistics.

"Will it change my playing?" she asked.

I closed my eyes and listened again through my stethoscope. The murmur had a rhythmic quality that seemed to want to resolve itself, like a dissonant chord seeking harmony.

"It might deepen it," I answered truthfully. "You'll feel the music differently. Not worse, but with more awareness of its fragility."

She nodded as if this were the most natural prognosis in the world, and perhaps between us, it was.

The heart reveals everything – anxiety, grief, joy, exhaustion, peace. A new mother's heart has a particular sound, a bit faster than normal but with a confident regularity that suggests both alertness and purpose. The hearts of the dying often develop a rhythm of resignation, a slowing that contains neither fear nor resistance, but rather a dignified preparation for silence. I've delivered terminal diagnoses to patients who nodded calmly while their hearts had already accepted what their minds were just learning.

Sometimes I think we have it backward in cardiology. We speak of the heart as a pump, a mechanical device whose purpose is mere circulation. But what if its primary purpose is musical? What if the blood moving through our bodies is secondary to the rhythm and resonance that establishes our place in the universal composition?

I will retire next spring, and Dr. Patel and his colleagues will continue without my esoteric observations. Their patients will receive excellent, evidence-based care guided by the latest research and technology. But I wonder if they will ever know what it means to close one's eyes and hear not just a heart, but a life story told in beats and pauses, in whispers and shouts, in the oldest language we know – the one we heard before we had words, when our mother's heart taught us the meaning of safety and love and connection through its steady, reassuring song.

Perhaps I'll take up piano lessons in retirement. My wife suggests I should find a hobby unrelated to medicine, but I disagree. Music and medicine have never been separate disciplines to me. They are merely different dialects of the same fundamental language – the language of rhythm and harmony that governs not just health, but existence itself.

The Cardiologist's Tale

There are moments in medicine when one is struck by the curious symmetries of human gratitude. Thirty-five years apart, two patients said nearly identical words to me: "Doctor, you are my best friend. You saved my life." The first came from a Presbyterian minister in the early 1980s; the second from a contemporary patient prescribed Viagra. Both for essentially the same problem. What connects them is not the malady but the relief – that particular lightness that comes when something thought irrevocably lost has been returned.

I was a young cardiologist then, freshly established in town, still finding my bearings in the peculiar intimacies that form the substrate of medical practice. The Reverend Williams (not his real name, of course) and his wife appeared in my office one Tuesday afternoon. He sat stiffly in the patient's chair, hands folded as if in perpetual prayer, while she occupied herself with the hem of her dress. The problem, when finally articulated after considerable throat-clearing and euphemism, was what we now call erectile dysfunction, though in those days it traveled under considerably less clinical nomenclature.

This was the dawn of the VCR age, that brief technological interregnum when the video cassette recorder represented the height of domestic entertainment. Being a doctor – and thus licensed to make suggestions that would have seemed impertinent coming from anyone else – I recommended they purchase such a machine and, in addition, procure what were then called "adult" videotapes, available at Crazy Eddie's, the local electronics emporium that advertised its "INSAAANE" prices on late-night television.

"To watch together," I added, in case my prescription required clarification.

They exchanged a glance whose meaning I could not decipher, nodded solemnly, and left.

A week later, they reappeared. The Reverend's posture had undergone a remarkable transformation. He sat now with the relaxed confidence of a man reconciled to his earthly vessel.

"Doctor," he said, leaning forward, "you are our best friend. You saved our marriage."

Mrs. Williams nodded vigorously, her face illuminated by what I can only describe as conspiratorial joy.

Several years after this small triumph of medical pragmatism, the Reverend suffered a myocardial infarction – a heart attack, in the vernacular. Upon his recovery, he insisted on telling me precisely what had precipitated his cardiac event. It wasn't cholesterol or heredity or stress, he maintained, but rather the young EKG technician, Miss Gladys Porter, who had leaned over him during his pre-admission examination, her uniform – he claimed – revealing aspects of her anatomy that proved too stimulating for his compromised heart.

"It was when she leaned over to attach the leads," he whispered from his hospital bed, with the urgency of a man imparting crucial scientific data. "That's when it happened."

Miss Porter was, in my estimation, a thoroughly pleasant young woman of unremarkable appearance, competent in her duties and universally regarded as professional. I nodded gravely at the Reverend's account, maintaining what I hoped was an expression of medical interest rather than skepticism.

These twin episodes bookend, in my mind, something essential about the practice of medicine: that our patients' most profound gratitude often follows not from our most sophisticated interventions, but from our recognition of their humanity in its full, complicated glory. The Reverend and my recent Viagra patient shared not only a complaint but a particular kind of loneliness, the specific isolation that comes when the body betrays a central human connection.

In medical school, they never teach you that sometimes the most effective prescription is permission – permission to acknowledge desire, to seek pleasure, to remain fully human even as the body falters. Both men called me their best friend not because I had done something particularly clever or heroic, but because I had granted them this permission when no one else would.

And if the Reverend believed Miss Porter's décolletage had nearly killed him? Well, there are worse ways for a man of God to rationalize the stubborn persistence of desire in the face of mortality. We physicians learn, eventually, that our patients' stories about their bodies are often more important than any clinical narrative we might impose upon them.

The Shifting Lens

It was an ordinary Wednesday afternoon in my practice. The rain tapped gently against the window as Dr. Milton Braithwaite – professor of economics, bow tie enthusiast, and my 3:15 appointment for the last twelve years – settled into the leather chair across from mine.

"I've been thinking about perception," he said without preamble. "Not the grand philosophical questions, mind you, but the small daily betrayals of our own eyes."

Milton had always possessed a certain professorial charm, the kind that made even his most mundane observations seem like revelations. Today was no exception.

"Last weekend, I attended a car show downtown. Vintage automobiles – primarily American, primarily mid-century. The kind my father used to point out on Sunday drives." Milton adjusted his glasses. "I found myself standing before a 1959 Cadillac – you know the one, with those outrageous tail fins that looked like something from a science fiction serial."

I nodded, though I knew nothing of cars beyond my sensible sedan that had carried me to and from this office for eight years without complaint.

"When I was twelve," Milton continued, "that car represented everything magnificent in the world. Those fins were promises of a future that never arrived. But standing there on Saturday, I found myself thinking how absurd they looked – excessive, almost embarrassingly so."

Milton paused, his fingers forming a steeple beneath his chin.

"And yet, the strangest thing happened. In the next room was a 1960 Cadillac – more restrained, more 'modern,' as they were calling it then. And I remembered how, when it first appeared, the '59 suddenly seemed gauche and outdated. My affections had transferred instantly to the newcomer."

He smiled wryly. "It's not just automobiles, of course. When slim-cut suits came back into fashion, I found myself looking at photographs from the seventies – my wedding, for instance – and wondering how I could have possibly thought those wide lapels flattered anyone. Now they only remind me of game show hosts and disco enthusiasts."

The rain intensified outside, creating a pleasant backdrop to our conversation. Milton wasn't seeking advice today; he was simply thinking aloud, working through something.

"It makes me wonder – what part of our preferences is truly ours? Every time the Range Rover releases a new model, the previous one – the very same vehicle I coveted last season – appears suddenly deficient. What mechanism in our brains allows this sleight of hand to occur? We become instantaneous converts to the gospel of the new, with hardly a backward glance at our former devotions."

I considered his question carefully. "Perhaps we're not just responding to the object itself, but to the narrative surrounding it. The new car isn't just a car – it's progress, innovation, status. We're social creatures, after all."

Milton nodded thoughtfully. "Yes, but there's something more fundamental at work. I genuinely perceive the older model as less appealing. My aesthetic judgment has been altered, not just my social understanding of what the object represents."

We sat in companionable silence for a moment.

"The trouble is," Milton finally said, leaning forward slightly, "I can't help but wonder what else in my life is subject to this same mutable perception. What truths have I held with certainty, only to discard when a newer version came along? What principles have I abandoned not because they were wrong, but simply because they went out of style?"

The question hung between us, unanswerable but essential.

As our session drew to a close, Milton stood and straightened his bow tie – narrow, currently fashionable, though I remembered when he had worn them wider.

"Perhaps," he said with a small smile, "the only constant is our capacity for self-deception. We believe our judgments are sound, even as they shift beneath our feet."

After he left, I found myself looking out at the rain-slicked street, watching umbrellas bloom like sudden flowers. I thought about perception and how easily it changes, how we convince ourselves that what we see now is what has always been true. There was something both troubling and comforting in the thought – that our certainties are temporary, but so too are our doubts.

The Long Rematch

The emergency room at Westlake Memorial never sleeps, though at 3 a.m. on a Tuesday in February, it had the drowsy quality of a train station between arrivals. I had been a cardiologist for nearly forty years, and the night shift, which I took monthly as penance for some forgotten professional sin, still felt like an ill-fitting suit.

The nurse handed me a chart. "Seventy-two-year-old male, chest pain radiating to left arm, minimal EKG changes." Her voice had the practiced flatness of someone who had announced a hundred such cases that month.

The patient sat upright on the examination table, a lean African American man with close-cropped silver hair and hands that looked as though they'd known labor. His name was William Thornton, and he regarded me with the calm wariness patients often adopt when they suspect bad news approaches but would prefer to face it with dignity.

"Good morning, Mr. Thornton. I'm Dr. Kaplan."

"Call me Bill," he said, and something in his voice tickled the back of my memory.

I proceeded with the examination, asking the usual questions about the nature of his pain, his medical history, his medications. His answers were precise, perhaps too precise – the narrative too rehearsed, the casual tone too deliberate. I've learned over decades that patients often try to negotiate with their symptoms through their descriptions of them.

"And where are you from, Bill?"

"Scotch Plains," he answered. "Been there most of my life."

I paused, stethoscope against his back. "Scotch Plains, New Jersey?"

"That's right."

"I grew up in Hillside," I said, the name feeling strange in my mouth, a childhood artifact suddenly unearthed.

His eyes narrowed slightly, recalibrating. "Hillside? What years?"

"Graduated high school in '70."

Something changed in his face, a kind of geological shift. "You didn't wrestle, did you?"

And suddenly, I was seventeen again, in a gymnasium that smelled of floor polish and adolescent anxiety. "152-pound weight class," I said quietly.

Bill Thornton began to laugh, a deep, knowing laugh that seemed to loosen something in his chest. "Well, I'll be damned. You're Alan Kaplan. I remember you."

I remembered him too, though the boyish face was buried beneath seventy years of living. William Thornton, state champion wrestler from Scotch Plains. I had faced him once in a regional match, an encounter that lasted an eternity of six minutes. I had joined the wrestling team on a whim, seeking some vague notion of toughness that seemed important at seventeen. Thornton had been wrestling since elementary school.

"You toyed with me like a cat with a half-dead mouse," I said, surprising myself with the lack of rancor in my voice. "Twenty-two to nothing, wasn't it?"

"Twenty-four," he corrected, then had the good grace to look embarrassed. "You know, I was showing off. Coach had scouts from Rutgers in the stands."

We shared a laugh, the kind that acknowledges the absurd persistence of memory and the way time renders even humiliations into anecdotes.

"I could have pinned you in the first period," he said, "but I was trying to demonstrate technique. Coach ripped into me afterward for not finishing it quickly."

"Small comfort," I replied, but I was smiling.

I ordered a nuclear stress test, though something about the presentation troubled me. The EKG changes were minimal, but his description of the pain had the authenticity that experienced physicians learn to heed. The stress test came back with subtle abnormalities that might have been dismissed by a less cautious practitioner.

"I'm sending you to the Cath lab," I told him. "Just to be certain."

My partner, Dr. Levinson, performed the catheterization. When she called me, her voice had the controlled urgency of someone delivering news they'd rather not.

"Left main coronary artery, ninety percent occluded," she said. "Left anterior descending, nearly as bad. I'm placing stents now."

The left main coronary artery – the Widowmaker. A complete blockage there leaves most patients with minutes, perhaps seconds. Thornton had been walking around with a bomb in his chest, its fuse burning invisibly short.

I visited him the following afternoon. He was sitting up in bed, looking remarkably improved, the gray pallor replaced by a healthier shade. His wife dozed in the chair beside him, her hand resting protectively on his arm even in sleep.

"Dr. Kaplan," he said, his voice stronger than it had been in the ER. "Seems I owe you one."

"Dr. Levinson placed the stents," I demurred.

"But you sent me to her. That hunch of yours..." He paused, looking down at his hands, which no longer trembled. "Doc, you know what this means? After all these years, you won."

I started to protest, but he raised a hand.

"No, I'm serious. I beat you back then. Beat you bad, and I knew it. But today? Today, you pinned me, fair and square. And saved my life doing it."

We regarded each other across the hospital room, two old men with more sand at the bottom of the hourglass than the top. I thought about telling him that medicine isn't a competition that we're all just trying to outmaneuver mortality for another day. But there was something in his eyes – a gleam of the seventeen-year-old champion acknowledging defeat with grace – that stopped me.

"Rematch in another fifty years?" I suggested.

Bill Thornton laughed, a sound full of life and promise. "You're on, Doc. But I'll be training this time."

His wife stirred at the sound, smiling in her half-sleep at hearing laughter where she had feared there might be none again.

Later, driving home, I thought about how strangely life measures victory and defeat. How a humiliation on a wrestling mat six decades ago could, through the long meandering of years, lead to being in the right place at the right time with the right knowledge. How losing thoroughly might be a precondition for saving someone, later, when it matters most.

In medicine, we speak clinically of "good outcomes," but what happened with Bill Thornton felt like something else, something older and more primal than professional satisfaction – a debt repaid, perhaps, or a circle closed. Or maybe just the recognition that in the longest matches, scored across decades rather than minutes, we all take our turns being pinned and being saved.

The Happiest Prescription

Sometimes I see patients together in the examining room: a husband and wife, a mother and daughter, and sometimes just two friends. Today, I saw two elderly ladies, both in their early to mid-eighties, longtime patients of mine. They were practically vibrating with enthusiasm, even more animated than usual.

Both women navigate the world with walkers or canes. One can hardly see, the other can hardly hear. Yet together they form a remarkably functional unit, each compensating for the other's deficiencies, their friendship creating something greater than its parts.

My medical assistant inquired about the source of their exuberant happiness, and they announced, almost in unison, "We're going to Atlantic City later today!"

Atlantic City – that faded jewel of the Jersey Shore with its famous boardwalk, once elegant hotels now converted to gambling palaces. They were bound for Valley's Casino, where they've achieved minor celebrity status. They're "comped," as the gambling parlance goes: free buffet meals, complimentary show tickets, beautiful hotel rooms – all the small courtesies extended to reliable customers.

"We go two or three times a month," the more talkative one explained, her rheumy eyes twinkling behind thick lenses. "It's the best thing in the world for us."

"Sometimes we win, sometimes we lose," her companion added. "Sometimes we just visit the money we left behind!" This set them both cackling with laughter.

They're well-known at the casino, fixtures at the slot machines. "They think we're lesbians down there," the first one confided with a conspiratorial wink, "but of course we're not. And if I were a lesbian," she added, pointing to her companion, "I could certainly do better than her!" More riotous laughter ensued, her friend swatting at her arm in mock offense.

I signed their prescriptions and wished them luck at the slots. As I watched them shuffle out – one guiding the other around obstacles she couldn't see, the second loudly repeating what the first couldn't hear – I reflected that I could prescribe the most advanced medications in the world, but nothing in my pharmaceutical arsenal could match what those flashing, dinging machines and that gaudy casino provided: purpose, excitement, community, and the most potent medicine of all – hope.

For three hours of dropping quarters into slots, they purchase what we all secretly crave: the sweet anticipation that perhaps today, against all odds, fortune might smile upon them.

VI. Vital Signs: Human Conditions

Thematic pairings exploring life's dualities

a. Mortality & Meaning

Time's Final Victory

Morris Lieberman defied time in ways that most of us never contemplate. When the doctors in '93 told him he wouldn't leave the hospital – that the damage to his heart was irreparable – he simply refused to accept their verdict. Not out of ignorance or denial, but because Morris had already faced death too many times to be intimidated by its latest messenger.

As I stood in the back of the chapel, observing the ritual of loss that has changed so little over the centuries, I couldn't help but note the bitter irony. The man who had escaped the unimaginable horrors of Auschwitz, who had rebuilt a life from nothing in a foreign country, who had stared down a massive coronary three decades ago and walked away, was finally defeated by the inexorable arithmetic of biology.

His wife, Sarah, sat in the front row, her small frame convulsed with grief that seemed too large for her body to contain. Married sixty-four years – a partnership that had witnessed history's darkest chapter and persevered. Their love story wasn't the Hollywood variety with swelling music and perfect lighting. It was forged in circumstances so grim that merely surviving together constituted a form of heroism.

"Morris, come back! Morris, come back to me now!" she wailed, her voice cracking with a desperation that silenced the room. Her words were not the dignified sorrow one expects at these occasions but the raw, unfiltered demand of a heart that cannot process its sudden solitude. Several relatives moved closer, enveloping her with protective arms, whispering consoling platitudes that bounced off her grief like rain off stone.

I had been Morris's cardiologist for the last fifteen years. When we first met, I had studied his medical history with professional fascination – how could someone survive that catastrophic event in 1993? His chart was a testament to medical improbability. "You know, Doctor," he once told me during a routine visit, his accent still thick after seven decades in America, "death has been chasing me since 1942. I'm very good at running."

But even Olympic runners eventually stop. Even the most determined hearts eventually falter.

As the rabbi spoke of Morris's remarkable resilience, his contributions to the community, his devotion to family, Sarah's sobs transformed into something more alarming. "I can't do this without you," she cried out, her hands clutching at her wrists in a gesture that sent a ripple of concern through the assembly. "What is the point now? What is left?"

The truth about profound love – the kind that spans continents and outlasts dictators – is that it contains within its depths the seeds of its own particular agony. The mathematics of devotion dictates that except in the rarest cases of simultaneous death, one partner must endure the unendurable: life without the other.

Morris had beaten death repeatedly. But death, patient beyond human comprehension, simply waited. It always does. And in its waiting, it ensures that even the most beautiful of human connections carries within it the certainty of devastating loss.

Later, after the service, I approached Sarah to offer my condolences. Her eyes, red-rimmed but suddenly clear, fixed on mine with surprising lucidity.

"You know what he said to me that morning? Before they took him to the hospital?" she asked, her voice now eerily calm. "He said, 'Sarah, I think I've finally run out of miracles.' Sixty-four years together, and he still found ways to prepare me."

I nodded, unable to find adequate words.

"But he was wrong," she continued, a ghost of a smile touching her lips. "The miracle was never that he survived. The miracle was that we found each other at all."

The Weight of Words

In the peculiar theater of medicine, where we doctors imagine ourselves as the principal actors, we often forget that our patients are watching us with the keen attention of critics. It is they who remember our lines long after we have forgotten the performance entirely.

I was rounding at St. Elizabeth's yesterday, shuffling through the corridor in my usual midday fatigue, when a nurse handed me a consult. "Cardiology issue, room 418," she said, already moving on.

Room 418 contained a woman who must have been in her eighties, though her hair – a shade of red so vibrant it practically hummed – suggested a certain defiance of time's conventions. The color was obviously from a bottle, and all the more charming for it.

"Doctor!" she exclaimed with unexpected delight. "Don't you remember me?"

I offered my standard apologetic smile, the one for these moments of failed recognition that increase in frequency as one's practice lengthens.

"You examined me thirty years ago," she continued. "I was much younger then."

I nodded politely, mentally calculating that I would have been early in my career at that point – a time when I saw so many patients that their faces blurred together like commuters on a passing train.

"What I remember," she said, leaning forward slightly, "is that you were sitting in your chair, and you looked at me and said, 'Get up on the table, Red.' Just like that. Period." She smiled at the memory. "To this day, I remember that phrase. I even think about it quite often. It was very nice, very casual. Put me quite at ease."

I felt a curious mixture of embarrassment and fascination. Here was a throwaway line, likely uttered without a moment's thought, preserved for three decades in the amber of this woman's memory.

"That's remarkable," I said, genuinely touched.

"That reminds me," I said, "of something else I heard over the weekend. We doctors don't realize that our words are listened to so closely and followed so faithfully." I paused, considering the weight of this realization. "A patient told me that I once advised her to drink a glass of warm water every night before bed to help her fall asleep and clear her nasal passages. For thirty-five years, that's exactly what she's been doing. Listening to the doctor's advice. Warm water before bed."

I sat down in the chair beside her bed, momentarily forgetting the consultation I was meant to perform. How strange to think that our casual prescriptions – these small, forgettable utterances – might be operating in the world long after we've moved on to other patients and other concerns. Like parents who discover, years later, that their children have been silently absorbing their offhand remarks, we doctors scatter our words like seeds, never knowing which will take root.

"It's amazing," I agreed, "the power of words."

"Yes," said the woman with the bright red hair. "Now, about my heart..."

And so we moved on to the business at hand, though I found myself choosing my words with unusual care, conscious that I might be writing a line that would echo for decades to come in this woman's private anthology of medical encounters. The thought was both humbling and oddly exhilarating – to imagine that in the vast and often cold machinery of modern medicine, such small human connections might endure.

The Shelf on the Wall

In the ICU, they all look the same. The human form, once distinct with its particular gait, gestures, and voice, is rendered anonymous by illness. Professor Joseph Halstein lies unresponsive on a respirator, one of twenty-nine patients in this ward. His skull, stripped of the silver hair that once crowned it with a certain professorial dignity, gleams under the fluorescent lights. A surgical wound across his abdomen seeps steadily, requiring frequent attention from the nurses who move efficiently between beds.

His lungs – those instruments that once projected lectures on Chekhov and Baldwin to the back rows of the university's largest hall – now struggle against the fluids drowning them. The machine beside him counts each mechanically assisted breath with quiet precision.

We know nothing of this man, not really. In the democratic republic of the critically ill, past accomplishments hold no currency. Yet his wife, Margaret, has attempted to assert his identity in this sterile space. She has papered the walls with photographs of Paris – the two of them smiling beneath the Eiffel Tower, leaning against the stone embankment of the Seine, sitting at a café on the Boulevard Saint-Germain. In these images, he stands tall and robust, his arm around her shoulders, his face animated in conversation.

Most telling is the Plexiglas display holder she has placed on the small table beside his bed. In it stand two books, their spines facing outward for all to see: "The Ironic Distance: Narrative Voice in Modern Fiction" and "Beneath the Surface: Essays on Literary Concealment." His name appears on both covers in raised lettering.

Margaret adjusts these books several times a day, ensuring they remain visible to anyone who enters. The medical staff – kind but necessarily detached – glance at them occasionally as they check his vitals and adjust his medications. Some pick them up, weighing them in their hands before returning them precisely to their display.

It is a quiet insistence: this man is not merely a failing body. He is Professor Joseph Halstein, who once stood before hundreds of students, who published in distinguished journals, who spent sabbaticals in Paris where he and Margaret walked for miles along narrow streets discussing the books they loved.

The monitors beep; the respirator hisses and clicks. His colleagues from the English Department visit in shifts, standing awkwardly at the foot of the bed, unsure whether to address him directly. They leave flowers and cards that Margaret arranges carefully. The department chair mentions that students have organized a reading of his work.

Margaret sits beside him, hour after hour, sometimes reading aloud from the dog-eared paperbacks she pulls from her bag. Her voice is steady as she recites passages he once underlined, though occasionally it catches on a particular phrase. When this happens, she pauses, sips water, and continues.

At night, when the ward is at its quietest, she leans close to his ear and whispers their private history – memories of their first apartment, the conferences they attended together, the garden he tended so meticulously. Whether he hears her is unknown. The machines continue their work, maintaining what remains of the man whose books stand sentry on the bedside table, asserting his identity against the tide of anonymity that illness brings to us all.

The Final Request

There exists in the small towns of New Jersey a particular intimacy between doctor and patient that the medical schools, with their emphasis on clinical detachment, neither teach nor perhaps even comprehend. I speak from my own experience, having practiced cardiology in such a town – let us call it Millburn – where the borders between professional obligation and personal affection grow indistinct over decades of shared medical crises and family milestones.

Stanley Greenberg was what my father would have called "a real character" – a phrase that, in the lexicon of men of my father's generation, could encompass everything from mild eccentricity to outright moral flexibility. Stanley inclined toward the latter end of this spectrum. He was what people once called "a man about town," driving a car slightly too expensive for his circumstances, frequenting restaurants where the maître d' knew to bring his preferred scotch without being asked.

Stanley had run into some trouble with the law. Nothing violent or depraved, you understand. White-collar improprieties: investment schemes that skirted regulations, tax maneuvers that caught the attention of authorities. The sort of transgressions committed in boardrooms rather than back alleys.

Yet despite these moral compromises, or perhaps because of them, Stanley possessed an extraordinary capacity for gratitude. I had guided him through a triple bypass, the installation of a defibrillator, and a valve replacement – the medical equivalent of renovating a house room by room over many years. After each procedure, his gratitude was effusive and persistent. Christmas baskets arrived at my office; invitations to his daughter's wedding and his son's bar mitzvah followed. His wife, Rebecca, a woman of quiet dignity and considerable intelligence, once confided to my own wife at a chance meeting in the supermarket: "Without your husband, I would have been a widow ten years ago."

In medical school, they warn against becoming overly attached to patients. "You cannot save everyone," the chief resident intoned during my internship, "and you must not try." But they never tell you about the opposite peril: that patients may become too attached to you, may invest in you powers that extend beyond the considerable but ultimately limited arsenal of modern medicine.

This truth revealed itself to me on a Tuesday evening in late October, when autumn had begun its rehearsal for winter. I was at home, reading a biography of Oliver Wendell Holmes, when my phone rang. It was the hospital. Stanley Greenberg had been admitted with massive cardiac arrest. CPR had been administered for nearly an hour. He was gone.

I drove to the hospital immediately – not because there was anything medically to be done, but because after twenty years as Stanley's cardiologist, I had become something beyond a doctor to his family. What precise role I played in their emotional ecosystem, I couldn't have articulated, but I knew my presence was required.

The scene at the hospital was one I had witnessed countless times: the harsh fluorescent lighting that seems designed to strip away not just darkness but any comforting illusion; the relatives clustered together, their faces bearing that particular expression of people trying to assimilate information that the mind instinctively rejects.

Rebecca saw me first. "Doctor," she said, and in that single word I heard both gratitude for my arrival and acceptance that it came too late.

Stanley's daughter, now a mother herself, embraced me. His son David, a man in his thirties with Stanley's prominent nose and receding hairline, stood slightly apart from the others, his posture suggesting that grief was a private business best conducted without witnesses.

I spoke the practiced words of condolence that doctors develop, like calluses, over years of delivering bad news. I answered their questions about Stanley's final moments with measured honesty. Yes, everything possible had been done. No, he would not have felt pain. The familiar liturgy of medical reassurance.

Then, as the conversation began to exhaust itself, David approached me. He had been silent until then, but now he placed his hand on my arm with an urgency that startled me.

"Doctor," he said, his voice low but perfectly steady, "can't you do something now and bring him back?"

The question hung in the air between us. Stanley had been dead for forty-five minutes. The family had already viewed his body. The hospital staff had begun the paperwork that transforms a person into a former person. Yet here was his son, a rational man with a degree from Rutgers and a position at an accounting firm, asking if I might reverse death itself.

"I'm sorry, David," I said. "I can't do that. Nobody can."

He nodded, not in acceptance but in the manner of someone filing away disappointing information. "I understand," he said, though his eyes suggested otherwise.

What struck me, driving home later through the dark suburban streets, was not the unreasonableness of his request – grief makes unreasonable demands of us all – but rather the extraordinary faith it revealed. Here was a man who had seen the full limitations of medicine throughout his father's long illness, who had presumably absorbed the bleak statistics and cautious prognoses I had delivered over the years, yet who still believed, at some level deeper than rational thought that a doctor's powers might extend to resurrection.

I felt, as I turned onto my own street, a complex emotion for which the vocabulary of medicine offers no term. Pride, certainly, at having earned such faith. Humility, that this faith was ultimately misplaced. But most of all, a profound sadness that after saving Stanley's life on three separate occasions, I had finally failed his family when it mattered most.

The following Sunday, at Stanley's funeral, David approached me again. "I want to apologize," he said, "for what I asked at the hospital. It was stupid."

"No," I replied, "it wasn't stupid at all. It was human."

What I didn't say, what perhaps I couldn't articulate even to myself until much later, was that his question had revealed something essential about the strange covenant between doctors and those who depend on them: that medicine, for all its scientific trappings, still exists in the realm of faith. That despite CT scans and artificial valves and the cold precision of surgical steel, what patients and their families truly seek from us is not merely technique but something closer to magic – the ability to say "no" to death itself.

It is a power no honest physician would claim to possess. Yet how much of my professional satisfaction, I wondered, had come from moments when I had seemed, however temporarily, to possess exactly that? And how much of my distress that night came from being forced, finally, to admit its limits?

The Invisible Victory

In the hospital's doctor's lounge, I was enjoying a roast beef sandwich when my phone buzzed. The resident's voice was calm but urgent – a new patient in the ER with chest pain and elevated troponin levels. I set my lunch aside, napkin still tucked in my collar, and headed down.

The young man looked too healthy to be there, his face drawn in pain but otherwise strong, vital. The EKG showed subtle changes, nothing dramatic, but combined with the enzymes and his story, my instincts flared. Twenty years of cardiology had taught me to trust that feeling.

"Let's take him to cath," I told the resident.

In the lab, the fluoroscopy revealed what I'd feared – a critical stenosis in the LAD, the artery we call the widow-maker. Ninety percent blocked. The team moved with practiced precision as we deployed the stent. The narrowed artery opened like a flower blooming in time-lapse, restoration of flow immediate and dramatic. The patient's face relaxed before we were even finished.

Victory. Silent, invisible to anyone outside that room, but victory nonetheless.

The next morning during rounds, I found him dressed, texting, eager to leave.

"Doc, I think this was all overkill. I'm fine now. Was this really necessary?"

I explained the blockage, what might have happened without intervention. He nodded politely, clearly unconvinced. To him, the disaster that never came might as well have never existed.

Walking back to my office, I passed a television showing some reality star's latest scandal. Three channels were covering it.

I smiled to myself. While cameras chased celebrities and the world obsessed over stock prices, I had reopened a human heart. No applause, no headlines, not even the patient's full comprehension. Just the quiet satisfaction of having turned death away from someone's door for another day.

This is the peculiar weight and grace of medicine – our most profound victories are the catastrophes that never happen, invisible to all, sometimes even to those we save.

b. Humor & Healing

A Condom Triptych

So, dear reader, in a previous confession I regaled you with the tale of my condom patent – that noble attempt at prophylactic innovation born from the complaints of go-go dancers whose customers lost tumescence at the crucial moment. My solution: a lust-support ring at the base. The patent office crushed my dreams with that most devastating of phrases – "prior art" – though I remain inordinately proud that when my name is Googled, there appears my patent application, complete with technical drawings, my modest contribution to mankind's endless struggle against unwanted conception.

But this reminds me of two other episodes involving that thin latex membrane that has preserved the social order and prevented countless hasty marriages.

I. The Hillside High School Fire Brigade

As a teenage boy roaming the hallways of Hillside High School, I carried a condom in my wallet for what seemed an eternity. It remained there, compressed into a perfect circle, creating a tell-tale impression in the leather – a secret badge of optimistic virility that remained, week after week, month after month, unused.

Its debut would come, not in some fevered backseat encounter, but in a New Jersey diner parking lot where we congregated on Friday nights, teenagers smoking cigarettes and pretending at adulthood. It was there that someone's carelessly discarded cigarette – perhaps mine, though I prefer to assign blame elsewhere – slipped between the vinyl seats of my friend's father's Oldsmobile. Within seconds, wisps of smoke began rising from the crack.

With remarkable presence of mind for a seventeen-year-old virgin, I extracted my wallet, retrieved my long-awaited condom, and sprinted into the diner's bathroom. There, at the sink, I filled the prophylactic with cold water until it hung heavy and distended, a water balloon of last resort. Back at the car, I ruptured my latex savior over the smoldering upholstery, extinguishing what might have been a catastrophic fire with this impromptu fire extinguisher.

And thus, with neither pleasure nor procreation, ended the long-awaited inaugural use of my condom.

II. The Operatic Finale in Bologne

Several years later, my European wanderjahr found me traversing Switzerland with a rucksack and the continental confidence of an American abroad. In a Zürich café, I encountered a University of Michigan soprano studying for the summer at the prestigious opera academy in Bologne. After an evening of conversation during which I feigned musical sophistication, she invited me to visit her at the academy's chalet.

This impressive edifice housed two dozen American vocal students in an atmosphere of Old World refinement. Crystal chandeliers hung from ornately plastered ceilings; heavy draperies framed tall windows; and at mealtimes, white-gloved staff served multicourse dinners on fine china.

That evening, after attending a student recital where my new acquaintance performed an aria from *La Bohème* with impressive technical skill if not emotional depth, we returned to her dormitory room. The night that followed was everything my seventeen-year-old self had imagined during those long months of wallet-carrying anticipation.

In the aftermath of passion, without thinking, I disposed of the spent latex evidence as seemed natural to me at that unrefined moment – I simply opened the leaded-glass window and tossed it into the darkness below, into what I assumed was a convenient shrubbery.

The next morning, I joined the academy students for breakfast in their formal dining room, where tall windows overlooked a manicured garden. As coffee was being served, a collective gasp arose from several students seated facing the windows. There, suspended from the lowest branch of a perfectly pruned linden tree, hanging like some obscene Christmas ornament, was my discarded condom, swollen and glistening in the morning sunlight.

The academy director, a severe Austrian woman with steel-gray hair twisted into a formidable bun, rose from her seat at the head of the table and stared pointedly first at the arboreal exhibition, then at me, then at my soprano friend, whose face had achieved a shade of crimson previously visible only in certain Renaissance paintings of martyred saints.

I departed within the half-hour, never to return, leaving behind both my dignity and that latex testament to youth's impulsivity. For all I know, it may still hang there, a cautionary decoration for subsequent generations of vocalists.

And there you have it – my condom triptych, tales neither of conquest nor of contraception achieved, but rather of American ingenuity and European mortification.

Coda: ***Fifty-Three Years Later***

As an aside – and here is where the true Rothian irony of Jewish-American experience reveals itself – some five decades after this ignominious departure, in a moment of nostalgic digital stalking that has become the pastime of our senescence, I Googled my operatic partner from that Swiss interlude. The soprano whose voice once aspired to La Scala now serves as a rabbinical cantor in Boise, Idaho. There, among the retired podiatrists and garment industry moguls, she teaches bar and bat mitzvah students the ancient melodies of our people, guiding them through the Hebrew passages that will mark their entrance into adulthood – presumably with more decorum than I demonstrated in mine. The voice that once filled a European concert hall with Puccini now intones "Baruch atah Adonai" to pubescent Jews in the air-conditioned comfort of a South Florida synagogue. Life, as they say, completes its circles, though rarely with the perfect symmetry of that condom's impression on my teenage wallet.

The Umbrella Incident

I was labeled mentally deficient at age six. Not my words – the New York City public school systems. My crime? Selecting "umbrella" on a standardized test asking what grows. The other options were a car, pants, and a tree. A tree seemed too obvious. I've always distrusted the obvious. The obvious is what gets you mugged in Central Park or married to your therapist's sister.

When my mother was summoned to P.S. 86 – a building that resembled a Soviet prison block designed by someone who'd never seen a Soviet prison block but had it described to them by a colorblind telegram operator – she found Miss Bernstein, my teacher, clutching my test paper like it contained launch codes.

"Mrs. Koenigsberg," she said, peering over glasses that magnified her eyes to the size of matzo balls, "your son selected 'umbrella' when asked what grows."

My mother, who believed intelligence came in precisely two varieties – "like your father" and "like your cousin Sheldon who went to Harvard" – looked at me with newfound suspicion, as if I might suddenly start collecting string or developing an unhealthy interest in fire.

"Regus," she said, using my full name, which only happened during tragedies or when company was over, "why would you pick umbrella?"

I remember looking up at these two women, these giants who controlled my access to recess and dessert, and saying with complete conviction: "Because when you open an umbrella, it gets bigger. It grows."

There was silence. The kind of silence that follows when you tell your analyst you've been dreaming about his mother.

Miss Bernstein looked at my mother. My mother looked at Miss Bernstein. I looked at my shoelaces, which I'd recently learned to tie using a method involving a rabbit going around a tree, which seemed unnecessarily complicated and possibly harmful to the rabbit.

"The child has a point," Miss Bernstein finally said.

It was my first experience with being right and wrong simultaneously – a condition I would perfect throughout three marriages and countless encounters with the IRS.

Years later, when my own son came home with a note saying he'd answered that the capital of Montana was "where the governor lives," I didn't panic. I simply told him the umbrella story, which has become our family's parable for lateral thinking, creative reasoning, and the dangers of standardized testing.

My analyst says this incident explains my lifelong tendency to search for complexity where simplicity exists, and my pathological need to open metaphorical umbrellas indoors. He charges $300 an hour to tell me this, which seems excessive, but he did go to Harvard. Like cousin Sheldon.

The Belt Buckle

Some stories arrive in a physician's examination room that have nothing to do with blood pressure or cholesterol levels. They arrive unannounced, carried in arthritic hands, preserved for decades in the quiet corners of memory.

Morris Lieberman was eighty-nine when I last saw him professionally. His daughter Rachel had scheduled the appointment – "just a check-up before the move," she'd said. Morris was relocating to Shalom Gardens, one of those places with carpeted hallways and emergency pull cords in the bathrooms. His colonial on Oakwood Drive, where he'd lived for fifty-two years, had become too much since Sarah passed.

"You'll like it there, Mr. Lieberman," I said, marking his chart. "They have bridge on Tuesdays."

"I never cared for cards," Morris said. "Sarah was the bridge player."

He had brought a small paper bag with him. While I checked his heart – still strong, still regular – he mentioned that he was sorting through his belongings.

"A lifetime of accumulation," he said. "Rachel says I can only take what fits in the new apartment. Two rooms and a kitchenette."

When I finished the examination, Morris reached for the paper bag.

"I found something, Doctor. Something I haven't looked at in years. Thought you might find it interesting."

From the bag he produced what appeared to be an ordinary belt buckle, tarnished with age. Nothing remarkable – oval-shaped, military issue by the look of it. Morris held it in his palm as if weighing it.

"I was an MP during the war," he said. "Military police. Stationed in Germany after we pushed through. Spring of '45."

Morris rarely spoke of the war. In fifteen years as his physician, I'd heard only fragments – a reference to Bastogne, a casual mention of having seen Patton once at a distance.

"A Nazi officer was brought in," he continued. "SS. Young fellow, maybe thirty. Arrogant. Even in defeat, so arrogant."

Morris turned the buckle over in his hand.

"I'm not proud of what I did next, but I was twenty-three and I'd seen things. My cousin Abe had been killed at Normandy. And my parents had family in Poland we never heard from again."

His voice remained steady, matter-of-fact.

"I took out my knife and cut his belt right off. Gave him a piece of rope and told him to hold his pants up with that. The other MPs thought it was funny. But I wasn't trying to be funny."

He handed me the buckle. It was heavier than it looked. Engraved across its face were the words "Gott Mit Uns."

"God is with us," Morris translated. "That's what it says. God is with us."

I felt a chill that had nothing to do with the office's aggressive air conditioning.

"The supreme irony," Morris said, reclaiming the buckle. "The most godless regime in history invoking divine partnership. And not just partnership – exclusivity. God is with *us*, not with *them*. Not with the people they were loading onto trains."

He returned the buckle to his paper bag with a small sigh.

"I kept it all these years as a reminder."

"Of what?" I asked.

"That the most dangerous people in the world are those absolutely certain that God approves of what they're doing." He smiled slightly. "Also, that I was once young enough to cut a man's belt off without throwing my back out."

We sat in silence for a moment. Through the examination room window came the sounds of the parking lot – a car alarm, someone's laughter.

"You see it today," Morris said finally. "Different uniforms, different languages, same certainty. Same belt buckles, just with different words."

He stood, joints protesting audibly, and placed the paper bag in his coat pocket.

"Anyway, I'm taking it with me to Shalom Gardens. Rachel says I can only bring what matters. This matters."

I wrote his prescriptions, scheduled a follow-up, and walked him to the waiting room where his daughter sat thumbing through a magazine.

"All set, Dad?" Rachel asked, not looking up.

"All set," Morris replied.

That was three years ago. Morris Lieberman died peacefully last winter. But I think often of that belt buckle, carried from a German battlefield to an American suburb, from one century into another. I wonder if Rachel found it among his effects at Shalom Gardens, if she understood its significance, or if it was simply discarded – a curious, tarnished relic without context.

Some patients leave you with more than medical histories. They leave you with stories that serve as their own kind of prescription against forgetting. Against the dangerous certainty that God – or history, or justice – belongs exclusively to any of us.

The Podiatric Magnate

I met him in the autumn of 1983, when a colleague suggested I speak with "the best businessman he ever knew." This was how I found myself riding an elevator to a suite at the Carlyle Hotel on the Upper East Side, where our friendship began almost instantly.

He was a podiatrist by training, raised in an immigrant Jewish household on the Lower East Side. His parents had fled Europe with little more than their suitcases and anxieties, and they pushed their son toward a profession that promised escape from the cramped confines of their tenement existence. Medicine was the dream, but podiatry school was the reality – a fact he never seemed to resent.

I complimented him on his Franck Muller wristwatch, admiring its elegant face and the way it caught the light. He winked conspiratorially and said, "I just bought that on Canal Street. It's not real, but everybody thinks it is since I'm wearing it." I found myself charmed by this casual admission of fraudulence, which seemed to contain a worldly wisdom I had yet to acquire.

He owned a Rolls Royce convertible, which he drove down Fifth Avenue with the top down, collecting stares like a child collects seashells – with unabashed delight. I later discovered that this automobile was not merely transportation but a statement, a raised middle finger to critics who had questioned his medical innovations.

The car had been purchased with proceeds from a controversial podiatric procedure he had developed – a technique for repairing the metatarsophalangeal joint that was supposedly revolutionary. He had made millions teaching this minimally invasive approach to hundreds of eager doctors, despite mounting evidence that it often caused more harm than good. National newspapers had published exposés about patients who couldn't walk properly after treatment, but he had already moved on, repositioning himself as an investor and entrepreneur.

His portfolio included a minority stake in a baseball team (which he mentioned at every opportunity), numerous office buildings throughout Manhattan, and various business ventures about which he was deliberately vague. He was a man about town, almost Mr. New York – though I never called him that to his face.

He wore a toupee that looked exactly like a toupee, yet somehow suited him perfectly. It was as if he were saying, "Yes, it's fake, and so what?" The same philosophy applied to his companions – always beautiful women who accompanied him to Elaine's, his favorite restaurant. They were introduced as secretaries, assistants, or simply "friends," though I suspected they were women he paid for their company. He was, to my knowledge, happily married with children in Westchester, but his urban persona required these decorative appendages.

I invested a modest sum with him and made a tidy profit. We became close – or I believed we were close. He attended my daughter's bat mitzvah, sent expensive gifts at appropriate occasions, and called me frequently to share medical concerns that he didn't trust to his regular physician.

After about five or six years of friendship, he began to change. His ankles swelled, his breathing became labored, and his exuberance dimmed. Here was a man who seemingly had everything – wealth, status, a beautiful family, and a Rolls Royce convertible – yet he grew increasingly despondent.

One Friday in late spring, he swallowed a bottle of pills. Just like that, he was gone. What puzzles me still is not the manner of his departure but the fact that a man who had so thoroughly created himself – from immigrant's son to podiatric innovator to Manhattan mogul – could discard it all so easily. It was as if he had finally recognized the emptiness behind his own performance, and finding no audience worth continuing for, simply closed the show. But I was his friend, and I will miss him.

The Doctor's Parrot

My readers have been persistent. "That parrot anecdote," they write, "tell us more about the parrot." As if I, a man of medicine who has spent forty-three years listening to the complaints of the human body, should now devote my literary efforts to ornithological curiosities. But the readers insist, and so I acquiesce. The parrot. Yes, the parrot.

We were discussing mortality that Tuesday afternoon, Lieberman and I. The shrinking arc of human existence and how, within my own lifetime, we'd managed to stretch it beyond recognition. I was telling him how my mother, at my grandfather's funeral, had whispered to me that he had "lived a good, long life." He was sixty-one. I am now seventy-four, thirteen years beyond what my mother considered the natural conclusion to a man's time on earth.

"In some parts of Africa," I explained to Lieberman, who sat picking at a thread on his sweater with the focused intensity of a man avoiding his own reflection, "to reach forty was to be ancient. Childhood mortality claimed half before they reached adolescence."

I was building toward some inevitably mundane observation about modern medicine – my profession's tiresome self-congratulation – when Lieberman interrupted with: "My parrot is probably forty."

The non sequitur hung between us like cigarette smoke in a sealed room.

"Forty years old?" I asked.

"At least. Maybe older. I've only had him six years. He belonged to others before me."

I nodded, waiting for him to return to our discussion of human frailty, but Lieberman had become entirely transfixed by his avian companion's longevity.

"When we first got him," Lieberman continued, leaning forward as if to share a state secret, "he would wake us up every night. Like clockwork. Two, three in the morning."

"Night terrors in parrots?" I ventured, my professional curiosity momentarily engaged.

"No, no," Lieberman waved dismissively. "Sex noises."

I must have raised an eyebrow.

"Moaning. Groaning. The whole performance. Christ, it was loud. Woke us from a dead sleep, every night."

"The parrot," I clarified, "made sexual noises."

"Yes," Lieberman nodded vigorously. "And I'll tell you something else, Doctor. Those sounds – they had an effect. On my wife and me. They would wake us up and then..." He trailed off, a slight flush rising from his collar.

"I see," I said, though I didn't entirely.

"It was like an alarm clock. A sex alarm. Two-thirty in the morning, like you could set your watch by it."

I maintained what I hope was a professionally neutral expression while inwardly calculating how many years of medical school had prepared me for a discussion about a lascivious parrot serving as an elderly couple's erotic timekeeper.

"We couldn't figure it out," Lieberman continued. "Why those noises? Why that specific time? Then we learned about the previous owner."

He paused dramatically.

"A policeman. Local cop. Worked the night shift. He'd come home around that exact time – two, three in the morning. Apparently, he and his wife would... you know. The parrot heard everything. Picked it up. They're mimics, you know."

"Yes," I said. "I'm familiar with the concept."

This reminds me, though I didn't tell Lieberman, of another patient of mine – Campisi, who made his fortune in waste management. I once visited his gaudy suburban mansion to deliver medication for an experimental trial. While sipping a Coke in his living room, which was decorated with all the restraint of a Vegas casino, I was startled by a harsh voice squawking: "Fuck you, Frankie! Fuck you, Frankie!"

Campisi – whose name was indeed Frank – had merely shrugged. "The bird's got opinions."

I find myself, at seventy-four, increasingly collecting these absurdities – human lives reduced to anecdotes that I scribble down and file away. The policeman's passionate nocturnal habits preserved in the syrinx of a tropical bird. Campisi's parrot hurling obscenities at its master. All of us leaving behind accidental legacies, recorded in ways we never anticipated.

And now, for reasons that escape even my analytical mind, I've written about a parrot's sexual vocalizations instead of finishing my treatise on renal function in geriatric patients. My readers will be delighted. My colleagues will question my sanity. My ex-wife would cite this as further evidence in the case she's been building against me since 1987.

But there it is – the parrot story, in all its absurd glory.

Make of it what you will.

VII. Consultations: Ethical Crossroads

Moral dilemmas and clinical decision-making

The Expert Witness

In the practice of cardiology, one occasionally finds oneself in situations that medical school – with its earnest focus on ventricles and valves – never quite prepares you for. My encounter with the American justice system as an expert witness for Vincent Calabrese was one such situation.

Calabrese was, by any medical standard, a desperately ill man. His heart had been comprehensively remodeled by modern medicine: a defibrillator nestled in his chest wall, an artificial aortic valve clicking with metronomic precision, and bypass grafts rerouting blood around the coronary arteries that had failed him. Congestive heart failure had left him perpetually short of breath, his ankles swollen, his life measured in pharmaceutical intervals. These were the clinical facts I was prepared to present, and did present, before the New Jersey Superior Court on that Tuesday in March.

What complicated matters – and complications, I've found, are as inevitable in law as they are in medicine – was my relationship with the patient. Calabrese was not merely a collection of symptoms and diagnoses that passed through my office every three months. He was a man of expansive charm, old-world courtesy, and dubious enterprises. Principal among these enterprises were several "gentlemen's clubs," as he insisted on calling them, scattered across the less scenic portions of northern New Jersey. He was also, the court had been informed, a real estate developer, though this description seemed to exist primarily for the benefit of his tax returns and social introductions.

I had known Calabrese for eight years by the time of the trial. Our relationship had evolved from the formal doctor-patient dynamic to something warmer and more complicated. He had invited me, on several occasions, to visit his establishments. I had accepted, on several occasions. We would sit at a reserved table, drink moderately good scotch, and discuss his health, his business concerns, New York sports teams, and occasionally politics, all while young women in minimal attire performed athletic routines on the stages around us. He would introduce me as "my doctor, the professor," a title I neither possessed nor corrected.

This background information was precisely what the distinguished criminal attorney, Harold Blumenthal, warned me about during our preparation session. Blumenthal was regarded as something of a legal magician in New Jersey courts – a man who could transform damning evidence into reasonable doubt through rhetorical alchemy.

"The prosecutor will try to discredit you," Blumenthal explained, pacing behind his mahogany desk. "They'll suggest your medical opinion is compromised by your personal relationship with Mr. Calabrese."

"I understand," I replied. "They'll want to know if I've socialized with him or frequented his businesses."

Blumenthal stopped pacing. "Exactly. And how will you answer?"

"Truthfully, but I'll emphasize that my medical assessment is based solely on clinical data."

He seemed satisfied with this approach, and we moved on to reviewing Calabrese's extensive medical records.

The courtroom itself was less imposing than television had led me to believe – a wood-paneled room with institutional carpeting and fluorescent lighting that did no one any favors. Judge Eleanor Hartmann presided with the weary efficiency of someone who had heard every possible human failing described in legal terminology.

For nearly an hour, I explained Calabrese's cardiac condition in terms that I hoped were both technically accurate and comprehensible to the jury. I described ejection fractions, New York Heart Association functional classifications, and medication regimens. I suggested that incarceration would present significant challenges to managing his condition and that house arrest might be medically preferable. I felt confident in my testimony – thorough, precise, professional.

Then Assistant District Attorney Michael Donovan rose for cross-examination. Donovan had the lean, hungry look of a man who had skipped lunch to review depositions. His questioning began predictably enough – establishing my credentials, confirming details of Calabrese's condition, probing for inconsistencies in my assessment. Finding none, he shifted tactics.

"Dr. Rosenthal," he said, "are you familiar with Mr. Calabrese's occupation?"

I maintained eye contact. "I believe he's involved in real estate development."

"Anything else?"

"I understand he owns several entertainment venues."

Donovan's smile didn't reach his eyes. "Entertainment venues. Is that how Mr. Calabrese describes his strip clubs?"

"I believe the term he uses is 'gentlemen's clubs,'" I replied, immediately regretting the precision.

"Have you ever socialized with Mr. Calabrese outside of your professional relationship?"

I glanced at Calabrese, who sat impassively beside Blumenthal. "Yes, on occasion."

"And have you ever visited Mr. Calabrese's, ah, gentlemen's clubs?"

The courtroom seemed to contract around me. I was suddenly, acutely aware of my yarmulke – a small circle of black fabric that, in that moment, felt like a spotlight. Dr. Joshua Rosenthal, graduate of Einstein College of Medicine, Assistant Professor of Cardiology, father of three, congregant at Beth Shalom, sitting in a strip club with a man on trial for racketeering. By morning, I would be "Dr. Go-Go" to every colleague at Mount Sinai.

If I denied it, I would be committing perjury. If I admitted it, I would be undermining my professional credibility and possibly embarrassing my family. Neither option seemed palatable.

"I don't see how that's relevant to my medical testimony," I said.

Donovan pressed: "Please answer the question, Doctor. Have you visited Mr. Calabrese's establishments?"

I turned to Judge Hartmann. "Your Honor, do I need to answer this question? I'm here as a medical expert."

Judge Hartmann regarded me over her reading glasses. "The question goes to potential bias, Doctor. Please answer it."

I looked to Blumenthal for objection, for rescue, but he was engaged in whispered conversation with his associate, seemingly unaware of my predicament.

"Your Honor," I said, "I respectfully decline to answer on grounds that it has no bearing on my medical assessment."

A small murmur ran through the courtroom. Judge Hartmann sighed. "We'll take that as a 'yes,' Doctor. But you're right – we've strayed from the medical issues at hand." She checked her watch. "It's nearly four. We'll adjourn for today and resume tomorrow morning."

As the courtroom emptied, I approached Blumenthal, anger rising in my throat. "You were supposed to object to that line of questioning."

He seemed unfazed. "Relax, Doctor. You did fine. Sometimes letting a prosecutor overreach works better than shutting them down. Trust me – this plays better in the press than you think."

Indeed, the next morning's *Star-Ledger* featured the headline: "PROSECUTOR HITS BRICK WALL QUESTIONING DOCTOR!" The article portrayed Donovan as overzealous and me as principled – a medical professional refusing to be drawn into sensationalism. Blumenthal, it seemed, had calculated correctly.

I never returned to court. Three weeks later, Calabrese suffered an acute myocardial infarction complicated by cardiogenic shock. Despite aggressive intervention, he died in the CCU at Mount Sinai. The case against him was posthumously dismissed.

At the funeral, Calabrese's wife – a woman of surprising dignity and restrained elegance – handed me an envelope. "Vincent wanted you to have this," she said. Inside was a handwritten note: "Doc – Thanks for everything. Sorry about the court business. You're a stand-up guy."

There was also a deed to a small property in Hoboken. Not one of his more colorful holdings, but a tidy commercial building leased to an accounting firm. The sort of straightforward, respectable real estate that requires no explanation at dinner parties.

I sometimes drive past it on my way into the city and think about Calabrese – about the strangeness of the doctor-patient relationship, about how we move through one another's lives in ways that medical charts and court transcripts can never fully capture. About how even the most compromised heart can, in its way, demonstrate a kind of honor.

The Cardiologist Who Wouldn't Pray

Joining Dr. Bernard Levine's cardiology practice in 1983 was, professionally speaking, something of a coup for a young physician like myself, freshly emerged from residency with the bloom of medical idealism still intact. Levine – I have changed his name, though I suspect he would have been flattered by the attention – was what people in our mid-sized Midwestern city called "an institution." His patients spoke of him with the reverence usually reserved for clergy. Hospital administrators straightened their posture when he approached. The nurses – ah, the nurses – responded to his presence in ways I found increasingly troubling as the months passed.

Levine had cultivated a persona with the careful attention of a botanist breeding orchids. The veneer was impeccable: Newark-born son of immigrants who had ascended to the heights of medicine, married well (the daughter of a prominent attorney whose name appeared on brass plaques throughout the city), and surrounded himself with the totems of sophistication. His office featured leather-bound medical texts that I never once saw him open, and a stereo system that quietly emitted Mahler or Brahms at precisely the right volume to seem cultured without being obtrusive.

He drove a Porsche, of course. Silver, always meticulously clean.

"European engineering," he would tell patients who admired it, as though he were speaking of Euclidean geometry or the Sistine Chapel – something timeless and profound rather than an expensive automobile that announced his success with the subtlety of a carnival barker.

It took me approximately three weeks to discover that Levine was conducting affairs with at least two nurses simultaneously. By the end of my first year, I had mentally cataloged at least seven ongoing dalliances. What struck me as peculiar was not the quantity – after all, medical practice has its share of philanderers – but his selection criteria, which seemed to defy conventional understanding of attraction.

"Martin," a surgeon once commented to me over coffee in the doctors' lounge, "have you noticed that Bernie only goes for the ones who look at him like he's Jonas Salk and Cary Grant rolled into one?"

It was true. Levine's conquests weren't chosen for their physical attributes – indeed, many were what unkind observers might call plain or even homely – but rather for their capacity for adoration. They were invariably women who seemed to have spent their lives waiting for someone to notice them, and Levine, with his practiced eye for vulnerabilities, noticed them thoroughly, temporarily, and destructively.

He preferred married women, he once confided during a moment of after-hours candor that I neither invited nor welcomed. "Less complications," he explained, swirling brandy in a snifter. "They have too much to lose to make scenes."

That he was wrong about this – that I witnessed the collapse of at least three marriages during my time in his practice – seemed not to trouble him. The scenes, when they came, were absorbed into the mythology of Levine. Everything fed his sense of himself as exceptional, even the wreckage.

Medically, Levine was competent but complacent, content to diagnose the obvious and refer the complicated. My arrival to the practice was like turning on a light in a dim room – suddenly, patients with conditions that had languished undiagnosed for years found themselves properly evaluated, treated, and in many cases, scheduled for life-saving interventions. Levine accepted my contributions with the magnanimity of a king tolerating a promising courtier, taking partial credit for my successes as though they reflected his mentorship rather than his neglect.

"That's why I brought you in, Martin," he would say, clapping me on the shoulder in the presence of others. "Fresh eyes! Fresh eyes!"

It was during a particularly grueling week – three difficult diagnoses and a patient lost on the operating table – that Levine shared the story about the war. We were reviewing EKGs late one evening, the hospital corridors emptied of all but the night shift. The rhythm of our work was occasionally interrupted by a nurse bringing coffee or updates on patients. Each time the door opened, I watched Levine's eyes assess the entrant with the calculating gaze of a man taking inventory.

Between charts, unprompted, he began to speak of his naval service in the South Pacific during World War II. His voice took on an unusual quality – stripped of its practiced charm, devoid of the Newark accent he normally suppressed.

"You know what I remember most? Not the combat. Not the noise. It was watching the other men pray." He set down an EKG, looking not at me but somewhere beyond the walls of the hospital. "Every last one of them, when the shells started falling, started bargaining with God.' Save me, Lord,' they'd cry. Right out loud, no shame about it. Grown men begging like children."

He paused, straightening a stack of charts with precise movements.

"I knew then that I was different. Special, maybe. I never prayed, not once. I just stood there and thought, 'This is happening, and either I live or I don't.' No pleading, no promises to be a better man if I survived. Just... acceptance."

The pride in his voice was unmistakable. He conveyed this anecdote not as a confession of spiritual emptiness but as evidence of exceptional character – a medal he had awarded himself for valor in the face of metaphysical temptation.

I said nothing in response, but I remember thinking that this absence of prayer revealed more about Levine than any psychological evaluation could have accomplished. Here was a man so complete in his self-regard that even under fire, he could not conceive of any power worthy of his supplication. His atheism wasn't philosophical but narcissistic – not "There is no God" but rather "There is nothing greater than myself to which I might appeal."

I remained in Levine's practice for seven years, eventually departing to establish my own. In the decades since, I've encountered him occasionally at medical conferences or charity events, always surrounded by admirers, always performing the role of distinguished physician with the same studied sophistication. I've heard that he's retired now, that his wife finally left him after a particularly public indiscretion with a pharmaceutical representative half his age.

What lingers with me isn't the memory of his infidelities or his medical negligence, though both were profound in their way. It's the image of a young sailor standing on a ship under attack, surrounded by praying men, feeling not fear but a cold, crystalline pride in his own exceptionalism. There is, I've come to believe, a particular kind of loneliness in believing oneself above the basic human impulse to cry out for help, a special isolation in the inability to conceive of one's own smallness in the face of forces beyond control.

In medicine, we speak often of heart disease – the blockages, arrhythmias, and structural failures that compromise the organ's function. What we discuss less frequently is the other kind of heart condition – the one that no stethoscope can detect, no EKG can display, no surgery can repair. In all my years of practice, I've never encountered a case as advanced as Bernard Levine's, the cardiologist who specialized in hearts but failed to understand their most essential function: the capacity to recognize that we are, all of us, desperately in need of something greater than ourselves.

The Ledger of Small Mercies

During my forty-odd years in cardiology, I've kept what I call a *ledger of small mercies* – a collection of patient encounters that, while perhaps mundane in the grand medical literature, strike me as worthy of preservation. Not for any scientific journal, mind you, but for that more personal accounting we physicians maintain to justify our choice of profession on days when the bureaucratic machinery threatens to grind us into fine powder.

My father, a reasonable man who sold insurance in Chicago for thirty-seven years, once told me that a man should be able to summarize his life's philosophy in a single sentence. Mine borrows liberally from the boxer Joe Louis and the writer Philip Roth: "I did the best I could with what I had to work with." This seems to me a fair assessment of both my career and character – neither heroic nor particularly distinguished, but earnest in its application.

The ledger began as a few scribbled notes in my desk drawer and has since expanded to fill several notebooks. Reading through these entries recently, I find myself particularly drawn to those collected during the pandemic – that surreal period when medicine briefly reclaimed its ancient status as a calling rather than a service industry.

A patient in her seventies arrived for her COVID vaccine, trembling at the sight of the needle.

"What about that tattoo on your other arm?" I asked. "Did that hurt when you got it?"

She gave me a look that suggested I had just played a very low card, but allowed us to proceed with the injection. Small victories constitute the bulk of a physician's daily triumphs.

Another patient, after receiving his vaccine, said something that stopped me in my tracks: "The only side effect I've had from this vaccine is that I cried. I cried because I was so happy."

I remember the day the vaccines first became available. I personally arranged for twenty-eight high-risk, disabled, elderly patients to receive their doses. I drove to the clinic myself to administer the shots, and witnessed what can only be described as a biblical awakening. After months of dread and isolation, here was this small vial of clear liquid offering salvation. Medicine rarely provides such clean narratives of deliverance.

An elderly Holocaust survivor, his voice still carrying traces of his native Germany, told me: "These COVID times remind me of when I was six years old with my little brother, being taunted by the Hitler Youth. I don't know why or what is similar, but the emotion is the same." Then, with impeccable comic timing, he added: "Thank God for Xanax."

During the worst of it, when the refrigerator truck morgues appeared in hospital parking lots, I experienced that familiar sinking feeling in my stomach – the same one I felt during my first week as an intern, when I realized that all the knowledge accumulated during medical school was merely prologue to the real education that awaited me.

"They shuffle the cards every morning," a patient with advanced COPD told me during this period. Indeed they do, and the dealer shows no favorites.

The ledger contains entries from before the pandemic as well, of course. Medical practice, when stripped of its technological trappings, remains fundamentally unchanged since Hippocrates – we listen, we observe, we comfort when we cannot cure.

A cancer patient, contemplating his prognosis, once offered this: "Doctor, a chicken only sees the ax when it is upon him. We people see the ax from the beginning. I wish we were more like chickens."

I've returned to this observation numerous times over the years, finding in it a peculiar wisdom. Our consciousness of mortality is both burden and gift – it allows us to prepare, to make amends, to complete the narrative of our lives with some measure of intention. Yet how much suffering comes from this foresight?

One of my favorite entries arrived unexpectedly in the mail: "Dear Doctor, today is 20 years since my heart surgery. Thank you for your help that I was given 20 years of life. Zei gezunt, and I wish many good years for you ahead." The patient had moved away two decades earlier, yet thought to mark this anniversary with me. Such gestures sustain a physician through countless insurance forms and electronic health record frustrations.

A similar note arrived on my birthday via Facebook, from the wife of a patient whose condition had been particularly challenging: "Had you not been born, I am sure Ben would not be by my side now. Happy birthday, Mensch." This use of **mensch** – that untranslatable Yiddish term suggesting a person of integrity and honor – meant more to me than any professional accolade I've received.

Recently, our new patient scheduling software showed that an appointment was canceled because the patient had died. We were, therefore, rather surprised when this same patient arrived for his visit, looking remarkably alive for someone the computer had already consigned to eternity. The incident provided a much-needed reminder that medicine, for all its technological advancements, remains an endeavor best conducted between human beings rather than algorithms.

Perhaps the entry that best captures the essence of this profession comes from a couple married fifty years. The husband, critically ill, refused the new hospital bed we offered because "there is not room for two on that bed." In that simple declaration lies a truth that no medical textbook addresses – that healing encompasses more than the mere repair of organs, that medicine at its finest acknowledges the human heart in all its metaphorical complexity.

The cynic might dismiss these collected observations as sentimentality, and perhaps they are correct. But after four decades of watching the human body in its remarkable resilience and inevitable decline, I've earned the right to a bit of sentiment. A local psychiatrist, whom I treated for atypical chest pain that I suspected represented significant heart disease, wrote to me years after his successful stent placement: "Thank you for saving my life." The note arrived out of the blue, on a day when I had spent more time arguing with insurance companies than caring for patients.

Such is the ledger of small mercies that justifies a life in medicine. Not the diagnoses made or procedures performed, but these human moments when the veil between doctor and patient temporarily lifts, and we recognize in each other fellow travelers on what is, after all, a rather brief journey.

The Physician's Pen

In the small hours between midnight and dawn, when even the most dedicated scholars of the Talmud have closed their books, I found myself unable to sleep. I, Dr. Benjamin Mendelssohn, a cardiologist who has witnessed the precise mechanics of the human heart for thirty-five years, am compelled to record an occurrence that defies all scientific explanation.

Two deaths have visited my family in recent days. My cousin Rivka, who survived the camps only to die peacefully in her Brooklyn apartment, and my uncle Morris, who passed away suddenly while reciting his morning prayers. Perhaps it was their departure that loosened whatever stitches hold our rational world together.

The pen in question is not merely a writing instrument but a Mont Blanc that has traveled twice to Europe for repairs. The nib, crafted by artisans whose skills predate this century of computers and digital signatures, has signed prescriptions that saved countless lives and, most recently, the documents for the Westchester medical center I have spent fifteen years bringing into existence.

On the morning of Tisha B'Av, the day we mourn the Temple's destruction, this pen – this extension of my rational self – vanished. Not misplaced, not fallen behind a desk or rolled under a car seat, but disappeared as completely as if it had never existed.

"Nonsense," I told myself. "There is always an explanation." Yet I searched my office, my car, my home, everywhere a pen might conceivably hide. My nurse Esther, whose grandmother was a famous matchmaker in Lodz, whispered about dybbuk and spirits, which I dismissed with the practiced smile I reserve for patients who believe their heart palpitations are visitations from deceased relatives.

That same morning, a black cat crossed before my car near the hospital. I, who have cut into the human chest and held beating hearts in my latex-gloved hands, found myself turning the car around to drive a different route. My colleague Dr. Friedman would have laughed until tears came to his eyes had he seen me.

Then came Leah, my oldest friend, returning from her spiritual pilgrimage to India with a gift – a black star sapphire that "dispels the evil eye and promotes healing." I accepted it politely, thinking how peculiar that a woman who once edited medical journals now speaks of gemstones and protective energies.

"Your aura is disturbed, Benjamin," she told me over coffee. "You've lost something important."

"A pen," I admitted, feeling foolish. "An expensive one, but still, just a pen."

"Nothing is just anything," she answered, placing the stone in my palm. It felt cool, like the skin of patients arriving in emergency.

Later that evening, exhausted from both the fast and the irrationality of my mounting obsession with the missing pen, I returned to my car. I placed Leah's stone on the passenger seat and thought, without much hope, that I would look once more.

The search lasted perhaps twenty seconds before I saw it – my Mont Blanc pen, resting atop last month's New England Journal of Medicine on the opposite seat, as visible as if it were illuminated by its own light. The same seat I had searched four times that very morning.

I sat motionless, the physician in me searching for the logical explanation, the grandson of Rabbi Mendelssohn of Cracow considering alternatives that my medical colleagues would find absurd. The pen had returned precisely when I had stopped believing in its return, exactly after placing down the sapphire stone.

As I drove home, the skies opened. First rain, then hail the size of frozen raisins pelted my windshield. "Like the plagues of Egypt," my grandfather would have said, though he would have added that God's miracles come not to punish but to remind.

What am I to make of this? That two worlds exist simultaneously – the world of echocardiograms and cholesterol levels, and another world where objects vanish and reappear, where black cats carry meaning and gemstones hold power? Or perhaps there is only one world, more mysterious than even we physicians, with our elaborate terminologies and advanced technologies, are willing to admit.

Tonight, I will use this twice-repaired pen to sign the charts of my patients. I will make my rounds tomorrow with the black sapphire in my pocket. Not because I believe, exactly – but because I no longer possess the certainty to disbelieve.

For what is a physician but a witness to mysteries? We give these mysteries names: myocardial infarction, ventricular fibrillation, cardiac arrest. But naming a mystery does not dispel it. Sometimes, between the beats of the heart, there are silences that belong to another realm entirely.

The Reluctant Knight

Some men fashion themselves as modern-day knights, though their windmills are often of their own imagining. Morris Kaplan was one such man – he had introduced himself to me during our first session as "Don Quixote ", with a wink that suggested I ought to be impressed by this literary allusion. "Always looking for the impossible dream," he added, as if I might have missed the reference.

Morris owned a string of parking lots in Chicago's Near North Side, a business that had apparently brought him into contact with certain individuals whose names he pronounced with a theatrical lowering of his voice. He had related to me, with no small measure of pride, an encounter with one such gentleman who had suggested that Morris might benefit from "protection."

"Go ahead," Morris had told the man, puffing up his chest in the retelling. "Do whatever you want. The worst you can do is kill me."

This pronouncement – delivered with the firm conviction of a man who believes himself to be the hero of his own story – had, according to Morris, sent the would-be extortionist retreating into the Chicago night, never to return. Morris had prevailed, David against the urban Goliath.

And yet today, Morris sat across from me, fidgeting with the crease in his trousers, explaining that he had canceled his colonoscopy appointment for the third time.

"I just don't see the point," he said. "If they find something, what good would knowing do?"

I recognized in Morris's demeanor none of the bravado that had animated his tales of standing up to organized crime. Here was a man who had stared down threats to his livelihood, his physical safety – if his stories were to be believed – but who now quaked at the prospect of a routine medical procedure.

"So you told a mafia enforcer to do his worst," I said, "but Dr. Greenberg and his fiber-optic camera are a bridge too far?"

Morris looked at me sharply. "That's different," he said.

"How so?"

"That was business. This is..." he trailed off, waving his hand in a circular motion as if to conjure the appropriate word from the air.

"Personal," I supplied.

"Invasive," he corrected.

It occurred to me then that perhaps Morris's courage had never been tested in the way he imagined. It is one thing to face a threat that may never materialize, quite another to willingly submit to an indignity that is guaranteed. The colonoscopy offered no glory, no story to tell over drinks. It promised only vulnerability – the very quality Morris had spent a lifetime armoring himself against.

"You know," I said, "Don Quixote's real heroism wasn't in fighting giants."

Morris looked at me expectantly.

"It was in being willing to look foolish in service of something greater than himself."

Morris nodded slowly, though I could see he was not entirely convinced. Our time was up, but as he left, he paused at the door.

"I'll think about rescheduling," he said. "But don't expect me to sing about it."

I smiled. Even reluctant knights can find their way to wisdom, though they rarely take the direct path.

The Specimen

So there I am, sitting in my examining room, with my stethoscope hanging around my neck like a sacred amulet – this ridiculous symbol of medical authority that allows me to peer into the private humiliations of my fellow human beings. Dr. Zuckerman, they call me. The great listener. The confessor of the geriatric set.

My patients, particularly the elderly women, they dress up for me. Can you believe it? Like I'm some kind of oracle they must impress. Blue-haired matrons with arthritic fingers struggling into their good pearls, their going-to-temple dresses, just to have me press my cold hands against their withered breasts and listen to the irregular rhythm of their aging hearts. I always make a point to notice. "That's a lovely brooch, Mrs. Goldstein." And watch their faces light up as if I've confirmed their continued relevance in a world that has long since moved on.

But this story isn't about the vanities of my elderly female patients. No, this is about a man – mid-fifties, balding, with the soft-around-the-middle physique of someone whose youth has abandoned him without warning. He's sitting on my examination table, and I'm supposed to be evaluating his cardiac function before his surgery. Cancer of the testicles. The ultimate cosmic joke on masculinity.

"Doc," he says to me, leaning forward with that conspiratorial air patients get when they're about to tell you something that has nothing to do with their medical condition. "I had to go to the sperm bank last week."

Of course he did. Before they slice into his scrotum and remove what's left of his manhood, he's hedging his bets against the future. A man in his fifties, probably already has children, grandchildren even, and yet here he is, acting as if his genetic material is some precious commodity that must be preserved at all costs.

"Beautiful nurse," he continues, his eyes alight with the memory. "Gorgeous. Brought me into this little room. Offered me magazines, videos. Then she left."

I nod, imagining the scene. Some poor nursing school graduate, probably twenty-five years his junior, trained to maintain a professional demeanor while escorting middle-aged men to masturbatoriums. Is this what Florence Nightingale had in mind?

"I picked a lesbian video," he tells me, as if this detail somehow elevates the sordid transaction. As if his choice of pornography reveals some sophisticated erotic sensibility.

"Seventeen seconds," he says, and I see the mixture of pride and embarrassment in his face. "That's all it took."

I think of the irony – this man with his cancerous testicles, producing what might be his final contribution to humanity's genetic pool in less time than it takes to recite the Pledge of Allegiance. The great male performance, reduced to its most efficient biological function.

But here's the kicker: "I stayed in there fifteen more minutes," he confesses, looking at me with what I can only describe as earnestness. "I was too embarrassed to come out so soon."

I'm fascinated now. Here's a man about to undergo surgery that might leave him permanently altered, worried not about his survival or his virility, but about what some nurse might think of his masturbatory efficiency.

"Weren't you concerned that the sample might deteriorate?" I ask, my medical training momentarily overriding my amusement.

He shakes his head, looks at me with absolute seriousness. "Doc, I didn't want the nurse to think less of me."

And there it is – the absurdity of the human condition distilled into one perfect moment. A man donating sperm, presumably hoping for its effectiveness, ejaculating with record speed, and then hiding in a room for fifteen minutes because he's worried about the professional opinion of a woman he'll never see again.

I laugh about it later, of course. After I've cleared him for surgery, after I've gone through the motions of evaluating his cardiovascular fitness. I laugh because what else can you do in the face of such perfect, unintentional comedy? But I also wonder, as I sit in my office surrounded by medical degrees and the accumulated wisdom of modern science, if I'm any different. Aren't we all just prisoners of our vanity, our desperate need to be thought well of, even in our most private moments of degradation?

The human brain – that magnificent organ that can contemplate the mysteries of the universe, that can perform complex mathematical calculations and compose symphonies – still, at its core, primarily concerned with what others think of our performance in small, private rooms.

The Stack of Photographs

Mrs. Abramson has been coming to my office every three months for the past seven years. Tuesday afternoons, 2:30 appointments. She is punctual, arriving precisely twelve minutes early, permitting herself exactly enough time to complete the paperwork my receptionist Sandra inevitably slides across the counter to her, despite my repeated instructions that we needn't put the poor woman through this exercise every visit.

Mrs. Abramson is ninety-two. Widowed twice. No children. A small apartment in Lakeview that she has lived in since 1973. Her medical chart contains the usual litany of the elderly: hypertension, osteoarthritis, mild heart failure, and the beginnings of macular degeneration. She takes her medications faithfully, walks daily when weather permits, and never complains about her various aches, which I know must be considerable.

She is, in short, a model patient. And if I am being completely honest, which physicians rarely are even with themselves, she has been, in my mind, little more than that: a model patient, a pleasant but unremarkable elderly woman who occupies the 2:30 Tuesday slot with reliable consistency.

Until last Tuesday.

Mrs. Abramson completed her paperwork in eleven minutes rather than twelve and was escorted to examining room number three. When I entered, I found her not perched on the edge of the examination table as usual but seated comfortably in the guest chair, her handbag open on her lap.

"Dr. Greenfield," she said, "before we begin, I've brought something to show you."

From her bag she withdrew a stack of photographs, black and white, held together by a faded rubber band that had long ago lost its elasticity. Her fingers, gnarled by arthritis into painful-looking angles, fumbled with the band until I offered assistance, which she declined with surprising firmness.

"I can manage," she said, and eventually did.

She handed me the first photograph. "Berlin, 1953," she said.

The young woman in the photograph stood beside a fountain, one hip cocked slightly, a cigarette held with impossible elegance between two fingers. Her face was striking – high cheekbones, a strong jaw softened by full lips curved into a knowing half-smile. Her eyes – even in black and white – seemed to contain both challenge and invitation.

"That's me," Mrs. Abramson said unnecessarily. "I was twenty-two."

I found myself staring at the photograph, then at Mrs. Abramson, then back again, attempting to reconcile the vibrant young woman with the diminished figure before me. The mathematics was simple – seventy years had passed – but the emotional calculus was bewildering.

She handed me another. "Paris, 1954. I had gone to study art." In this one, she leaned against a railing along the Seine, laughing at something beyond the frame. Behind her, Notre Dame rose in misty grandeur.

Another: "Rome, 1955. That's Giorgio, my first husband." A handsome couple at a sidewalk café, her head thrown back in laughter as a dark-haired man whispered in her ear.

And another: "New York, 1957. I had just sold my first illustration to a magazine." Standing proudly outside a brownstone, portfolio clutched to her chest, that same confident smile.

For twenty minutes, Mrs. Abramson led me through her youth – through Europe and America, through love affairs and professional triumphs, through a life so vivid and expansive it made my own seem pale by comparison. In each photograph, she was stunning, not merely in the conventional sense of physical beauty, but in the more profound sense of a person fully alive.

When we finished, she carefully re-banded the stack and returned it to her handbag.

"I thought you should see," she said simply. "That I wasn't always just an old lady with pills."

I attempted a protest, but she waved it away.

"It's all right, Dr. Greenfield. It's what happens. We all become invisible eventually. But I wanted someone to know that I wasn't always..." she gestured vaguely at herself, "...this."

We proceeded with the examination. Blood pressure 138/82. Lungs clear. Heart regular but with the expected murmur. Arthritis in the hands progressing but still manageable. I renewed her prescriptions. I advised her, as always, to continue her daily walks.

But something had fundamentally changed. As I examined her spine, noting the pronounced kyphosis that had bent her once-straight posture into a question mark, I no longer saw merely the physical manifestation of osteoporosis. I saw the woman who had once stood tall beside a fountain in Berlin, cigarette held aloft, the world spread before her like a banquet.

As I checked her reflexes, I found myself wondering about the hands that had once created illustrations good enough for New York magazines, which had caressed Giorgio's face in Roman twilight.

After she left, I sat for a long while in my office, thinking about Mrs. Abramson and all my elderly patients – how I had reduced them, in my mind, to their medical conditions and appointment slots. How I had failed to see the full arc of their humanity.

The next morning, I instructed Sandra to include a new question on our intake forms: "Would you be willing to bring a photograph of yourself from your youth to your next appointment?"

Sandra raised an eyebrow but said nothing. She has worked for me long enough to recognize my occasional eccentricities and to indulge them accordingly.

Yesterday, Mr. Wojciechowski, age eighty-seven, COPD and peripheral vascular disease, brought in a photograph of himself at twenty-four, standing beside a B-17 bomber in England, 1944. His crew all around him, young men with unlined faces and untroubled eyes, four of whom would not survive the next three months.

This morning, Mrs. Delgado, age seventy-nine, diabetes and rheumatoid arthritis, showed me herself at nineteen, dancing at a club in Havana before the revolution, her body a sinuous flame in a red dress.

Medicine, I was taught, is a science. We diagnose pathology, we prescribe treatment, and we monitor progress or decline. But medicine, I am learning seventy years too late, is also an act of witnessing – bearing witness not just to illness and aging, but to the full measure of our patients' lives.

I have been practicing medicine for thirty-seven years. I will retire in less than two. I cannot help but wonder how many ghosts I have failed to see, how many vibrant twenty-two-year-olds have sat before me, invisible within their aged bodies, waiting for someone to recognize that they are still there, still themselves, still holding within them all that they have ever been.

Mrs. Abramson returns next Tuesday at 2:30. I will see her differently now. And for the first time in many years, I find myself looking forward to a Tuesday afternoon appointment.

The Last Barber Visit

There are certain patients for whom one develops a genuine fondness, often unexpected and arriving through some small, repeated ritual of acknowledgment. In my twenty-seven years of practice, I have found that a well-placed compliment, judiciously offered to the right patient, can be as therapeutic as any prescription I might write. This is not the empty flattery of department store clerks, but rather the honest recognition of those small vanities that sustain us all.

Mr. Levinson – whom I called "Elvis" – was one such patient. He was seventy-eight when I first met him, suffering from the usual potpourri of geriatric complaints: hypertension, mild congestive heart failure, a touch of diabetes. But what distinguished him was his magnificent head of hair – thick, silver-white, and impeccably combed back with a subtle pompadour that indeed suggested a senior version of the King of Rock and Roll.

"Here comes Elvis," I would say when he shuffled into my examination room, and he would straighten slightly, pat his coiffure, and offer a close-lipped smile that contained both embarrassment and pleasure. The joke was sweeter, perhaps, because of my own follicular inadequacy – my hair having begun its retreat sometime during my residency and now reduced to what charitable observers might call "distinguished thinning."

During our appointments, I would inquire about his grandchildren, his bowling league (which he attended faithfully until his recent hospitalization), and only then about his various physical complaints. He always answered the medical questions with impatience, as if they were irrelevant intrusions on our more important social exchange.

Yesterday, his son Martin came to my office. I had not seen Mr. Levinson for nearly a month, not since his discharge to Lakeside Gardens Nursing Center following a bout of pneumonia.

"Dad passed away," Martin said, settling heavily into the chair across from my desk. He looked exhausted, his tie loosened and his eyes rimmed with red. "Two weeks ago."

"I'm very sorry," I said, meaning it. "Your father was a wonderful man."

Martin nodded, then seemed to struggle with something. "There's something else," he finally said. "Something that's been bothering me. It's silly, really."

"Go on," I encouraged.

"When they moved him to Lakeside, they have this barber who comes around once a week. Gives everyone the same haircut. A crew cut." He made a chopping motion with his hand. "They didn't ask. Just sat him down and-" The chopping motion again. "All that beautiful hair. Gone."

I felt a peculiar hollowness in my chest.

"Dad was so proud of his hair. You know that. That's why you called him Elvis." Martin looked at me imploringly, as if I might retroactively intervene. "He was too weak to object. Or maybe too confused by then. But when I visited him after, he just kept touching his head, over and over. He wouldn't look in the mirror."

I thought of Mr. Levinson's elegant hands, spotted with age, patting the stubble where his proud mane had been.

"He died two weeks later," Martin continued. "And now he's buried like that. For eternity. Not as himself. Not as Elvis."

Martin's voice cracked on the nickname, and I understood that he had come not for medical advice but for a kind of absolution – or perhaps merely for someone else who would recognize the peculiar cruelty of this final indignity.

What is it about human vanity that makes it simultaneously ridiculous and sacred? We physicians like to believe we deal in the substantive matters of life and death, yet here was a reminder that sometimes the deepest wounds are inflicted upon our most trivial pretensions. Mr. Levinson had endured heart failure, diabetes, and pneumonia with stoic resignation. But the loss of his hair – this cosmetic detail – had somehow violated his essential dignity.

I have often thought that the true measure of civilization might be found in our capacity to honor the small vanities of others, especially as age and illness strip away so much else. The nursing home barber, performing his efficient hygienic function, had inadvertently committed an act of existential violence.

"Your father was always Elvis to me," I told Martin. "Hair or no hair." This was not entirely true, of course, but it seemed the kindest fiction. "And I suspect he knew that what made him Elvis wasn't just what sat atop his head."

Martin nodded, though without much conviction. We both knew that Mr. Levinson had died feeling diminished – not by disease but by this casual aesthetic assault. The son rose to leave, our conversation having accomplished nothing except perhaps the sharing of this peculiar grief.

Later, examining my own sparse reflection in the bathroom mirror, I found myself wondering what small vanity of mine, if violated, would feel like the final unbearable insult. We are, all of us, more fragile than our medical charts suggest.

The Weight of Saving

Lying in bed, the autumn sun filtering through my window in Princeton, New Jersey, I remembered something from long ago. Forty-three years had passed since that day, yet the memory returned with the clarity of yesterday.

It was September 1981, my first month at medical school. I was young then, nervous, wearing a starched white coat that still smelled of the store. We knew students were to be examined by a physician working at the school as part of the orientation process.

Dr. Finkelstein was an old man with hands spotted by age, but steady. His eyes, behind thick glasses, remained sharp. When I entered his office, he glanced down at my forms.

"Goldstein," he said, considering my name. "A good Jewish name." He nodded approvingly. "You know, as you begin your studies, remember what the Talmud teaches us: if you save one life, it is as if you save the entire world."

I had heard such things before – in synagogue, from my grandfather – but never had those words carried such weight. In that moment, they became more than a saying. They became my calling.

"Yes, sir," I answered, my voice catching slightly.

"You come from a long line," he continued, adjusting his glasses. "The Jewish doctor is not just a profession, it's a tradition. From Maimonides to now, we heal not just because we can, but because we must."

That night, I studied with new purpose. The exuberance I felt cannot be properly described – like I had found my place in an unbroken chain stretching back thousands of years. Every diagram I memorized, every Latin term I struggled to pronounce, connected me to generations before.

But there was something else Dr. Finkelstein said that day, something that has followed me like a shadow through my career. "Save a life," he told me as I was leaving, "and you are now responsible for it."

At the time, I didn't fully understand. Only years later, when I stood exhausted in emergency rooms, when I delivered difficult news to families, when I watched patients I had saved return again and again with new ailments – only then did I grasp his meaning.

Why these memories returned to me today, lying in bed at eighty-six years old, I cannot say. Perhaps it was the call yesterday from Mrs. Abramowitz, a patient I had treated for heart trouble thirty years ago. She still sends me cards on Rosh Hashanah. Or perhaps it was the dream I had of my father, who never lived to see me graduate.

My hands shake now. I can no longer perform surgery. My office has been closed for a decade. But when young Dr. Levy from down the street comes to check on my arthritis, I see in his eyes the same fire I once had. Last week, I told him the same words Dr. Finkelstein told me. He nodded politely, but I wonder if he truly understood.

The world has changed since my days in medical school. Computers now know more than any doctor could memorize. Machines can see inside the body without cutting. But some things remain unchanged – the responsibility that comes with the power to heal.

Lying here, I feel the weight of all the lives I've touched. Some I saved, others I couldn't. For each one I saved, I became, in some small way, responsible for the world they continued to inhabit. A frightening thought, perhaps, but also a comforting one.

The sun is setting now. Soon my daughter will come with dinner. She became a doctor too. The tradition continues, the chain unbroken.

Why these memories returned today, I don't know. But somehow, they all connected, like sutures drawing together the different parts of my life into a single, healing whole.

VIII. Afterglow: Reflections at Dusk

Contemplative closure and philosophical resonance

The Mirror

Very often in my examining rooms patients complain about how old they're getting. Today I had a woman who turned 70, and she complained, "I'm so old, doc," and for some reason I remembered an instance from my childhood.

"I remember when I turned 10," I said. "It was double digits, and I was so wistful. You know, I thought to myself I was no longer a little boy. I was growing up."

I have this conscious memory. I went into my parents' bedroom, and in the bedroom was this big mahogany dresser with a huge mirror that spanned half the length of the room, and I looked in the mirror and I looked at myself, and I remember feeling that my childhood was over and I was no longer my mother and father's little boy, but I was grown-up, growing up, and I was old.

I tried to point out to this woman that the emotion that I felt at age ten is similar to the emotion she's feeling at age 70, and everything is relative. Just amazing what one can pull out of their memory banks and make it appropriate for the moment at hand.

The Tailor of Possibilities

The journalist who interviewed Professor Amos Steinberg – winner of the Nobel Prize in Physics for his work on quantum entanglement – expected grand philosophical reflections on destiny and historical inevitability. Instead, when asked where he might be had the Holocaust not occurred and his parents never fled to Palestine, the professor adjusted his wire-rimmed glasses and answered with disarming simplicity.

"I would probably be a tailor in some small Polish village," he said, his hands – those instruments that had written equations reshaping our understanding of the universe – making a small gesture as if threading an invisible needle.

I found myself thinking about Steinberg's answer months after reading the interview. There is an entire literature devoted to alternative histories, to the grand what-ifs of human existence: what if Napoleon had won at Waterloo, what if the Spanish Armada had succeeded, what if Kennedy had lived? But Steinberg's counterfactual was intimate, modest – a tailor in rural Poland, snipping and stitching, perhaps humming Hasidic melodies while creating wedding suits for local farmers' sons.

What fascinated me was not the dramatic difference between being a Nobel laureate and being a village tailor, but rather the professor's lack of sentimentality about the matter. There was no suggestion that the universe would have been poorer for the absence of his contributions to theoretical physics. No hint that his alternative life would have been less worthy or less complete.

I had the opportunity to meet Steinberg at a university function some weeks later. He was smaller than I expected, with that particular energy one often finds in the very intelligent – a kind of coiled alertness behind calm eyes.

"Professor," I said, after the obligatory pleasantries, "I was struck by something you said in your interview. About being a tailor in Poland."

"Ah, yes," he replied, a slight smile forming. "My grandfather was a tailor. And his father before him."

"So you really think that's where you would have ended up? Not perhaps as a physicist in Warsaw or Krakow?"

He considered this for a moment, sipping the mediocre wine provided at such functions.

"In my family's shtetl, there was little opportunity for formal education. The yeshiva, perhaps, for religious studies. But physics? No, I don't think so." He paused. "Besides, there is something to be said for making clothing. You create something tangible. Something that protects people, makes them feel dignified. My equations? They exist on paper, in computers. Sometimes I envy my grandfather."

Later, watching him accept an award from the university president, I thought about how history moves through us, redirecting our lives like water flowing around rocks. Some are swept to higher ground, others to lower. Steinberg had been carried to Israel, to the Hebrew University, to Princeton, to Stockholm. But in his mind, there remained this other self – the tailor who might have been – cutting patterns in wool rather than discerning patterns in the cosmos.

What wisdom there is in acknowledging such alternatives without resentment or inflated self-importance. To understand that in some other configuration of history, one might be measuring inseams instead of measuring quantum states, and to see dignity in both occupations.

I wonder if, in his private moments, Professor Steinberg ever takes needle and thread to repair a button or mend a tear, his fingers remembering skills they never learned, connecting him to that other self who exists only in the realm of possibility – that ghost who sits cross-legged on a wooden table in Poland, squinting in the late afternoon light, carefully guiding thread through the eye of a needle.

The Heart's Compass

Dr. Lerner had been practicing cardiology for twenty-six years, and in that time he had developed the habit of talking to his patients about matters that extended well beyond the parameters of their cardiovascular health. Some of his colleagues found this unprofessional, though none said so to his face. They made jokes instead. "Lerner thinks the heart is an emotional organ," they would say. But Lerner knew better. The jokes simply confirmed his suspicion that most doctors were afraid of the very human elements that made medicine worthy of being called a practice rather than merely a science.

It was Thursday afternoon, and Mrs. Abramowitz was sitting across from him in his examining room, her chart showing the same steady improvement in her numbers that had been evident for the past three visits. A widow of seven years, she had weathered the initial medical setbacks following her husband's death and now maintained what Lerner considered an impressive regimen of moderate exercise, Mediterranean diet, and social engagement through her synagogue and book club.

"You know," Lerner said, closing her file, "I've been thinking lately about nostalgia."

"Nostalgia?" Mrs. Abramowitz repeated, her eyebrows rising slightly above her tortoiseshell glasses. "What brought that on?"

"I've come to believe it might be the most underrated emotion in the human repertoire," he said, leaning back in his chair. "Everyone dismisses it as sentimental indulgence, but I'm convinced it serves a profound evolutionary purpose."

Mrs. Abramowitz tilted her head. "How so?"

"It's our heart's compass," Lerner said. "Not the anatomical heart, of course – that's my professional territory – but the metaphorical one. Nostalgia is what pulls us home, what makes us want to return to the people and places that gave us our bearings in the first place."

As he spoke, he noticed a subtle shift in Mrs. Abramowitz's expression, a softening around the eyes that suggested she was no longer entirely in his office but had begun traveling inward.

"I still smell Morris sometimes," she said quietly. "Not his cologne, but that other smell – the one that was just him. I'll be folding laundry or making a cup of tea, and suddenly it's there, and for a moment, I'm certain he's just walked into the room."

Lerner nodded. "The olfactory sense is perhaps the most powerful trigger for nostalgia. There's a direct neural pathway from the nose to the limbic system – no intellectual processing required. The smell bypasses our rational filters and delivers us straight to memory, to emotion."

"And why would that be evolutionary?" she asked, her practicality reasserting itself.

"Think about our ancestors," Lerner said, warming to his subject. "Before GPS, before maps, before even written language – how did they find their way back to safety, to community? They followed sensory cues. The smell of cooking fires, the familiar songs echoing across valleys, the visual landmarks that signified home."

"So nostalgia kept us from getting lost?" A smile played at the corners of her mouth.

"More than that," Lerner said. "I think it kept us from wanting to stay lost. It's the emotional counterpart to our physical homing instinct.

When we feel that pull toward what we've known and loved, when we experience that bittersweet longing, we're being guided by evolutionary wisdom thousands of years in the making."

Mrs. Abramowitz considered this. "That might explain why my daughter calls me every Sunday at exactly six o'clock, even though she lives in Seattle and has two children and a demanding job. She says it grounds her."

"Precisely," Lerner said. "And I'd wager those conversations give her a particular kind of peace that nothing else in her busy life can provide."

"But what about when home is gone?" Mrs. Abramowitz asked, her voice dropping slightly. "What happens to nostalgia then?"

Lerner paused, recognizing the delicate territory they were entering. "That's where I think nostalgia reveals its deepest function. When home as we knew it disappears – through death, disaster, or simply the passage of time – nostalgia becomes both the wound and the balm. The longing can trigger depression, yes, even anxiety. But it also provides the blueprint for what we need to rebuild or discover anew."

"A blueprint," she repeated, trying the word out.

"I've noticed that patients who allow themselves to feel nostalgia, who don't run from it or dismiss it, often find their way to new forms of belonging. They recognize the elements of home when they encounter them, even in unfamiliar settings."

Mrs. Abramowitz nodded slowly. "After Morris died, I couldn't bear to hear the Gershwin songs we used to dance to in our living room. Now I play them deliberately, usually on Friday evenings before I light the candles. It hurts, but it's... orienting, somehow."

"You're using nostalgia as it was meant to be used," Lerner said. "As a compass rather than a cage."

She smiled then, a full smile that reminded Lerner why he practiced medicine the way he did. "And is that what you tell all your cardiac patients, Dr. Lerner? That their metaphorical hearts need tending as much as their physical ones?"

"Only the ones who I think will take it seriously," he said, standing to open the door. "See Nancy at the front desk to schedule your next appointment in six months. And Mrs. Abramowitz?"

She looked up at him.

"Keep playing those Gershwin songs."

After she left, Lerner made notes in her chart, adding a line that no other doctor in the practice would have included: "Patient demonstrates healthy integration of grief through structured nostalgia practices."

He knew it sounded pretentious, perhaps even unprofessional. But after nearly three decades of watching hearts fail and recover, he had developed an unshakable conviction that the emotional patterns we establish are as crucial to our survival as any artery or valve. Nostalgia, with its bittersweet tugging at our consciousness, might just be what keeps us tethered to ourselves when everything else threatens to sweep us away.

Before his next patient arrived, Lerner found himself thinking of his father's bakery. Growing up as the son of a Jewish baker had left him with an indelible olfactory memory – the characteristic scent of buttercream that clung to his father's clothes when he came home each evening. Even now, forty years later, he could conjure that smell with perfect clarity. It was the scent of safety, of sweetness, of a world where love was expressed through the careful crafting of nourishment.

Just last week, Mrs. Goldstein had come in for her quarterly checkup. She worked at the local supermarket bakery, and every time she entered his office, she brought with her that same unmistakable aroma of buttercream.

"You know," he had told her, "every time you come to see me, I feel a particular kind of happiness. You smell exactly like my father did when he came home from his bakery. That buttercream scent – it's like a time machine."

Mrs. Goldstein had laughed, pleasantly surprised. "Most doctors tell me to change before my appointments. They say the sugar smell makes them crave sweets."

"Never change it," Lerner had replied. "It's the best medicine I get all day."

He made a mental note to call his son that evening, to ask about the grandchildren, to listen for the echoes of his own voice in the boy's deepening tenor. Another kind of nostalgia, he supposed – one oriented toward the future rather than the past. The compass working in both directions, always guiding us home.

The Humming Heart

In my examining room in Brooklyn, where the sunlight filters through blinds like the stripes of a prayer shawl, I listen to the hearts of strangers. I, Dr. Mendel Feinberg, have heard thousands of hearts, each with its own rhythm, its own story.

When Mrs. Goldstein comes with her chest pains that appear every Tuesday ("Never on Shabbos, Doctor, the Holy One blessed be He gives me rest then"), I place my stethoscope and hear beneath her complaints the steady drumbeat of a heart that has survived Poland, two husbands, and a daughter who married a gentile from Connecticut.

While I listen, I often think of my mother, Rivka. She would sit at our kitchen table on Ocean Parkway, her fingers always busy with something – peeling potatoes, folding napkins, or simply tapping out an invisible melody on the oilcloth. "Mendeleh," she would say, "remember what the old ones taught. Bullets kill people close to them. Words kill people across the ocean."

In the neighborhood where we lived, words traveled faster than the trolley cars. One whisper about a girl seen talking to the wrong boy, and her prospects for marriage would wither like flowers in winter. One rumor about a man's business dealings, and his customers would disappear like dreams upon waking.

My mother never participated in such talk. When Mrs. Himmelfarb came to gossip about the rabbi's wife, my mother would offer tea and change the subject to the weather or the price of herring. If pressed, she would say, "From such talk, what good comes? Better to use the mouth for prayer or for eating my strudel."

When patients tell me of their troubles – the daughter who doesn't call, the son who married out of the faith, the neighbor who plays the radio too loud – I hear my mother's voice. I have become a doctor of hearts partly because of her. She knew that the heart could be injured not just by disease but by the sharp edges of words.

My sister Sarah and I, we were not so wise as children. We would laugh at old Mr. Pinsky with his crooked back, or mock Miss Teitelbaum who spoke with a stutter. But our mother would look at us with eyes that carried all the sadness of the shtetl and say nothing. Her silence was more powerful than any scolding.

When she died – on a Tuesday, also the day she was born – Sarah and I stood by her grave at the cemetery in Queens. The rabbi asked what inscription we wanted on the stone. Sarah looked at me, and I knew what we both were thinking. Not the usual phrases, not "beloved mother" or "she will be missed."

"She saw life with a good eye," I told him, quoting from the Mishnah. The rabbi nodded, understanding immediately. In those six words lay the essence of our mother – her refusal to judge, her ability to find goodness even in the darkest corners.

My grandmother, my mother's mother, I remember less clearly. She came from Lublin to New York when I was five or six. She lived with us for three years before she died. What I recall most vividly was her constant humming – niggunim, wordless melodies that followed her like shadows.

She hummed while cooking, while sweeping, while sitting by the window watching the world pass by on Ocean Parkway. If she stopped humming, it was only to speak, and when the words ended, the humming began again.

As a child, I thought perhaps she was simple-minded. "Why does Bubbe always make noise?" I asked my mother once.

My mother smiled. "In the old country," she said, "your grandmother lost everything – her parents, her brothers, her first husband. She had reasons to cry all day. Instead, she hums. This is how she keeps the darkness away."

Now, in my examining room, between patients, I sometimes find myself humming. The melodies come unbidden – old synagogue tunes, fragments of Yiddish songs, sometimes just notes strung together like beads on an invisible thread. When my nurse, Miss O'Reilly, gives me a curious look, I smile and say, "Just checking my own heartbeat."

And perhaps this is true. Perhaps the humming is a way of listening to one's own heart, of reminding oneself that beneath all the words and worries, there is still rhythm, still music.

When I place my stethoscope on the chest of Mr. Abramowitz, who complains of palpitations every time the stock market dips, I listen not just for murmurs or arrhythmias but for his humanity. And sometimes, in the spaces between heartbeats, I hear my grandmother humming and my mother saying, "See with a good eye, Mendeleh. Always with a good eye."

In this way, the wisdom of the women travels through generations, not through blood or genes, but through stories and silences, through the heritage of seeing the world not as it is, but as it might be if we all listened more carefully to the humming beneath the noise.

In the Shadow of Days: Chronicles of a Doctor's Patients

In the world of medicine, there are no strangers, only people whose stories you haven't yet heard. As I sit in my office each evening, transcribing notes about the day's patients, their voices echo in my mind like whispers from a forgotten synagogue. I am merely the keeper of these tales, a collector of human moments that might otherwise vanish into the air.

An old man visited today, his body seemingly diminished since our last appointment.

"Looks like you've lost some weight," I observed.

He adjusted his glasses, revealing a glimmer of mischief in his rheumy eyes. "No, Doc. I didn't lose anything that my wife didn't pick up."

Such is the nature of long marriages – nothing truly disappears, merely changes hands.

Another patient, Mr. Goldstein, complained about his parrot. "Every night at 3 AM, the bird makes these noises... like deep breathing, sexual breathing." He leaned forward, embarrassed yet needing to share this peculiarity. "I didn't understand until I learned I bought that parrot from a policeman who visited his wife at exactly that hour every night. The bird was merely echoing what it had heard."

In this way, we all become mimics of our circumstances.

Mrs. Feingold spoke of her mother with such devotion it was almost religious. "Fathers leave you for other women, brothers and sisters go away. Even your wife and children go away, but your mother is your best friend," she insisted. "You could be a serial killer, but she would still be there."

I nodded, thinking how faith and motherhood share this quality of unconditional love.

The unexpected often reveals itself in my examination room. A woman with a prominent nose requested plastic surgery, and I assumed I knew her concern. "Doc, it's my breasts," she said, upending my expectations. We see what we expect to see until someone shows us otherwise.

Sisters carry peculiar burdens. One patient told me about her sister's visit to a plastic surgeon who remarked, "One breast is smaller than the other." Now she cannot look at her sister without this knowledge intruding. Our perceptions of others can be permanently altered by a single careless observation.

The nature of worry transforms with illness. "Doc, I used to worry so much every day," confessed a cancer survivor. "Now I only worry that my cancer will return." Suffering distills our anxieties to their essence.

This morning, before work, I realized that the tenth commandment – thou shall not covet – and Buddha's teaching that craving causes misery are essentially identical. Different traditions circle the same human truths, like planets around a hidden sun.

I marvel at rebirth in medical form: the oncologist who received a twenty-year-old's heart after his own failed him. For twenty-three years he'd been dying slowly, and now he lives again. What wisdom might come from carrying another's heart within your chest?

Time collapses in unexpected ways. A seventy-year-old patient asked what he should do about a Facebook friend request from his childhood enemy. "I haven't seen or heard from him in fifty years. Still hate him very much." Some grudges we carry like precious heirlooms.

Families misunderstand in ways both painful and comical. The reformed alcoholic fuming because his sister gave him wine for Christmas. What was she thinking? Perhaps that change is something we cannot always recognize in those we've known the longest.

Priorities reveal character. My patient refused knee surgery until after seeing "Hamilton" on Broadway. "I waited a year for those tickets. My knee can hurt another two months," she declared. Pain is relative to what brings us joy.

Mr. Cohen proudly told me he belongs to the "ROMEO Club." When I inquired, he explained with a wink: "Retired Old Men Eating Out." In our later years, we create communities around whatever pleasures remain.

The longtime smoker with emphysema showed rare self-awareness. "Every time I begin to whine about my shortness of breath, I remember who did it," he wheezed. Self-inflicted suffering carries its own particular sting.

Another philosophical patient with chronic illness said, "No one takes medicine in the cemetery, Doc. I'm glad to take the pills. I'm coughing, but it's better than being in a coffin." Perspective is the most potent medicine I cannot prescribe.

Some stories end too quickly. Eight weeks ago, a nasal lump. Seven weeks ago, a biopsy revealing metastatic melanoma. Today, he died. Like a candle snuffed by an unseen wind.

The patient covered in cancer knew his fate but focused only on the immediate concern. "Doc, if you can get rid of my pain, I would be the happiest man alive." In suffering's presence, our horizons contract to the moment at hand.

Human contradictions never cease to amuse me. The patient terrified of a vaccine needle while sporting an elaborate tattoo on his arm. We fear what we choose to fear, regardless of logic.

When a radio interviewer asked why I enjoy being a doctor, I answered simply, "It's like visiting old friends." Each patient brings their history into the room with them.

Wisdom sometimes arrives in unexpected packages. My 89-year-old patient offered this: "If you lose today, it's because you worry about yesterday or tomorrow." The elderly often understand time's true nature better than the rest of us.

A harried woman complained of palpitations. "I have two daughters living with me, along with their husbands and intermittent boyfriends. One has an autistic child." She looked at me expectantly. "Do you think that's from stress?" Some questions answer themselves.

Coincidence reminds us how connected our lives truly are. I called American Express about a billing matter, and the operator recognized my name. "Pardon me, sir. Are you the Doctor who saved my mother's life?" The world contracts in such moments.

Touch becomes precious with age. "You are the only one who puts his hands on me," an elderly woman said during her examination. Later, I learned her husband had been dead for eleven years. Her children lived across the country. Her neighbors waved from a distance. The home health aide helped with bathing, but always wore gloves. My clinical touch – checking her pulse, palpating her abdomen, listening to her lungs – was the only human contact that reached her skin directly. In this way, the routine of medicine sometimes serves needs beyond the physical diagnosis. How strange that in our crowded world, simple touch has become so rare, like a language nearly forgotten.

Our work echoes through generations. I examined the daughter-in-law of a patient who died four decades ago. I shared with her how he had called out for his "mother" during a painful episode with kidney stones. She smiled knowingly. "He always called his wife 'Mother.'" Context changes everything.

No one is immune from fate's arbitrary hand. The dean of our medical school – brilliant, accomplished, seemingly invincible – was found unconscious from a massive stroke. No position protects us from our mortality.

Simple pleasures sustain us. A patient continuously hummed during her appointment, reminding me of my grandmother sixty years ago, humming comfortably as she worked in her kitchen. Some habits transmit joy across generations.

Gratitude appears in unexpected follow-ups. "Doctor, you saved my life twice," declared a patient. "In 1982 during my heart attack, and six months ago when you noticed my anemia, which led to finding my rectal cancer early." He grinned. "See you again in 34 years."

Modern problems require creative solutions. The woman who requested weight loss medication explained her psychiatrist's unusual advice: masturbate when hungry. "I was hungry in the waiting room," she added matter-of-factly. "Even now." Some confidences I am unsure how to receive.

Life circles back upon itself. A young man announced his wedding would be held in the same hotel ballroom as his bar mitzvah twelve years prior. He showed me photos of his fiancé – another young man with kind eyes and a brilliant smile. The invitation described their journey from childhood friends to lovers. Looking for my reaction, I simply said, "That's wonderful." What else can one say to love's perfect symmetry? Some circles complete themselves in ways our ancestors could never have imagined.

At the local Veterans Home, I meet an 86-year-old Korean War veteran, philosophical despite his confined circumstances. "One half of a room here, Doc, is my home and my whole world now." His words remind me that our universe is as large or small as we perceive it to be.

Mrs. Abramowitz came in for her regular checkup accompanied by her husband, a frail man with a pharmacy of pill bottles in a plastic bag. As he complained about his various specialists, she turned to him with the sharp wit only decades of marriage can hone. "You have so many doctors and you complain so much. Be careful! I'm going to bring you to the only one you're missing, and that's a gynecologist." Even in his discomfort, he laughed. Sometimes humor is the most effective medicine.

An overweight Russian doctor became my patient after a serious car accident. During her follow-up, she proudly showed me her $1,000 Chanel sneakers. "I only had one pair of shoes as a child," she explained, eyes distant with memory. I glanced down at my $19 Walmart rubber-soled sandals and thought about how we measure distance traveled in life. Some journeys are measured in miles, others in the space between a single pair of worn shoes and a closet of designer footwear.

Mr. Petersen, a retired fisherman, surprised me with his contentment. "Doc, I am so happy in life. I made it to 70. I can walk my dog and I can go fishing anytime I want. That's all I need or want in life."

I watched him leave, whistling, and thought: this is the richest man alive. We search for wisdom in ancient texts, but sometimes it arrives wearing faded jeans and carrying a tackle box.

In the complex terrain of human dignity, I've learned that suffering takes many forms. A middle-aged man whispered his confession: "Doc, before my penile implant, I was going to kill myself. Now I want to live." His eyes brimmed with tears of relief. Some despair runs deeper than we can see, hiding in places medicine traditionally overlooks. How many conditions dismissed as merely "quality of life" issues actually stand at the precipice between existence and oblivion?

These stories – fragments really – form a mosaic of human experience. I collect them like precious stones, each one containing its own light. In the examining room, I am both doctor and witness, keeping small records of lives that might otherwise pass unnoticed, unseen. This is the privilege of my profession: to stand at the intersection of science and story, of medicine and meaning.

Two Doors

In the practice of medicine, as in life itself, one develops a knack for spotting patterns in seeming randomness. After thirty-five years of maintaining patient journals – a habit I picked up from my mentor at Northwestern – I sometimes find myself leafing through old entries with a mixture of nostalgia and professional curiosity. Last evening, I came across a notation from April 2005 that gave me pause.

The morning had begun with Mr. Schlesinger, a financial advisor who's tailoring always struck me as being slightly more expensive than his conversation merited. He settled into the examination room chair – avoiding the table, as the successful often do – and launched into the usual preludes about his golf game and the market's performance before I could inquire about his blood pressure.

"Doc," he said, leaning forward conspiratorially, "my son-in-law cleared a million last year. Thirty-nine years old! Working at Morgan Stanley. Brilliant kid, really. Elizabeth sure knows how to pick them."

I nodded appreciatively, having learned long ago that patients require physicians to play audience to more than just their physical complaints.

"The thing is," he continued, his voice dropping slightly, "they've had some... difficulties recently." He adjusted his French cuffs, revealing monogrammed links. "Elizabeth was expecting their second. The tests showed Down syndrome."

The room seemed to contract slightly.

"They're good Catholics, of course," he added quickly. "Abortion was out of the question. But when the baby was born, they... well, they arranged an adoption immediately." Mr. Schlesinger's gaze drifted toward the window. "They felt it would be detrimental to their first child. Confusion, you understand. Resources diverted."

I maintained my professional neutrality, though I noted how his confident posture had subtly collapsed.

"Elizabeth tells me they made the right decision," he said, not quite meeting my eyes. "The practical decision. But you know, Doc, I can see it – a kind of shadow on their faces now. I suspect it will always be there."

After he departed, I had precisely twelve minutes to document his visit, order his lipid panel, and prepare for my next appointment.

They were new patients – two sisters, the Rogers women, referred by a colleague. The elder, Margaret, was sixty-four; the younger, Susan, sixty-one with Down syndrome. They entered the examination room with the synchronized movements of people who have shared living quarters for decades.

"We've been together since our parents passed," Margaret explained, her hand resting lightly on her sister's arm. "Twenty-seven years now."

Susan beamed at me. "I make the coffee every morning," she offered proudly. "Margaret burns it."

The elder sister laughed with genuine delight. "She's right. I'm hopeless in the kitchen. Susan keeps us fed and organized."

As I proceeded with the examination, I observed their interactions – the small gestures of consideration, the private jokes, the way they anticipated each other's thoughts. My nurse later commented that she'd never seen such patience between siblings.

The affection between them was palpable, radiating from their matched postures and complementary stories. It filled the sterile examination room with something rarely found in medical settings – a sense of contentment so profound it bordered on wisdom.

Before they left, Susan took my hand in both of hers. "You're a good doctor," she declared with absolute certainty, though I had done nothing yet to earn such an assessment.

After they departed, I sat in the sudden silence of the examination room, struck by the juxtaposition fate had arranged in my schedule that day: two doors to the same circumstance, opening onto profoundly different moral landscapes.

In my journal that evening, I wrote only: "The Schlesingers believe they have made a sacrifice. The Rogers sisters have discovered a sufficiency."

The older I grow in this profession, the more I understand that medicine's greatest insights rarely come from textbooks or laboratories, but from these accidental collisions of human stories, these unplanned experiments in contrast that the examining room witnesses daily.

The Miracles of Trikosi

In the small Ukrainian town of Trikosi, where the old synagogue had been converted into a granary during the Soviet years and then abandoned after the empire's fall, there lived people who had forgotten what they once knew. Memory is a curious thing, like a bird that flies away and sometimes returns when you least expect it.

I, Dr. Menachem Birnbaum, tell this story not for glory but as testimony to the strange ways the Holy One, blessed be He, moves through our world, sometimes with thunder and sometimes with the smallest whisper, sometimes even through a little blue pill.

When my patient Rebecca Goldstein spoke to me about her work with the Chesed Society at her synagogue, visiting the elderly mother of the congregation's president, her words transported me across oceans and decades. As I examined her thyroid, my mind wandered to Ukraine, to dust-covered roads and eyes that had seen too much suffering.

"You know," I said to her, placing my stethoscope back around my neck, "what you tell me of this Chesed, this loving-kindness, reminds me of something that happened long ago, after the Soviet darkness lifted."

Twenty-five years earlier, when the walls between East and West had crumbled like the ancient walls of Jericho, I joined a medical mission organized by the Jewish Federation. We journeyed to help the remnants, the She'erit, of Eastern European Jewry who had survived first the Nazis and then the Communists – both demons of different faces but similar appetites.

The Federation had established a clinic in Trikosi – the Chesed Medical Clinic – where any person with at least one Jewish grandparent could receive care. This was the law of return applied to medicine, you understand. In those days, many who had hidden their Jewishness for generations were beginning to remember, like seeds that had waited decades for the right season to sprout.

I arrived on a Thursday, my suitcase heavy with medicines, particularly samples of the new miracle drug called Viagra, which had just been approved in America. In those days, this medicine cost more than gold and was said to restore a man's vigor like the staff of Moses.

The people of Trikosi regarded our medicines with the reverence usually reserved for holy relics. But when whispers spread about the Viagra, something truly remarkable occurred. By Friday evening, as Shabbos approached and the women of the town were covering their eyes to welcome the Sabbath bride, sixteen men who had never before acknowledged any connection to Judaism suddenly discovered their heritage.

They came to the clinic one by one, these sixteen souls, each with a story more fantastical than the last.

"My grandmother," said Dmitri Petrovitch, a blacksmith with hands like shovels, "her mother lit candles every Friday night behind closed shutters. She would whisper strange words. Only now do I understand they were prayers."

Boris Mikhailovich, who had been the Communist Party secretary for the region, arrived with an old spoon he claimed had belonged to his great-grandfather. "See these markings?" he said, pointing to what might have been Hebrew letters or might have been scratches from decades of use. "My ancestor brought this from Jerusalem."

Sixteen men, sixteen stories, sixteen pairs of eyes that avoided mine when I asked specific questions about Jewish traditions. What is the blessing over bread? When is Yom Kippur observed? These questions were met with silence or creative misdirection.

"In my family," said Leonid, a potato farmer, "we have always believed the most important thing is not words but the heart." He thumped his chest for emphasis. "And my heart is very Jewish. Very, very Jewish."

Rabbi Himmelfarb, who accompanied our mission, was suspicious but also moved. "Who are we to judge?" he whispered to me. "The Talmud says that even the sincerest conversion begins with ulterior motives. Perhaps the Holy One works through many vessels, even pharmaceutical ones."

I distributed the samples according to medical need, not religious conviction. Yet I could not help but notice how fervently these new Jews studied the directions on the packages, with more devotion than many study the Torah.

Six months later, we received a letter from Trikosi. There had been seven weddings and nine pregnancies announced. The Chesed Clinic now had a regular minyan for the first time in sixty years. The letter was signed: "The Jewish Community of Trikosi, remembered and renewed."

Was it wrong, what happened? Who can say? In the small Ukrainian town where my grandparents were born, before pogroms and death camps emptied it of Jews, there was a saying: "God creates the cure before the affliction." Perhaps sometimes He creates the affliction to lead us to remembrance.

When I finished telling this story to Rebecca Goldstein, she was silent for a long moment. Then she laughed – not mockingly, but with the laughter that acknowledges the absurdity and wonder of human existence.

"So," she said finally, "you're telling me that Viagra brought Jews back to Judaism?"

"Not Viagra," I corrected her. "Desire. Desire and memory. They are often the same thing."

As it is written in the Psalms: "If I forget thee, O Jerusalem, let my right hand forget its cunning." Sometimes the body remembers what the mind has forgotten. And sometimes, in the most unexpected ways, we find our way back to who we always were.

The Miracle in His Pocket

In Brooklyn, where I practiced the healing arts, the winters were harsh and unforgiving, like God Himself had turned His face away until spring. I, Dr. Mendel Kirschbaum, was known as a good doctor, perhaps the best cardiologist in three provinces. But even the best doctor is nothing without knowledge of his patients' sufferings.

Before the cellular telephone came to us in 1983, oy, such troubles I had! Every moment away from my office was a torment. The beeper – that small black box which would wail like a dybbuk at all hours – it gave no peace. It would cry out while I stood on the Verrazano Bridge, where the wind cuts through even the thickest wool coat, and what could I do? Pull my automobile to the roadside and search like a beggar for coins to feed the public telephone.

Five minutes I would wait! Five minutes while somewhere a heart might be stopping. And for what? To hear Mrs. Goldstein complain of gas pains that she was certain would kill her before morning? Or Mr. Abramowitz, who needed a prescription for sleeping pills because his wife's snoring kept him awake? How was I to know until I reached the telephone? Such was a doctor's life.

The public telephone booth was like a confessional box – cold, smelling faintly of urine, with strange numbers scratched into its walls by people I would never meet. Inside it, I would speak with operators and nurses, all while watching my breath form clouds in the winter air.

But God, in His mysterious wisdom, allowed men to create miracles from metal and glass. The cellular telephone! When it came, it changed everything. No more did I stand shivering on roadsides. No more did I wonder if a patient lived or died while I searched for coins.

Today, a Thursday in late autumn, an old patient of mine, Chaim Leventhal, came to my office. With him was his granddaughter, Shayna – a beautiful child with eyes like dark cherries and the impatience of youth in every movement. While I examined Chaim's heart, my cellular telephone made its musical sound three times. With a touch, I spoke to the hospital, dictated notes that appeared immediately in my records, even showed Chaim photographs of my own grandchildren.

Chaim, not to be outdone, removed from his pocket a cellular telephone of his own. Older than mine, yes, but still a marvel.

"Doctor," he said, "I wanted to show you a video of my grandson Moishe at his bar mitzvah, but this miserable thing, I think I erased it."

At this, Shayna made a sound like air escaping a balloon. "Zayde, that phone belongs in a museum! You should get one like Dr. Kirschbaum's. I would die of shame to be seen with such an antique."

Something in her words pierced me more sharply than winter wind ever could. I looked at this child, born into a world of wonders she had never learned to see.

"Shayna," I said, setting down my own telephone, "what you call an antique, in the shtetl where I was born, they would have called divine."

Her eyes widened slightly, disbelief written across her smooth face.

"Forty years ago, not so long in God's eyes, if a man carried in his pocket a box that could capture moving pictures, speak across oceans, and hold more wisdom than all the yeshivas in Lakewood, New Jersey – do you know what would happen? They would think him a prophet, or perhaps the Messiah himself!"

Chaim chuckled softly, his old eyes twinkling.

"If Moses had shown Pharaoh such a device," I continued, warming to my subject, "the children of Israel might have walked from Egypt without a single plague. More impressive than parting the Red Sea! At least water we understand – it rises and falls by laws we know. But this?" I tapped Chaim's telephone gently. "This would have been beyond understanding."

I leaned toward the girl, my voice dropping as though sharing a secret. "Before 1983, I stood on the Verrazano Bridge in snowstorms, feeding coins into telephones, not knowing if my patient lived or died while I waited. Your grandfather's 'antique' can still save lives, show bar mitzvahs, and connect people across the world. The miracle isn't having the newest. The miracle is having it at all."

Shayna looked at her grandfather's telephone with new eyes, perhaps seeing for the first time not an embarrassment but a wonder.

"In the difference between your grandfather's telephone and mine," I told her, "there is only a small distance. But between either of them and the public telephone on the Verrazano Bridge? Between them lies the distance from darkness to light, from exile to redemption."

Chaim nodded slowly, his hand covering his granddaughter's. "This the child should understand," he murmured. "That even the smallest miracle is still a miracle."

And so it is with all God's gifts. We forget their wonder until someone reminds us to see with fresh eyes. Even a telephone, that small box of metal and glass, contains within it echoes of divine creation – voice from nothingness, light from darkness, connection where once there was only silence and waiting.

The Miracle in My Hand

In the small examination room, where the scent of antiseptic mingled with the whispers of human frailty, Dr. Mordechai Weintraub held up a device no larger than a slice of challah. His patient, an elderly woman with eyes that had witnessed the transformation of worlds, listened with the patience of generations.

"Bubbie," he said, his voice soft yet vibrant with wonder, "do you know what this is?"

The woman adjusted her glasses, her wrinkled hands folded neatly on her lap. She had seen much in her lifetime – pogroms and migrations, wars that consumed continents, technologies that would have seemed like sorcery to her parents.

Dr. Weintraub tapped the screen, and it illuminated like a magical window. "Fifty years ago, this would have been considered a miracle beyond comprehension. With a touch, I can speak to my daughter in New York, see a map of the entire world, read the wisdom of sages from centuries past – all in this small device."

He thought of Moses standing before Pharaoh, performing miracles to demonstrate divine power. How different would that ancient confrontation have been with such a device? Would the magicians of Egypt have been more impressed by video calls or GPS navigation than by staffs turning into serpents?

The elderly patient smiled, a knowing curve of her lips. "Miracles," she said, "are not in the device, but in the eyes of those who see them."

Dr. Weintraub nodded. His daughter, with her constant desire for the newest phone model, would never understand the magic that resided in these small technological wonders. To her, they were mundane, disposable – each new version quickly replaced by another.

But to him, each device was a testament to human imagination, a small miracle that connected souls across impossible distances that held the accumulated knowledge of humanity in a palm-sized rectangle.

"A miracle," he murmured, more to himself than to his patient, "is simply a wonder not yet understood."

The woman's eyes twinkled. She had seen enough of life to know that wonder was the truest form of faith – whether in technology, in God, or in the endless human capacity for transformation.

The Forgotten Glasses

It's the small things that alter the course of our lives, isn't it? The forgotten item, the chance encounter, the random book pulled from a shelf. Looking back, we see these moments for what they were – hinges upon which entire lives pivot.

I'm driving between hospitals on a crisp Saturday morning. At my age, I've become something of a relic – one of the last working cardiologists in our community. My contemporaries have mostly retired, died, or relocated to Florida's warmer climes. I remain, partly out of love for the profession, partly because I've somehow become the adhesive holding our cardiology department together at Locum Hospital.

The rhythm of the highway lulls me into reflection. My thoughts drift to my wife of nearly 49 years. We first reconnected in Northwestern University's library in Chicago. I was trudging through medical school; she was navigating the labyrinth of law school. That evening, I offered her a ride home in my prized possession – a used red Volkswagen that I had lovingly maintained.

The interaction was strained, awkward. She wore striking blue aviator frames that accentuated her features, but our conversation stumbled along. By the time I dropped her off, I was certain nothing would come of our meeting. There was posturing, defensive attitudes – the careful dance of two young people unsure of themselves or each other.

The next morning, I noticed them – her beautiful glasses, abandoned on the floor of my back seat. Those blue aviator frames had slipped from her possession into mine, creating an obligation, a reason to see her again.

When I returned them, something shifted. The awkwardness dissolved, and a spark ignited that would burn for almost five decades.

My mind shifts to another fortuitous accident. 1988. We were trying to have a child without success. Planning to host family, we needed new silverware and found ourselves at a New York City store selling gold flatware. They accepted only cash – a common policy in those days. We retrieved the money from an ATM, only to return and find the store unexpectedly closed.

With cash in hand and time to spare, we wandered to a Barnes & Noble at the edge of Greenwich Village. Despite being a cardiologist, I found myself inexplicably drawn to a gynecology text. There, on a random page, was information about progesterone suppositories to sustain pregnancies.

The very next day, my wife mentioned this to her fertility specialist, who agreed it was worth trying. As it happened, she was already pregnant – a fact we didn't yet know – and the progesterone prevented what might have been another miscarriage. Our daughters, now in their thirties, owe their existence to that closed silverware shop and a randomly selected medical text.

Both stories – the forgotten glasses and the serendipitous fertility book – are carefully recorded in my little book of miracles that I keep hidden in the bottom drawer of my desk. It's a small, leather-bound journal where I document the inexplicable turns of fate that have shaped my existence. I rarely show it to anyone; it remains my private catalog of wonder, a testament to life's mysterious workings that science cannot explain.

As I pull into the hospital parking lot, I marvel at life's capriciousness – forgotten glasses and closed shops, small incidents cascading into marriages, children, and grandchildren. These are the invisible hinges of fate, the tiny inflection points that, in retrospect, reveal themselves as the architects of our greatest joys.

The Class Reunion

Shortly after what I believe was my 20th high school reunion, I saw one of my former high school acquaintances as a patient. I knew him, but wasn't terribly friendly with him in those days. We recognized each other, nodded in the hallways, but traveled in different orbits, had different sets of friends – his, I recall, the livelier bunch.

He appeared deeply troubled when the subject of the reunion arose. Since I had attended the same gathering, I inquired about the source of his distress.

"When I got home," he said, "my wife yelled at me."

"Why would she have yelled at you?" I asked.

"You know those guys I used to hang around with," he said. "Well, my wife claims that the moment I joined their circle at the reunion, I immediately reverted to being a high school kid again."

I waited for him to continue.

"Back then, I was always the butt of their jokes, always being mocked. Now I run my own successful sales company. But at this reunion – my God – I slipped right back into that old pattern. Not exactly being picked on, but joked on, if you know what I mean."

He shifted in his chair, his expensive suit suddenly seeming to sit awkwardly on his frame.

"I'm upset about two things, Doc," he said. "First, that it happened at all – that I reverted back to my old high school self, my old high school posture, my old high school personality, my old high school subordinate situation to these so-called 'cool kids.' And second – this is worse – I'm angry at myself because my wife saw it. She witnessed it. She had never seen me like that before."

He looked at me with the expression of a man who had inadvertently revealed a shameful secret he'd successfully concealed for decades.

"What do you think?" he asked.

What did I think? I thought about how the hierarchies of youth never fully dissolve, how they crystallize in our memories and resurrect themselves at the least provocation. I thought about how we construct elaborate adult personalities that can be undermined by a single knowing glance from someone who knew us when. I thought about the disappointed look on his wife's face when she realized the powerful man she married could be reduced to an anxious adolescent by the casual teasing of men whose peak achievements quite possibly occurred when they were seventeen.

But I said none of this. Some wounds require careful probing before treatment can begin.

The Doctor's Philosophy

Two complaints dominate my examining room with a regularity that borders on the comical. The first arrives with a sheepish glance toward the floor: "Doctor, once I start eating, I simply cannot stop. I stuff myself until discomfort becomes my companion." The second comes with furrowed brow and restless hands: "Doctor, anxiety is my constant shadow. I worry about everything – absolutely everything."

Over thirty years of practice, I've developed what my wife fondly calls my "jungle philosophy." Not quite Schweitzer in Africa, but perhaps useful nonetheless.

When Mrs. Abramson, a retired librarian with immaculate posture and a fondness for statement brooches, laments her inability to resist second helpings, I invite her to imagine her distant ancestors.

"Consider, Mrs. Abramson, that we are merely sophisticated animals with ancient programming. When our ancestors brought down a wild boar – no small feat with primitive weapons – the entire tribe gorged themselves. They ate until their stomachs distended, until the very thought of food became momentarily repulsive."

"But why, Doctor?" she asks, adjusting her brooch – today a silver owl with sapphire eyes.

"Because, my dear Mrs. Abramson, they never knew when the next substantial meal might present itself. Feast or famine – a rhythm as old as humanity itself. Our bodies developed this imperative: eat to fullness when food is available."

She considers this, nodding slowly. "But now all I need to do is open my refrigerator."

"Precisely," I tell her. "Evolution hasn't caught up with our convenience. We have Stone Age bodies wandering through supermarkets stocked with more calories than our ancestors saw in a decade."

Mr. Goldstein, a tax accountant whose anxiety peaks with such reliable seasonality that I could mark tax deadlines on my calendar by his appointments, receives a similar explanation.

"Anxiety," I tell him, "is nature's motivational tool. The lioness feels it when her cubs are hungry – this drives her to hunt. When they're fed, she lounges on sun-warmed rocks, magnificently unconcerned about tomorrow's meals. Anxiety compels necessary action."

His eyebrows rise above his wire-rimmed glasses. "But I'm anxious even when nothing threatens me."

"Ah," I say, "therein lies our modern predicament. We've inherited the mechanism but lost the off-switch. Anxiety made our ancestors study their surroundings, anticipate danger, prepare for scarcity. It made them run when chased, fight when cornered, and work when hungry. But they could also rest when safe."

I lean forward slightly. "Your task, Mr. Goldstein, is not to eliminate anxiety – it's hardwired, after all – but to recognize when it's serving no purpose and gracefully walk away from it."

These explanations – simplistic perhaps, but containing kernels of evolutionary truth – bring noticeable relief to my patients. There's comfort in understanding that what feels like personal failure is often biological programming running its ancient scripts in a world that no longer requires them.

Modern medicine has begun to catch up. The weight-loss medications now prescribed target those very hormones that once told our ancestors to eat until the last morsel was gone. Perhaps someday we'll have similar elegant solutions for anxiety – though I suspect we'll always need some of it to get our taxes filed on time.

In the meantime, I offer my patients this modest consolation: their struggles aren't moral failings but evolutionary hangovers. We're all just cave people in clothes, trying to adapt our Stone Age wiring to a world of refrigerators and tax deadlines.

Sometimes, understanding is the best medicine I can prescribe.

The Examining Room Proverbs

My mother, may she rest in peace, knew the secret shape of wisdom. Not the kind found in journals or textbooks, but the deeper truths handed down through generations of shtetl ancestors who understood life's fundamental rhythms.

Dr. Goldstein – that's what they call me now, with my framed diplomas and cardiac monitoring equipment – sits in his examining room and becomes, in small moments between EKGs and prescription renewals, his mother's son again.

"Mrs. Abramson," I say to the worried woman clutching her test results, "we all make plans and God laughs." I pause, letting the words settle. In my mind, I hear it in my mother's Yiddish cadence – "Mentsh trakht un Got lakht" – how the syllables would dance from her lips while she kneaded dough or folded laundry.

Mrs. Abramson's shoulders relax slightly. "My daughter wanted me to ask about this new procedure she read about online."

"Of course she did," I say. "Everyone plans. But medicine, like life, rarely follows our exact blueprint."

My mother arrived in America with little more than a suitcase and those proverbs. The daughter of immigrants who fled the pogroms, she carried their words like amulets. English eventually replaced Yiddish in our home, but those sayings remained, linguistic heirlooms more valuable than silver.

When Mr. Stein frets about the cost of his heart medication, I lean forward and share her second gift: "If money can fix it, it's not a problem." His expression shifts as the perspective realigns. What is a co-payment compared to a beating heart?

I find myself repeating this wisdom often. My patients nod solemnly, immediately grasping its profound truth. They think of the neighbor's child born with severe disabilities, or the colleague battling late-stage cancer, or their own family member slipping away through the fog of dementia – problems that no amount of wealth can truly solve. In these moments, their own financial concerns recalibrate against life's genuine hardships. The burdens that money can address suddenly appear manageable, even trivial.

"Doctor," a patient once told me after I shared this bit of maternal wisdom, "I've been losing sleep over my mortgage. But my sister's son – no fortune in the world could make him well." Her eyes had welled with tears of recognition.

For forty-three years I've practiced cardiology, peering into the physical mechanics of human existence. Yet my most effective medicine often comes not from pharmacology but from my mother's philosophy, distilled through centuries of Jewish pragmatism and delivered in her voice, which somehow never fades despite the passing of two decades.

The stethoscope around my neck is American, but the wisdom in my examining room crossed oceans. We doctors may repair valves and clear blockages, but it's these inherited truths that heal the deeper anxieties of living.

My mother would smile knowingly at this – her son the doctor, still her student after all these years.

About the Author

Aaron J. Feingold, M.D. has dedicated over four decades to the practice of cardiology, bringing compassion and expertise to countless patients throughout his distinguished 43-year career. He serves as the longtime Chairman of the Division of Cardiology at Hackensack Meridian JFK University Hospital and is President of the Raritan Bay Cardiology Group.

A New Jersey native, Dr. Feingold has deep roots in the community he serves. He and his wife, Brenda, are the proud parents of two daughters: Zara and Rachel and two grandchildren.

The recurring motif of hands throughout this book's imagery carries profound meaning that extends beyond mere artistic choice.

In many cultures, the hand serves as a powerful symbol of protection – worn as amulets or talismans to guard against harm. The physician's hand upon his chin on the book cover represents the contemplative nature of medical practice, the pause for thought that precedes healing action.

The third hand visible on the cover symbolizes the extra dimension that distinguishes exceptional healthcare – that transcendent quality that moves beyond the standard two-dimensional interaction between doctor and patient. This additional hand represents the deeper connection, the intuitive understanding, and the spiritual dimension that transforms medical care from mere treatment into genuine healing.

The hand cradling the anatomical heart on the back cover embodies the central truth this book seeks to convey: that medicine, at its essence, is about one human being holding the life and wellbeing of another with the utmost care and reverence. These hands are not merely appendages but instruments of connection, protection, contemplation, and ultimately, love made manifest in the sacred act of healing.

Lastly, the first pulse is taken while holding the hand , a reminder that life itself flows through these instruments of touch and care.

www.ingramcontent.com/pod-product-compliance
Lightning Source LLC
Chambersburg PA
CBHW071751110726
47908CB00006B/1764
9798999507006